The Illustrated Dictionary of
KNITTING

For Mary More of Hopeman and all knitters like her,
who share their knowledge that the next generation may
know more

Rae Compton

The Illustrated Dictionary of

KNITTING

B.T. Batsford Ltd, London

ISBN 0 7134 4863 6

Typeset by Tek-Art Ltd, Kent
and printed in Great Britain by
The Bath Press, Bath
for the publishers
B.T. Batsford Ltd
4 Fitzhardinge Street
London W1H 0AH

**The Publishers would like to thank Angela ffrench for her expert advice
and help in preparing this book for publication.**

Introduction

Knitting is one of the most popular hobbies in the world and appeals to a wide range and to many nationalities. Such diversity and universal appeal makes a dictionary of hand knitting essential for anyone interested in the craft. With all the varieties of stitches, patterns, styles and designs in mind, this easy-to-use guide has been compiled to satisfy both beginners and more experienced knitters. Used as a manual, it will provide you with the groundwork information to learn a new technique, perfect an old one, or, in fact, learn how to knit from scratch. Used as a reference book, the dictionary will teach you about the more popular knitting styles, national knitting preferences, types of yarn, the history behind the craft and the culture and traditions that still survive in knitting communities.

As well as the more universal techniques and terms, I have also included some of the more unusual and have explained how they are carried out. Indeed, it is the very fact that so many of the more unusual terms have been forgotten that encouraged me to compile this volume. Knitting is such an important part of our heritage that it would be a great misfortune for some of the more exotic and impressive styles to be lost. The patterns I have included, therefore, will not only teach you today's methods but those that previous generations thought important, and which may be the knitting heritage of the future.

Since knitting, in effect, has only two basic stitch forms – knitting and purling, and purling is only the reverse of knitting – there is, hopefully, no end to the designs that you can make and the opportunities the craft of hand knitting affords.

Added width should not be placed at any one point such as centre front, unless the neck shaping is also going to be repositioned. Decide on the number of stitches to be removed or added, then divide that number so that they reduce or add to the number of stitches inside the five vertical double lines on fig. 5. This will automatically spread the alteration and will mean adjusting the armhole depth or shaping, the number of stitches on the shoulders and the number of stitches at centre neck.

On sleeves or shaped sides first calculate the number of rows to be subtracted or added. Make a small diagram on squared paper showing the shaping with the number of rows between increases or decreases on the original design. Divide the amount of the alteration so that instead of working a decrease or increase on every 8th row it will be every 7th row if it is to be shortened, every 9th row if it is to be longer. In this way, instead of altering one area only, the finished slope of side or seam will be retained without an alteration in shape (see fig. 6).

Altering sleeve width

Where additional width is required in the sleeve it must be dealt with in two ways.

The sleeve must be drawn out on graph paper so that the original sleeve top is copied for the number of rows required but the shaping must be altered to dispose of the altered number of stitches (see fig. 7).

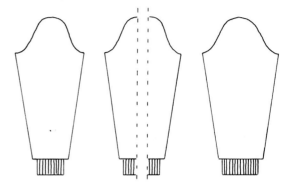

7 Altered sleeve width means a re-arranged shaping

If the sleeve shaping is not altered the sleeve will require an alteration of half of its added width made to both front and back armhole, so that it will again fit properly.

For all alterations, consider, by making a small diagram, if one alteration causes another and which way causes least alteration to all the other sections.

Button strips and borders

Length alterations to garments with fastenings will also need adjusting and should be dealt with in the same way as shaped sides in order to fit the new line.

American knitting terms

Although American knitting terms are easily understood by an experienced knitter used to British instructions, there are certain words and phrases that can cause doubt for a first time reader. Finishing may well include simple crochet stitches so crochet terms, which can be very misleading, have been included.

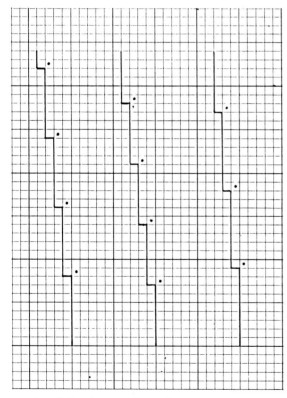

6 Altered distribution of rows between increases

US	UK
afghan	small blanket
argyle	argyll-patterned garment
bind off	cast off
double crochet	treble crochet
double rib	knit 2, purl 2 rib
duplicate stitch	Swiss darning
every other row	every alternate row
gauge	tension
half double crochet	half treble crochet
make 1	increase 1 stitch
pailettes	large sequins
pat	abbreviation for pattern
placket	opening, often at neck or waist, usually with overlapping closure
reverse stockinette stitch	reverse stocking stitch
schematic	diagram, layout
scrap	contrast yarn (to be discarded
seed stitch	moss stitch
shell	loose-fitting sleeveless top
single crochet	double crochet
single rib	knit 1, purl 1 rib
skip	miss, pass over
slip, slip, knit (SSK)	slip next 2 stitches singly and knitwise, to the right needle, insert tip of left needle, into front of both slipped stitches and knit together in this position. (used to replace sl1, K1, psso as much neater)
stitch glossary	stitches used
stockinette stitch	stocking stitch
throw	light, small blanket
tote	bag
vest	waistcoat, also sleeveless top

wrap yarn over (yo)	wind round or over yarn over needle, also used in place of yrn, yfwd when a stitch is made.

Angora

See **Yarns**

Appliqué

Knitted or fabric shapes can be sewn on to the surface of knitted garments to emphasize the stitch pattern or to give a plain surface added interest, decoration and a texture change.

Day wear can have shoulder areas or elbows decorated with toning or contrasting patches of smooth fabric, leather, or knitted tweed. Evening wear can shimmer with simple shapes of soft kid – or metallic yarn knitted shapes.

Choice of material

The material used for appliqué is very important and must not be too heavy for the base fabric. Fabrics like kid, leather, felt and non-fraying dress materials are easiest to handle and can be stitched in place with matching thread or sewn on with contrast embroidery yarn as additional decoration. Dress fabric must be pre-hemmed or the edge securely covered by the method of attaching.

Cleaning

The finished garment must be capable of being cleaned and is best dry-cleaned, unless the added fabric and yarn will not be spoilt by hand washing as in the case of added knitted sections.

8 Appliquéd elbow patches

Motifs

Pre-formed dress motifs can often be purchased from specialist shops or haberdashery departments and bright, machine-embroidered symbols or characters can give an individual touch to the plainest garment. Lace and sequin or bead-decorated motifs can be sewn on to evening wear with as few stitches as will hold them evenly in place to be removed for laundering, and replaced afterwards.

Picture making

Appliqué also offers a unique way of picture building and can be used for sweater decoration, household articles such as cushions, wall hangings or for pictures. Many stitches are fascinating to knit and have interesting textures. They may be difficult to use unless a garment is designed particularly for them but can fit together, appliquéd to a base, forming a pattern of geometric shapes – a stone and tiled house with surrounding trees and flowers, a bead encrusted lizard, or a Christmas scene for a personalized greetings card. A list of suitable stitches and their uses is endless, and you can be quickly stimulated to new ideas by turning the pages of a stitch dictionary.

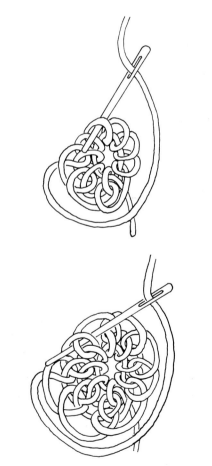

9 Needle-made stitches (*see* **Arabic knitting**)

Arabic knitting

Arabic knitting with twisted stitches that appeared to be worked by knitting into the back of every stitch were once thought to be the earliest form of knitting. Remnants of such fabrics were discovered in Egypt, dated fourth to fifth centuries AD, and showed an understanding of structure and form.

Later research, however, shows that these socks and sandal-type items were constructed by a form of needle weaving akin to a form of netting. Worked with a rough darning needle, the short lengths of yarn were woven in much the same way as Swiss darning is worked, except that they were made without the background fabric to follow.

Starting from a circle of yarn, the first round of stitches is worked through the circle, forming a base for future rounds (see fig. 9 *Top*).

Into the base round other rounds are worked, increasing or decreasing as required to build up as complex a shape as a foot and ankle with separate toes (see fig. 9 *Bottom*).

Aran knitting

Off the west coast of Ireland, in the mouth of Galway Bay, lie the islands of Aran, the home of Aran knitting, so popularized since the middle of the twentieth century. It was from Inishmore, Inishmaan, and Inisheer, the three main islands, that the creamy, undyed wool, knitted into the intricate patterns after being handspun by the island women, first came. It has been written that the fascinating patterns, known now by romantic and symbolic names, are thousands of years old. It is true to say that characters, twining their way round illustrated manuscripts, are clad from head to toe in garments decorated with similar coils and twists but were these garments knitted?

It is not until the twentieth century that there is any photographic evidence of Aran knitting and even in 1907 J.M. Synge writing of the islanders who came to mean so much to him said, 'The men wear three colours; the natural wool, indigo and a grey flannel that is woven of alternate threads of indigo and natural wool. In Inishmore many of the younger men have adopted the usual fisherman's jersey; but I have only seen one in this island.' However, by 1943 Mary Thomas, in her *Book of Knitting Patterns*, published a photograph of intricate cross-over patterns 'traditional of Aran, and worn by the Irish fishermen'.

Fishermen, for over a century had been wearing jerseys, often called frocks, shirts, ganseys or guernseys. These were more often of dyed wool and seldom handspun, but the patterns were similar, of rope and coil, diamond and zigzag. Ideal for contact with water, the wool was water repellent because of its lanolin content and was not harmful to the wearer when it did become wet, drying from the body heat in the same way as a cold compress. Like Shetland and Iceland the islanders, in the first instance spinning their own sheep's wool, used it undyed, *bainin* in their own vocabulary.

Unlike other fishermen's guernseys Aran knitting has always been presented to the knitters of today as being worked in sections, back, front and sleeves; other traditional knitting of this type is worked seamlessly, on sets of needles or on a circular needle.

The Aran islanders, with roots in a Celtic lineage, used stitches and patterns to indicate their links through trade or heritage with the settlers of Bohemia and Austria, where similar patterns have been in use for many centuries and where hand-knitted stockings were known as long ago as the sixteenth and seventeenth centuries.

Tradititionally, the Aran sweater, where back and front are related in pattern but may not be identical, has a wide central pattern, with side panels always carrying cable patterns or rope-like patterns (see fig. 10). The variation of these patterns is endless and is witness to the ingenuity and skill of the knitters who could always find a new way of interpreting the well-known stitches.

Stitches were often given religious names; Trinity stitch for its formation of three-in-one; the Tree of Life and the Ladder of Life; and the Honeycomb pattern and Trellis, said to be a link between God and man. Popularization of Aran knitting, so endlessly complex to the non-knitter, has added to the source of patterns, which today may be likened to lobster-claws or wishbones, Irish moss and knots, sheaves, leaves

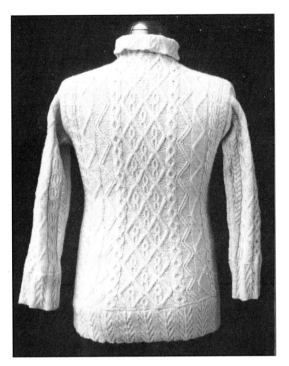

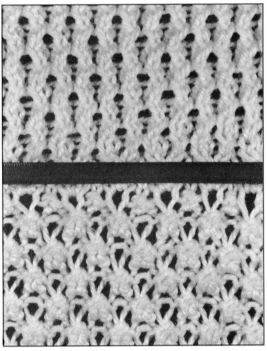

10 Aran sweater back

11 (*Top*) Honeycomb pattern.
(*Bottom*) Trinity stitch

and twigs. One pattern is even supposed to symbolize the small Donegal fields.

Aran patterns

Honeycomb pattern

This is often used as a filler between cables, allowing the same basic design to be knitted in many different sizes, by increasing the number of stitches used between the panels (see fig. 11a). Work on a number of stitches divisible by 4.

1st row (RS facing) * Tw2R, Tw2L, rep from * to end.
2nd and every alt row P.
3rd row * Tw2L, Tw2R, rep from * to end.
4th row As 2nd.
Rep rows 1–4 as required.

Ribbon cable pattern

(illustrated at side of central panel in fig. 10)

This cable, which turns on the surface but never actually twists, is often used along with more rope-like cables to form a panel.

Worked over a number of stitches divisible by 12.

1st row (WS facing) K2, P8, K2.
2nd row P2, K8, P2.
3rd row As 1st row.
4th row P2, sl next 2 sts to CN, hold at back, K2, K2 from CN, sl next 2 sts to CN, hold at front, K2, K2 from CN, P2.
5th row As 1st row.
6th row As 2nd row.
7th row As 1st row.
8th row P2, sl next 2 sts to CN, hold at front, K2, K2 from CN, sl next 2 sts to CN, hold at back, K2, K2 from CN, P2.
Rep rows 1–4 as required.

The Tree of Life pattern
(pattern shown on welt in fig. 10)

This has many uses and can be used to form centre panels or, as in fig. 10, for welt and cuffs. It seems too often in present day garments that this delightful character of early Aran garments, patterned cuffs, welts and collars, is overlooked. Worked over a number of stitches divisible by 13.

1st row (RS facing) * K4, P3, Kb3, P3, rep from * to end.

2nd row * K3, Pb3, K3, P4, rep from * to end.

3rd row * K4, P2, sl next st to CN, hold at back, Kb1, P st from CN, Kb1, sl next st to CN, hold at front, P1, Kb st from CN, P2, rep from * to end.

4th row * K2, [Pb1, K1] twice, Pb1, K2, P4, rep from * to end.

5th row * K4, P1, sl next st to CN, hold at back, Kb1, P st from CN, P1, Kb1, P1, sl next st to CN, hold at front, P1, Kb st from CN, P1, rep from * to end.

6th row * K1, Pb1, [K2, Pb1] twice, K1, P4, rep from * to end.

7th row * K4, sl next st to CN, hold at back, Kb1, P st from CN, P1, Kb3, P1, sl next st to CN, hold at front, P1, Kb st from CN, rep from * to end.

8th row * Pb1, K2, Pb3, K2, Pb1, P4, rep from * to end.

9th row * K4, P2, sl next st to CN, hold at back, Kb1, sl next st to CN, hold at front, P1, Kb st from CN, P2, rep from * to end.

Rep 4th–9th rows as required.

Diamond and bobble pattern

Many Aran patterns make use of travelling stitches, which move position but may not actually cross each other. This design outlines diamonds with three lines of travelling stitches, each worked through the back of the knit stitches to give them an extra twist. Texture is also added by bobbles which could be said to be emphasizing the fact that the lines do not cross (see fig. 12).

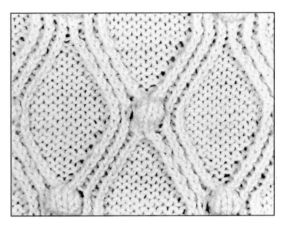

12 Diamond and bobble pattern

Special abbreviations
C2B – sl next st to CN, hold at back, Kb1, P1 from CN

C2F – sl next st to CN, hold at front, P1, Kb1 from CN

MB – * K4, turn, P4, turn, K4, turn, P4, turn. With K side facing, K tog 1st st with 1st st of 1st bobble row 6 rows below, K2, K tog last st with last st of 1st bobble row 6 rows below.

Worked over 42 sts.

1st row Kb1, P5, [Kb1, P1] twice, Kb2, [P1, Kb1] twice, P10, [Kb1, P1] twice, Kb2, [P1, Kb1] twice, P5, Kb1.

2nd row Pb1, K5, [Pb1, K1] twice, Pb2, [K1, Pb1] twice, K10, [Pb1, K1] twice, Pb2, [K1, Pb1] twice, K5, Pb1.

3rd row Kb1, P5, Kb1, P1, Kb1, MB, Kb1, P1, Kb1, P10, Kb1, P1, Kb1, MB, Kb1, P1, Kb1, P5, Kb1.

4th row Pb1, K5, [Pb1, K1] twice, Pb2, [K1, Pb1] twice, K10, [Pb1, K1] twice, Pb2 [K1, Pb1] twice, K5, Pb1.

5th row Kb1, P4, C2B 3 times, C2F 3 times, P8, C2B 3 times, C2F 3 times, P4, Kb1.

6th row Pb1, K4, [Pb1, K1] twice, Pb1, K2, [Pb1, K1] twice, Pb1, K8, [Pb1, K1] twice, Pb1, K2, [Pb1, K1] twice, Pb1, K4, Pb1.

7th row Kb1, P3, C2B 3 times, P2, C2F 3 times, P6, C2B 3 times, P2, C2F 3 times, P3, Kb1.

8th row Pb1, K3, [Pb1, K1] twice, Pb1, K4, [Pb1, K1] twice, Pb1, K6, [Pb1, K1] twice, Pb1, K4, [Pb1, K1] twice, Pb1, K3, Pb1.

9th row Kb1, P2, C2B 3 times, P4, C2F 3 times, P4, C2B 3 times, P4, C2F 3 times, P2, Kb1.

10th row Pb1, K2, [Pb1, K1] twice, Pb1, K6, [Pb1, K1] twice, Pb1, K4, [Pb1, K1] twice, Pb1, K6, [Pb1, K1] twice, Pb1, K2, Pb1.
11th row Kb1, P1, C2B 3 times, P6, C2F 3 times, P2, C2B 3 times, P6, C2F 3 times, P1, Kb1.
12th row [Pb1, K1] 3 times, Pb1, K8, [Pb1, K1] 3 times, [K1, Pb1] 3 times, K8, [Pb1, K1] 3 times, Pb1.
13th row Kb1, * C2B 3 times, P8, C2F 3 times, rep from * once, Kb1.
14th row Pb2, * [K1, Pb1] twice, K10, [Pb1, K1] twice, Pb2, rep from * once.
15th row Kb1, MB, Kb1, P10, Kb1, P1, Kb1, MB, Kb1, P1, Kb1, P10, Kb1, MB, Kb1.
16th row Pb2, * [K1, Pb1] twice, K10, [Pb1, K1] twice, Pb2, rep from * once.
17th row Kb1, * C2F 3 times, P8, C2B 3 times, rep from * once, Kb1.
18th row [Pb1, K1] 3 times, Pb1, K8, [Pb1, K1] twice, Pb1, K2, [Pb1, K1] twice, Pb1, K8, [Pb1, K1] 3 times, Pb1.
19th row Kb1, P1, C2F 3 times, P6, C2B 3 times, P2, C2F 3 times, P6, C2B 3 times, P1, Kb1.
20th row Pb1, K2, [Pb1, K1] twice, Pb1, K6, [Pb1, K1] twice, Pb1, K4, [Pb1, K1] twice, Pb1, K6, [Pb1, K1] twice, Pb1, K2, Pb1.
21st row Kb1, P2, C2F 3 times, P4, C2B 3 times, P4, C2F 3 times, P4, C2B 3 times, P2, Kb1.
22nd row Pb1, K3, [Pb1, K1] twice, Pb1, K4, [Pb1, K1] twice, Pb1, K6, [Pb1, K1] twice, Pb1, K4, [Pb1, K1] twice, Pb1, K3, Pb1.
23rd row Kb1, P3, C2F 3 times, P2, C2B 3 times, P6, C2F 3 times, P2, C2B 3 times, P3, Kb1.
24th row Pb1, K4, [Pb1, K1] twice, Pb1, K2, [Pb1, K1] twice, Pb1, K8, [Pb1, K1] twice, Pb1, K2, [Pb1, K1] twice, Pb1, K4, Pb1.
25th row Kb1, P4, C2F 3 times, C2B 3 times, P8, C2F 3 times, C2B 3 times, P4, Kb1.
Rep rows 2–25 as required.

Trinity stitch (see fig. 11 *Bottom*)

Trinity stitch, so named because three stitches are made from one and three stitches become one, is also known as blackberry stitch and bramble stitch. It is suitable for both thick and fine yarns.
Worked on a number of stitches divisible by 4, plus 2.
1st row (WS facing) K1, * (K1, P, K1) all in next st, yarn to front, P3 tog, yarn back, rep from * to last st, K1.
2nd row P.
3rd row K1, * P3 tog, yarn back, (K1, P1, K1) all into next st, yarn to front, rep from * to last st, K1.
4th row P.
Rep rows 1–4 as required.
Note The larger the needles used the more open the finished pattern will be.

Argyll pattern

The Argyll pattern is very distinctive and was originally used in the handknitting of tartan hose for Scottish military bands and uniform wear (see fig. 13).

13 Argyll-patterned socks

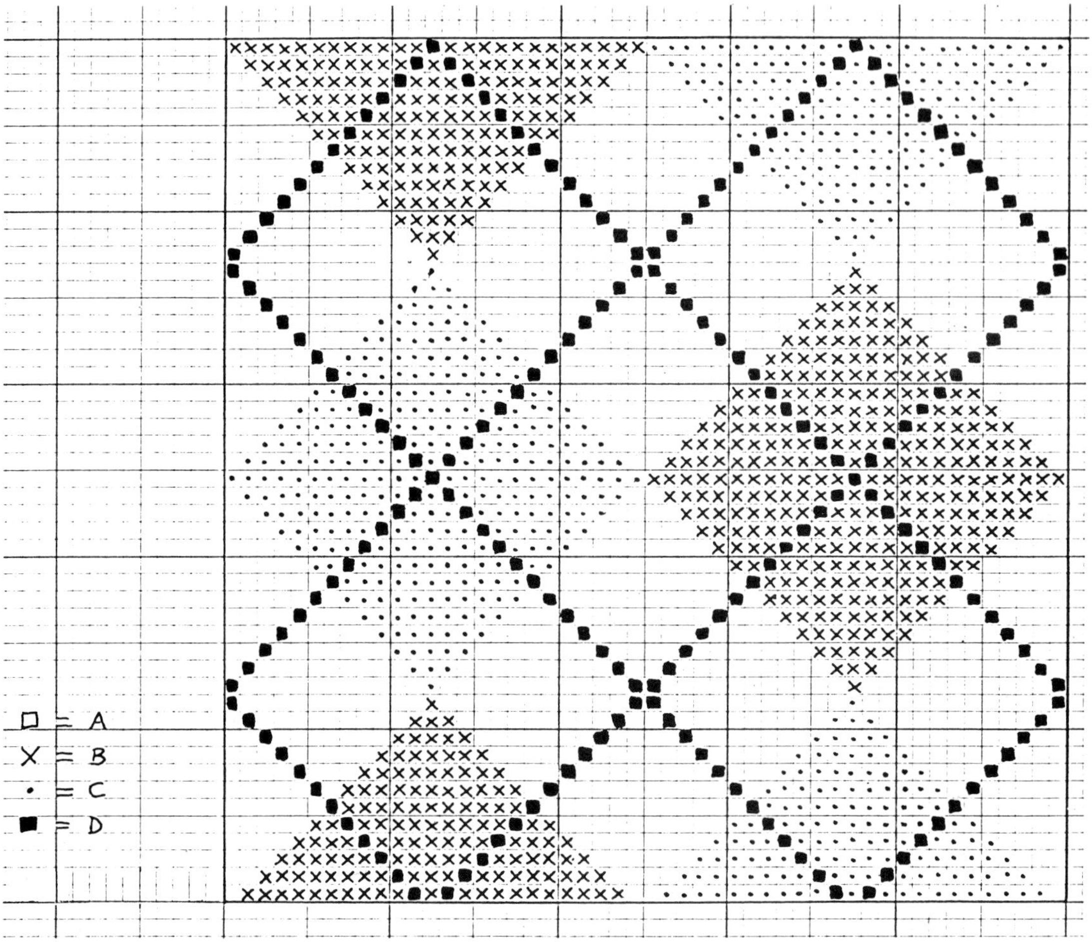

14 Chart for Argyll pattern

The pattern is never worked in less than three colours and can be designed to use more. The secret of knitting it successfully is to use small, separate balls of yarn for each colour area, twisting one yarn over the other at every colour join to avoid holes (*see* **Coloured knitting**). Even the single stitch lines should use a separate thread for each line so that the yarn is not stranded or carried across the back of the work (see fig. 14).

Asterisk

See **Reading instructions**

Austrian knitting

For many centuries the knitters of Austria have produced knitting that is both skilled and highly technical. As in most folk knitting, stockings were one of the earliest items knitted and became very decorative, with beautifully-placed leg shaping and an endless variety of patterns on the tops. Later, other garments became popular, and jerseys and jackets also carried the decorations of intricate cable patterns, travelling stitches and geometric designs (see fig. 15).

Many of these patterns are given an extra clarity by having the stitch used for the pattern worked through the back of the stitch. So lines of twisted knit stitches might well be used to

15 Austrian sock

part of the traditional costume and are mentioned in B. Geramb's *Steirisches Trachtenbuch*, written in the eighteenth century. It is not difficult to find evidence of the growth in popularity of knitting during the eighteenth and nineteenth centuries, and many samplers of stitches remain as proof.

In Austria there are many patterns which are interlaced and twisted, benefiting from the natural form of knitting, which, worked round, allows the right side of the work always to be facing the knitter. In this way, twisted and interlaced patterns are worked only on right side rounds, and the pattern can evolve visually without the need to constantly refer to instructions.

The number of abbreviations for these patterns is reduced, as there is no need for wrong side row stitch movement, which can be more awkward to work, and is an adaptation made for working on two needles.

Austrian stitch patterns

Most of the traditional Austrian patterns are designed to be knitted round, and the instructions below are given in this form. A chart has also been provided to help in the adaption to two-needle knitting. For details of the various twisted or travelling stitches and how they are worked without the help of a cable needle see **Twisted stitches**. For those who prefer a cable needle when moving stitches, the chart shows the direction of the twist.

Round knitting improves the regularity of the fine twisted lines of the stitches because they are always worked in the same direction. All patterns of this type and Aran-type patterns are easier to work. It is also easier to design in round knitting where the right side of the work is facing and the twists and interlacings can be placed as the work grows.

Arrowtail pattern

This pattern is worked over only 6 rounds or rows and can be used as a vertical panel or repeated all round the fabric (see fig. 16a).

outline a shape or to frame a patterned stitch, standing clear and slightly proud of purl background stitches.

By the end of the nineteenth century and in the early part of this century there was a great revival in lace knitting particularly for household items, tablecloths, mats and doilies.

In Austria, as in southern Germany and surrounding areas, men's knitted stockings were

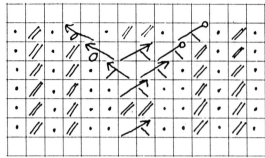

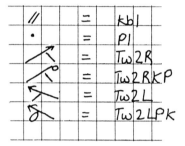

17 Chart for arrowtail pattern

Interlaced diamonds

By Austrian standards, this is a simple pattern and many diamonds and half diamonds use the central interlacing over larger areas (see fig. 16b).

Worked over a number of stitches divisible by 18.

1st round * P1, Kb1, P3, Kb1, P2, Tw2R, P2, Kb1, P3, Kb1, P1, rep from * to end.
2nd round * P1, Kb1, P3, Kb1, P1, Tw2RKP, Tw2LPK, P1, Kb1, P3, Kb1, P1, rep from * to end.
3rd round * P1, Kb1, P3, Kb1, Tw2RKP, P2, Tw2LPK, Kb1, P3, Kb1, P1, rep from * to end.
4th round * P1, Kb1, P3, Tw2R, P4, Tw2L, P3, Kb1, P1, rep from * to end.
5th round * P1, Kb1, [P2, Tw2RKP, Tw2LPK] twice, P2, Kb1, P1, rep from * to end.
6th round * P1, Kb1, P1, [Tw2RKP, P2, Tw2LPK] twice, P1, Kb1, P1, rep from * to end.
7th round * [P1, Kb1] twice, P4, Tw2R, P4, [Kb1, P1] twice, rep from * to end.
8th round * P1, Kb1, P1, [Tw2LPK, P2, Tw2RKP] twice, P1, Kb1, P1, rep from * to end.
9th round * P1, Kb1, P2, [Tw2LPK, Tw2RKP, P2] twice, Kb1, P1, rep from * to end.

16 (*Top*) Arrowtail pattern.
(*Bottom*) Interlaced diamond pattern

Worked over a number of stitches divisible by 13.

1st round * [P1, Kb1] twice, P2, Tw2R, P2, Kb1, P1, Kb1, rep from * to end.
2nd round *[P1, Kb1] twice, P2, Kb2, P2, Kb1, P1, Kb1, rep from * to end.
3rd round As 1st round.
4th round * [P1, Kb1] twice, P1, Tw2R, Tw2L, [P1, Kb1] twice, rep from * to end.
5th round * [P1, Kb1] twice, Tw2RKP,Tw2R, Tw2LPK, Kb1, P1, Kb1, rep from * to end.
6th round * P1, Kb1, P1, twice, Tw2RKP, P1, Kb2, P1, Tw2LPK, P1, Kb1, rep from * to end.
Rep rounds 1–6 as required.

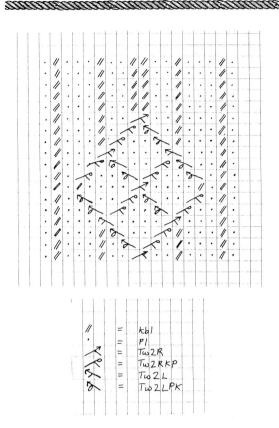

18 Chart for interlaced diamond pattern

10th round P1, Kb1, P3, Tw2L, P4, Tw2R, P3, Kb1, P1.

11th round * P1, Kb1, P3, Kb1, Tw2LPK, P2, Tw2RKP, Kb1, P3, Kb1, P1, rep from * to end.

12th round * P1, Kb1, P3, Kb1, P1, Tw2LPK, Tw2RKP, P1, Kb1, P3, Kb1, P1, rep from * to end.

13th round * P1, Kb1, P3, Kb1, P2, Tw2L, P2, Kb1, P3, Kb1, P1, rep from * to end.

14th round * P1, Kb1, P3, Kb1, P2, Kb2, P2, Kb1, P3, Kb1, P1, rep from * to end.

15th–18th rounds As 14th round.

Rep rounds 1–18 as required.

Panelled serpentine pattern

For a panel or repeating pattern this makes an outstanding design (see fig. 19a).

Worked over 22 stitches per panel or a number of stitches divisible by 22.

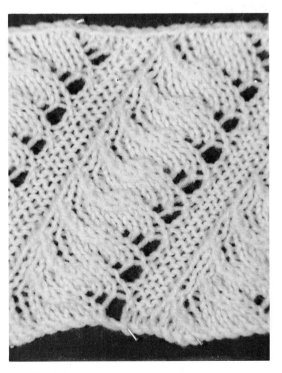

19 (*Top*) Panelled serpentine pattern. (*Bottom*) Lace spiral pattern

1st round * P2, yon, K4, K2 tog, P2, Tw2R, P2, yon, K4, K2 tog, P2, rep from * to end.
2nd–6th rounds As 1st round
7th round * P2, SSK, K4, yon, P2, Tw2R, P2, SSK, K4, yon, P2, rep from * to end.
8th–12th rounds As 7th round.
Rep rounds 1–12 as required.

Lace spiral

This unusual lace spiral makes a beautiful sock top pattern but can be used on fine yarn as an all over pattern or in panels one, two or three patterns deep (see fig. 19b).
Worked over a number of stitches divisible by 13.
1st round * yon, K5, K2 tog tbl, K3, P3, rep from * to end.
2nd round * K1, yon, K5, K2 tog tbl, K2, P3, rep from * to end.
3rd round * K2, yon, K5, K2 tog tbl, K1, P3, rep from * to end.
4th round * K3, yon, K5, K2 tog tbl, P3, rep from * to end.
Rep rounds 1–4 as required.

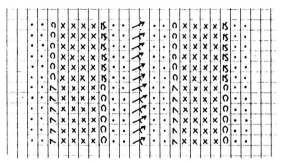

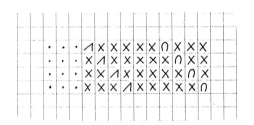

20 Chart for panelled serpentine pattern

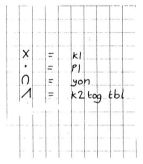

21 Chart for lace spiral pattern

Basic shapes

Understanding shape is important, even if designing is never attempted and printed instructions are always followed. To know before starting what shapes are to be knitted and how they are to be pieced together is helpful and can make adjustments or alterations easier to place.

Using 'exploded' diagrams

However rough, a small diagram 'exploded' or with the sections laid out as if they are about to fit together, gives a reasonably close idea of the finished shape. In designing it is a very useful way of checking that all the necessary decisions have been made; whether the proportion of armhole to body, or neck to shoulder is correct or whether the sleeves have shaped armholes.

Minimum shaping

Rectangles provide the simplest garments, but with the addition of a little shaping can add to the shape interest. A straight-sided sweater

requires no armholes, and you can avoid neck shaping by leaving the centre of the shoulder edge open to form the neck.

In fig. 23 the sleeves could be rectangular, drawn in at the cuff with ribbing. The black line shows a sleeve which increases slightly towards the top, the dashed line shows how this must be altered for a dolman sleeve, and the dotted line increases the sleeve for a batwing design. The diagram shows increases on the sleeve forming a diagonal line from wrist to top that can be altered to give the same total width from above elbow to top, but which can have fewer shapings from cuff to elbow making the sleeve less full in the lower section.

Adding shaping

Armholes can be added in many shapes. The slightly indented but otherwise straight armhole shown in fig. 24 is the first step towards a more tailored shape. The depth of indentation must be echoed in the straight section at the sleeve top, which should then slope gradually to the wrist. The slope may be varied from the line shown,

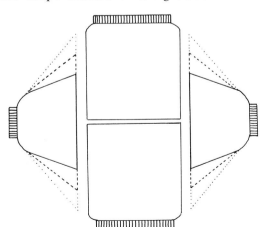

23 Basic shape without armholes

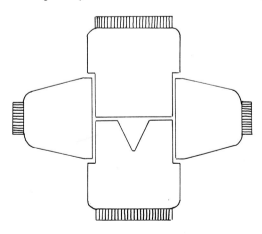

24 Slightly indented armholes

being gradual up to the elbow and increasing more rapidly from that point to the top (see fig. 24).

A more fully-shaped armhole brings with it the need to alter the top of the sleeve which must now have two measurements to give its total length: the length from cuff to start of top shaping and the length from the start of the shaping to the top. The top of the sleeve is called the head and should measure approximately the same as the depth of the armhole (see fig. 25).

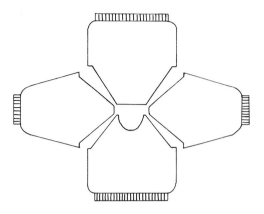

26 Alterations for raglan seams

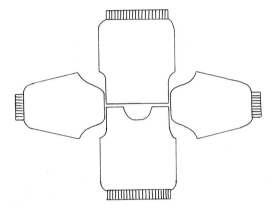

25 Curved armholes and set-in sleeves

The armhole indentation can be calculated from the total width across back or front at the bust or chest line and the required width across the back or front at a straight shoulder line. Subtract one from the other and the result will be the amount that has to be reduced between both armholes. The shaping is usually worked within the first 5–7cms and the top of the armhole is straight to the shoulder.

Raglan shaping

Raglan shaping forms the armhole into a sloping line and is matched with a similar sloping line on the sleeve head. Fashion may determine the width at the top of the raglan shapes.

In fig. 26 the raglan seams on the sleeves decrease to only a few stitches, sufficient only for the seam on either side to be made neatly.

The slope may be altered so that the sleeve top is wider. This, in turn, makes the neck wider; the top when worn will thus sit lower on the

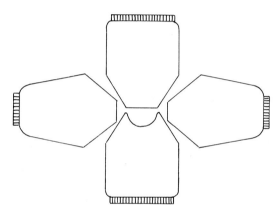

27 Altenative raglan version

shoulders; illustrating that change made to one part of a design must be compensated for in another section (see fig. 27).

Outlines

The outline of any basic shape shows the relation between sections. Figure 28 shows an outline which can be achieved in many different ways.

As the black lines show, it can be knitted from the base up to the shoulder line (dotted). Back and front can both be worked in this way. Alternatively, the back or front can be carried across the shoulder, after you have worked the neck, and be knitted downwards to the other lower edge.

Another way is to cast on at one sleeve edge and work across to the other sleeve edge, working back and front sections separately only

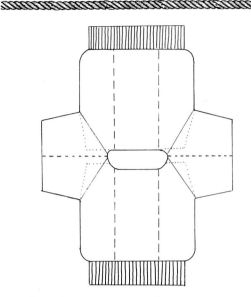

28 A basic shape can be altered in many ways

Ultimate shape

A basic shape may, therefore, be divided and subdivided many times. There is also no sense in making sections just for the sake of dividing up a diagram.

Using a stitch which must be knitted in one direction only for best results may add to the number of seams but it may be worth while for the effect gained. Figure 29 shows how a basic outline was cut to add a complex but very effective neckline.

The rule to remember is that, whatever is done to one section must be reflected by the other shapes. Form a central panel that does not take in the side sections and they may well become part of the sleeves, as shown by the coloured dashed lines in fig. 28.

Skirts

Skirt shapes can be dealt with in exactly the same way. A rectangle with ribbed top edge can become a skirt and requires only two measurements for success: the width at the hips and the finished length (see fig. 30a). The other extreme in skirts is a circular skirt with the centre

until the neck shaping is complete. This cuff to cuff, or sideways knitted style can be split into two sections from sleeve to sleeve, a front and a back, with seams from wrist to shoulder as well as underarm seams.

The solid coloured lines show how this basic shape can be divided further to make a raglan top. The dotted coloured line shows how a saddle-topped sleeve might be cut into the shape.

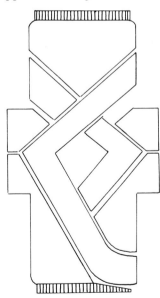

29 A garment divided in unusual ways for specific design

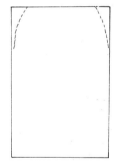

30a Rectangular skirt showing changes for shaping

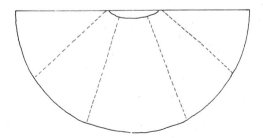

30b Circular skirt showing altered lines for panels or gores

wide enough for the waist edge and the length determining the width of the circle at the hem edge (see fig. 30b). The dotted coloured lines on both basic skirts show how the rectangle can be given side shape and the circular skirt can be reduced to a gored pattern. On this the gores can be worked separately and seamed, or the increases or decreases (depending on whether it is worked upwards or downwards), can be placed along the gore lines; the work, however, can still be made with only side seams or with no seams at all.

Collars

Collars can be planned in much the same way. The neck edge provides the necessary measurement but depth may be no more than a neckband, or the collar may be large, widening to the outer edge and intended to be folded once or more.

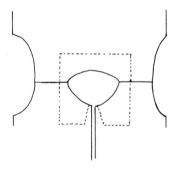

31a Collar planned over back and front shapes

A sailor collar may require to begin at either side of a centre front opening and extend over the shoulders to the back. It has to lie over the knitted garments and so can be shaped over the front and back sections placed together (see fig. 31a).

A shawl collar will also take its neck edge measurement from the back and fronts of the jacket it is to be stitched to, but may have

31b Shawl collar showing curved edge worked with short rows

additional depth added by your working it in short rows over the centre back area, keeping the fronts less wide. This cannot adequately be shown on the same diagram but can be added as a small extra detail; place the collar on a straight line and show the curve of the added short row depth by the dotted line below the original neck edge measurement line (see fig. 31b).

Basic stitches

Knitting may look complex but it is not so, and once casting on and off are learnt there are only the two ways of working stitches to learn. Other techniques are all used in pattern and texture making, but there are only two ways in which to work all stitches – to knit or to purl.

To knit

Cast on several stitches by either of the first two casting-on methods.

Place the needle with the stitches in the left hand and wind the yarn to the ball round the right hand fingers as given for thumb casting on.

Insert the right needle tip through the 1st stitch on the left needle from front to back and with the right forefinger bring the yarn round under the right needle tip (see fig. 32a).

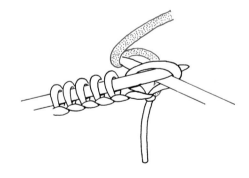

32a Bring yarn under tip of right needle

Use the right needle to draw the yarn through the cast-on stitch so that it forms a loop round the right needle tip (see fig. 32b).

Withdraw the left needle. This completes

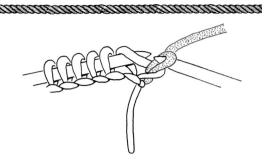

32b Draw through new loop

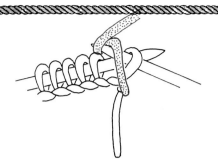

33a Put yarn over and round needle tip

knitting one stitch which should be on the right needle.

Continue knitting each cast-on stitch in the same way until all the stitches have been knitted and are on the right needle (see fig. 32c).

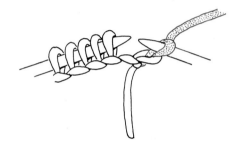

32c One knitted stitch on right needle

To work the next row place the needle with the stitches in the left hand with the yarn close to the tip. Wind the yarn over the right hand fingers as before and work each stitch in the same way until all the stitches have been knitted, thus completing two rows.

To purl

Cast on several stitches.

Place the needle with the stitches in the left hand and wind the yarn to the ball round the right hand fingers as you do for thumb casting on.

Insert the right needle tip through the 1st loop on the left hand needle from back to front and bring the yarn over, round behind and under the right needle tip (see fig. 33a).

Use the right needle tip to draw the yarn through the cast-on stitch so that it forms a loop round the right needle (see fig. 33b).

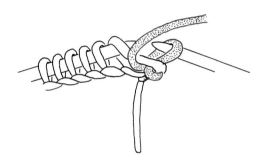

33b Use right needle to draw through new stitch

Withdraw the left needle. This completes purling one stich, which should be on the right needle. Continue purling each stitch in the same way until all the cast-on stitches are purled and are on the right needle (see 33c).

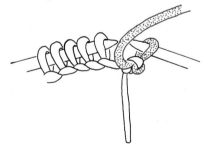

33c One purl stitch on right needle

To work the next row place the needle with the stitches in the left hand with the yarn close to the tip. Wind the yarn round the right fingers as before and work each stitch in the same way to complete the 2nd row.

Garter stitch

A piece of knitting which has had every row knitted is said to be worked in garter stitch. It has one row forming a smooth line on the side facing and a row of raised bars on the other side. The next row will repeat this but, because the work has been turned, gives the effect of alternately ridged rows and smooth rows. A piece of knitting worked with every row purled will give the same effect – alternate ridges of smooth and ridged lines – and is also called garter stitch (see fig. 34).

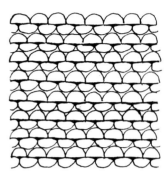

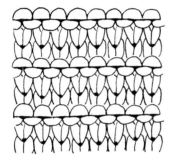

34 Garter stitch

Stocking stitch and reverse stocking stitch

When knit rows and purl rows are alternated a different appearance is obtained. A smooth fabric will show on the side that is knitted and a ridged surface will show on the purl side. When all the smooth stitches are placed on one side and it is used as the right side of the work, it is called stocking stitch (see fig. 35a). Alternatively, the

ridged side may be used as the right side and is then called reverse stocking stitch (see fig. 35b).

Moss stitch and single rib

Garter stitch lies flat because the ridges and smooth stitches are equal in number each side of the fabric. When equal numbers of ridges and smooth stitches are placed differently they will also form fabrics which do not curl as both stocking stitch and reverse stocking stitch do. Arranged alternately they give a fabric called moss stitch (see fig. 36a). Moss stitch is a very

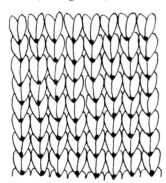

35 (*Above*) Stocking stitch.
(*Top right*) Reverse stocking stitch

36 (*Top*) Moss stitch.
(*Bottom*) Single or knit one, purl one rib

valuable stitch and has many other names. In America it is known as rice stitch or grain stitch but in Scotland it becomes cat's teeth, in the Yorkshire Dales hit and miss, on the Yorkshire coast bird's e'en and in Norfolk, hailstones.

Moss stitch worked over an even number of sts is worked thus:

1st row * K1, P1, rep from * to end.
2nd row * P1, K1, rep from * to end.
Rep these 2 rows as required.

Moss stitch worked over an odd number of stitches alters to this:

1st row K1, * P1, K1, rep from * to end.
Rep this row as required.

Stitches can be alternated in another way than in moss stitch. The knit stitches can be arranged so that they come above each other, and the purl stitches also can be in vertical lines. This fabric too will lie flat because it has an equal number of smooth stitches and ridges on both sides, but it changes slightly in width and is narrower than the same number of moss stitches would be. This makes for a very elastic fabric which is why ribbing, as vertical lines of stitches are called, is used at the base of sweaters and at cuff edges.

Single ribbing on an even number of stitches is worked as follows:

1st row * K1, P1, rep from * to end.
Rep this row as required (see fig. 36b).
On an odd number of stitches it becomes:

1st row K1, * P1, K1, rep from * to end.
2nd row P1, * K1, P1, rep from * to end.
Rep these 2 rows for length required.

Double moss stitch

Variation of basic stitches always includes repeating some rows more often than in the original. Thus moss stitch varied becomes a

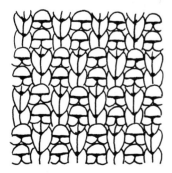

37 Double moss stitch

small 4-row pattern in place of a 2-row pattern. This stitch is also sometimes known as Irish moss stitch and in America as the true moss stitch (see fig. 37).

Worked over a number of stitches divisible by 2.

1st row * K1, P1, rep from * to end.
2nd row As 1st row.
3rd row * P1, K1, rep from * to end.
1st row As 3rd row.
Rep rows 1–4 as required.

Check stitch

Doubled again in width this time instead of in height, double moss stitch becomes a small checked or diced pattern (see fig. 38).

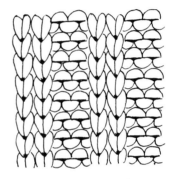

38 Check Stitch

Worked over a number of stitches divisible by 4.

1st row * K2, P2, rep from * to end.
2nd row As 1st row.
3rd row * P2, K2, rep from * to end.
4th row As 3rd row.
Rep 1-4 rows as required.

The arrangement of smooth stitches and ridged stitches is what all textured patterns are based on. More examples are to be found in the other stitch pattern groups. Knit and purl stitch patterns use no other techniques but knit and purl stitches.

Double rib

Stitch patterns can be doubled in width as well as in height. Arranged vertically like 1 and 1 rib but with two knit stitches beside two purl stitches, the rib is called K2, P2 rib or double ribbing (see

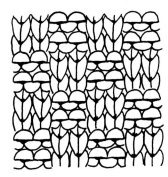

39 Double or knit two, purl two rib

fig. 39). Over a number of stitches divisible by 4, plus 2.
1st row K2 * P2, K2, rep from * to end.
2nd row P2 * K2, P2, rep from * to end.
Rep these 2 rows as required.

Working stitches through back of loop

Both basic knit and purl stitches can be given an additional twist by being worked through the back, instead of through the front, of the loop. Used for stocking stitch, with all knit and purl stitches twisted or crossed in this way, the fabric is similar in appearance to textiles made in the East, possibly 16 centuries ago. At one time all rows would be worked with twisted stitches because knitting was worked in the round, making every row a right side row.

The twisted purled row, worked on flat knitting, makes working every row much more difficult and today it is usually used on right side rows only or, if on both rows, then only on specific stitches as in Austrian knitting.

To twist knit stitches

Insert the right needle tip through the stitch from right to left but through the back loop. Pass the yarn under and in front of the needle tip (see fig. 40a). Use the right needle tip to draw through a new loop on to the right needle (see fig. 40b).

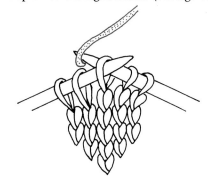

40a Insert needle through back of loop

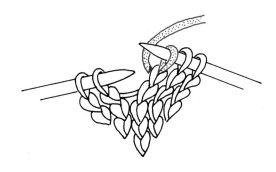

40b Draw through new stitch

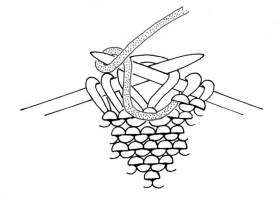

41 Insert needle through back of stitch

To twist a purl stitch

Insert the right needle tip through the stitch from left to right but through the back loop. Pass the yarn over and round the tip of the needle back to the front (see fig. 41).

Use the right needle tip to draw a new loop through on the right needle (see fig. 42).

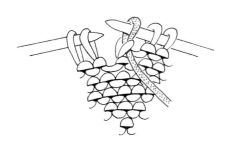

42   Draw through new stitch

Twisted or continental stocking stitch

Stocking stitch can look uneven if the tension of knit rows differs from purl rows. This can be altered by using needles differing in size or by substituting twisted or continental stocking stitch (see fig. 43).

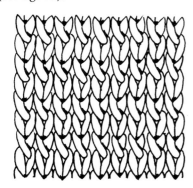

43   Continental stocking stitch

Worked over any number of stitches.
1st row (RS facing) K each st through back of loop.
2nd row P in usual way.
Rep these rows as required.

True twisted stocking stitch, seldom used, is worked by twisting every stitch on every row.

Twisted rib

Twisted rib is often used along with other patterns and is worked so that the knitted stitches are emphasized, seeming to stand out more than an ordinary rib. The stitches are worked so that the knit stitches are twisted on every row (see fig. 44).

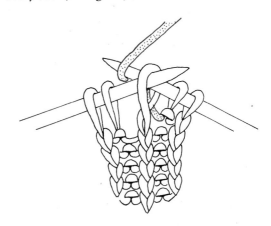

44   Twisted rib

Worked over an odd number of stitches.
1st row (RS facing) Kb1, * P1, Kb1, rep from * to end.
2nd row Pb1, * K1, Pb1, rep from * to end.
Rep these 2 rows as required.

Beaded knitting

Bead-trimmed knitting is nearly always in fashion, particularly for evening wear. In the eighteenth century beads were used, not just for single motifs, but for areas such as collars and cuffs, or shimmering glass was lightly scattered across the entire garment. The actual fabric of knitting was completely covered with the beads which were used to form flowers, geometric designs, small pictures and even romantic scenes (see fig. 45).

Where beads are used as closely as this they must be exceedingly carefully threaded as one colour out of place would spoil the shading of the whole design. First the design must be charted, then the beads laid on a tray in the exact

45   Beaded bonnet

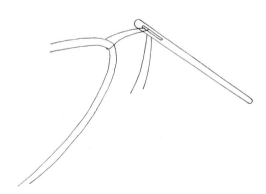

46   Place yarn into looped cotton

order in which they are to be knitted. Starting with the bead in the left hand top corner, the last bead that will be knitted in, they must each be threaded on to the yarn retaining the order.

To thread beads

Beads are much too small to be threaded directly on to knitting yarn, however fine. Instead the yarn is looped through a fine cotton thread doubled through the eye of a fine sewing needle that will pass through the bead (see fig. 46).

The bead will pass over the needle and will allow the double cotton loop holding the start of the knitting yarn to be drawn through the bead (see fig. 47).

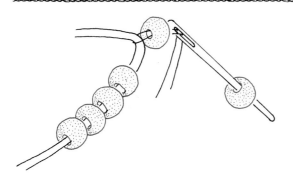

47 Threading beads

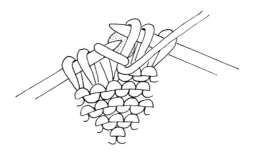

48b Put bead through stitch and have left needle ready to be withdrawn

Bead knitting

The eighteenth century method of placing beads so closely that the background yarn does not show through meant that beads were knitted into the actual stitches on both right and wrong side rows, using stocking stitch with both knit and purled rows worked through the back of the loop. This twist helps to keep the beads in place. The knit row bead is helped through the hole of the stitch before the left needle is withdrawn moving the bead from the yarn through the stitch to the front. On the purl row the bead is moved up to the stitch opened with both needles and is helped through the stitch to the right side (see fig. 48).

Beaded knitting

When the beads decorate only the surface but do not cover it, as in the old bead knitting, different methods of placing the bead can be used.

Between stitches

The most usual way of placing beads is to place them on the right side during the working of the wrong side row. The yarn can be either purled or knitted for a stocking stitch or garter stitch fabric. Beads should not be placed more closely together than on alternate stitches and rows. Fig. 49 shows rather open stitches, but the actual fabric needs to be sufficiently close to keep the beads from slipping through on to the wrong side of the fabric.

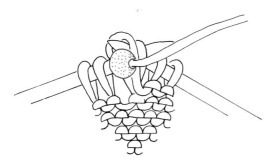

48a Bring bead up to stitch on wrong side

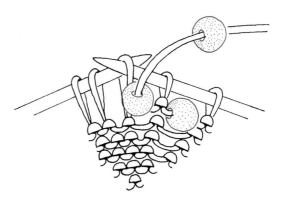

49 Leave bead between stitches

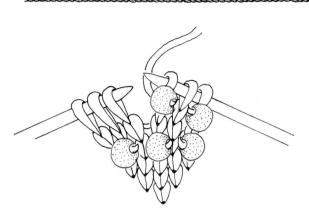

50 Place bead in front of slipped stitch

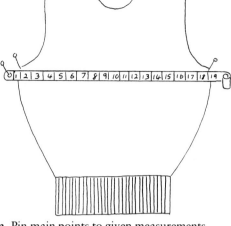

51a Pin main points to given measurements

Slipped stitches and bead placing

Beads can also be left on the right side in front of a stitch that has been slipped (see fig. 50).

Decorative clusters

Both of these methods can be used to create groups of more than one bead, provided the beads are kept to the smallest size.

Placed between stitches, imitate the Victorian knitters and push three or four small beads together between stitches so that they sit above the surrounding stitches. Alternatively, strand the yarn in front of three or more stitches so that the yarn left on the right side can hold several beads in a swag (a line or bar). Both methods are only suitable for small beads that do not weigh heavily or drag the stitches at their sides.

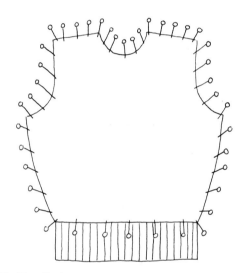

51b Pin all edges

Blocking and pressing

Blocking and pressing is an important stage of finishing a garment, provided the yarn is suitable. Check the ball band and the instructions before starting to block or press to see if either carries a warning against pressing.

Blocking

For all wool garments or yarns with high wool content blocking is particularly necessary as it evens out the lines of stitches and the fibres of the yarn itself.

Pin out each section of knitting, wrong side up. This is easiest to do if worked on a padded ironing board or table. Under a covering sheet place a flannel pad or folded blanket, something firm yet soft enough for pins to be stuck into firmly. Draw the garment or garment section out to the correct measurements and hold in place at the corners with pins placed through the knitted edge and directly into the pad (see fig. 51a).

Before pinning finally check that the vertical lines are vertical and the horizontal lines are horizontal. Place pins around all the edges not more than 5cm (2in.) apart. The sections are now ready for pressing (see fig. 51b).

Blocking for non-iron yarns

Where knitted sections of man-made fibre yarns, or yarns marked as unsuitable for pressing, seem to require drawing into position, blocking can be carried out without having to be followed up with pressing. Dampen the sections by rolling in a wet towel. Leave for a short time so that the moisture can soak into the yarn.

Pin out as for blocking the section that is to be pressed but with the right side up. Leave in the pinned position until the sections are completely dry, then unpin and continue to make up.

Pressing

Pressing is a misnamed procedure for knitting as the weight of the iron should never touch the knitted sections. It should be termed steaming, because it is the steam caused by holding a hot iron immediately over a wet cloth that straightens the yarn fibres. Pressing, with weight on the iron, only flattens the stitches, spoiling the roundness and softness of the yarn.

Wring out a clean cloth in warm water and lay over the knitted sections. Hold the iron immediately above the cloth so that the heat will make the cloth steam. Move the iron from section to section by lifting it directly up. Do not push the iron along as in ordinary ironing or the stitches will be pushed out of position. Continue until the complete section has been covered. Allow to dry before unpinning and completing making up (see fig. 52).

Steaming

When work has become over-pressed and flattened by the iron, particularly garter stitch and ribbing which need no pressing, it can be unflattened by steaming.

Place a very wet cloth over the section to be raised and hold the iron over the cloth, allowing the steam to work on the yarn.

Alternatively hang the garment where the steam from a kettle can circulate round it. Take care that the jet of steam does not damage the garment or yourself.

Re-pressing

After seams have been made up they need to be pressed again.

Place a wet cloth over the seam and, using only the iron tip, hold the iron against the cloth until it is dry. If at all possible this should be worked from the wrong side.

Bobbins

Bobbins are the answer to tangle-free yarns when you are working with more than one

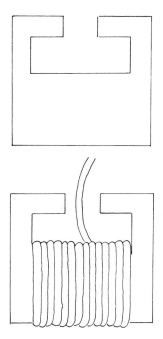

52 Hold iron over wet cloth

53 Card bobbins unwound and wound

colour. A card bobbin will hold several yards of yarn and will hang close against the work without unwinding. The size of the bobbin will depend on the quantity of yarn to be wound on and the thickness of the yarn in use. Quite large bobbins will still prevent tangling as they are lighter than a ball of yarn and tend to hang with the yarn in one of the angles, rather than unwinding before they are in use (see fig. 53).

Bobbles

Bobbles are made in several ways and can vary considerably in size. Some of the smaller bobble patterns are, in fact, popcorn patterns. The difference between popcorns and the bobbles is found in the method of working.

Bobbles are raised knots, made out of one stitch and returning to a single stitch, but are usually worked for several rows before they are completed. They are not worked at the same time as the rest of the row. Each bobble is worked individually as it is reached, and several rows are worked on the bobble stitches only until the width of the bobble is drawn in and the bobble is complete (see fig. 54a).

A popcorn is usually made out of one stitch and is drawn together into one stitch again on the following row. Sometimes, however, popcorns are worked with one row between the row they are made on and the row on which they are completed (see fig. 54b). *See* **Knot stitch patterns** for working instructions.

Bobbles are large or small, and usually worked with the right side as stocking stitch, if the background is reverse stocking stitch, or in reverse stocking stitch, if the bobbles are placed on a stocking stitch area. The number of rows worked on the actual bobble stitches between increase and decrease may vary, but are usually 4. The method of increasing and decreasing may vary and can affect the way in which the bobble lies against its background as well as the roundness of the finished bobble. Instructions usually give details of how the bobble is worked.

54 (*Top*) Boxed bobble pattern. (*Bottom*) Puff stitch, a popcorn pattern

Making a popcorn

Work in stocking stitch to the popcorn position, then knit into front, back and front of next stitch (see fig. 55a).

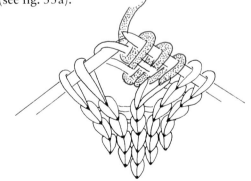

55a Knit into front, back and front of stitch

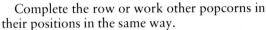

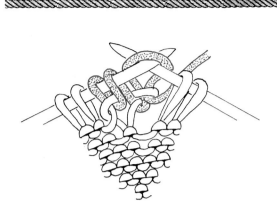

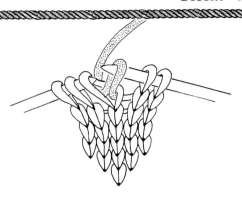

59a Knit one into bobble stitch

55b On next row slip one, knit one and psso

Complete the row or work other popcorns in their positions in the same way.

On the next row purl to the popcorn (the 3 made stitches) and slip the 1st; knit together the remaining 2 stitches and pass the 1st stitch over the 2 knitted together and off the needle (see fig. 55b).

This decrease might, alternatively, have been worked by purling all 3 stitches together (see fig. 56).

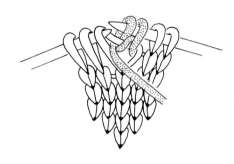

59b Purl one into same stitch

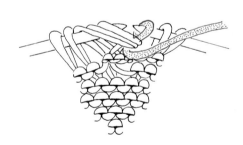

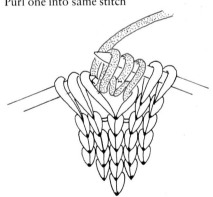

56 Purl three together

Making a small bobble

This small bobble is worked in reverse stocking stitch against a stocking stitch background.

Knit to the bobble position. Into the next stitch work K1, P1, K1 (see fig. 57).

Turn and knit each of the 3 bobble stitches.
Turn, P3, turn, K3, turn (see fig. 58a).
Turn, lift 2nd st over 1st, then last st over

59c Knit into same stitch again

remaining st (see fig. 58b) and off the needle to complete the bobble.

Work to the next bobble and work it in the same way or knit to the end of the row.

Two other increases may be used to make the bobble: it may be worked by knitting into the front, (see fig. 59a) then the back (see fig. 59b) and then the front of the next stitch (see fig. 59c),

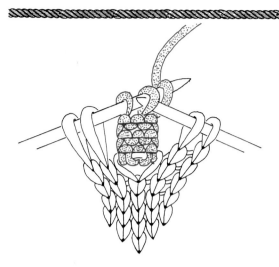

58a Knit one row, purl one row, knit one row

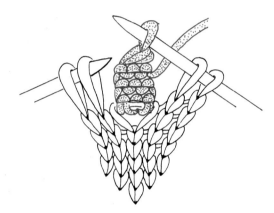

58b Knit three together

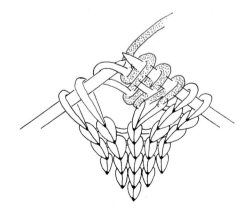

57 Knit into front, back and front of bobble stitch

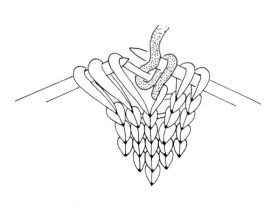

60a Knit one, yarn over needle

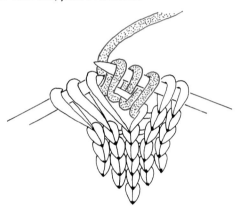

60b Knit same stitch again

or it may be worked by knitting the 1st stitch, putting the yarn over the needle to make another stitch and knitting into the same stitch again, so forming 3 stitches (see fig. 60).

The width is determined by the number of stitches increased and, of course, by the thickness of the yarn.

Making a large bobble

A large bobble usually has 5 stitches made out of one stitch or even more. The increases are worked in any of the ways already given. Where very large bobbles are required, the last method of increasing is less bulky and it is easy to work K1, yon, K1, yon, K1, or even more repeats, into any one stitch. The decrease of so many stitches may be given as slip 2 stitches, knit or purl 3 stitches together, then lift both slipped stitches over the other and off the needle tip. The alternative for a bulky knot is to lift each stitch over the last singly, but this does tend to turn the bobble sideways. If this method is to be used, the last row must be worked before the stitches are lifted so that the yarn is at the left edge of the bobble, ready to work to the next bobble or the end of the row.

Another way of making a very firm bobble can be found in **Aran patterns** on the diamond and bobble panel pattern.

Brioche knitting

Brioche patterns are particularly pliable because of their construction, which includes a floating thread caught in with every stitch or every alternate stitch. This strand is made by being worked as a yon or strand which is carried over the top of the needle but not worked. On the following row it becomes part of a worked stitch.

To work brioche stitch

Use a needle 2 sizes larger than would be normal for the type of yarn. Cast on an even number of stitches.
Preparation row (WS facing) * Yarn over needle, sl1 purlwise, K1, rep from * to end.

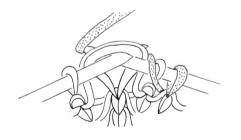

61a Yarn over needle, slip one purlwise and knit together with next stitch

1st pattern row * Yarn over needle, sl1 purlwise, K2 tog, rep from * to end (see fig. 61a).
Rep 1st row to form pattern (see fig. 61b).

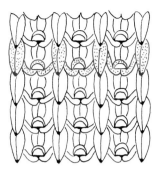

61b Brioche stitch

Casting off on the pattern can be difficult so work 1 knit row then cast off normally.

Brioche stitch looks very similar to continental or fisherman's rib although the actual working method is different. In that case you form the floating stitch by knitting a stitch on the row below and allowing the upper stitch to unravel to form the loop (*see* **Knitting below stitches**).

Brioche stitch patterns

Their light, almost fluffy stitches, make brioche patterns fun to work and delightful to wear. The degree of laciness will depend on the size of needles used.

Syncopated brioche stitch

This pattern is the same on both sides and so has many uses. Although perfectly suitable for use as a solid fabric, it is even better when worked on larger needles than usual (see 62a).
Worked over a number of stitches divisible by 2.
Preparation row (WS facing) * Yon, sl1 with yarn back, K1, rep from * to end.
1st row * Yon, sl1 purlwise, K2 tog, rep from * to end.
2nd, 3rd, 4th, 5th, 6th and 7th rows As 1st row.
8th row Yarn to front, * sl1 purlwise with yarn forward, yon, P2 tog, rep from * to end.
9th, 10th, 11th, 12th, 13th and 14th rows As 8th row.
Rep rows 1–14 as required.

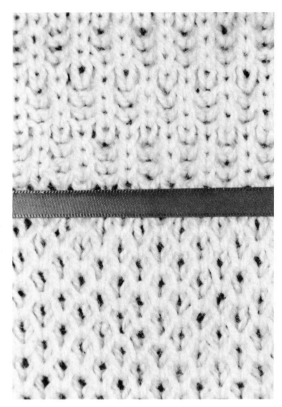

62 (*Top*) Syncopated brioche stitch.
(*Bottom*) Double English brioche pattern

Double English brioche pattern

This version gives the fabric the appearance of double honeycomb.
Worked over a number of stitches divisible by 2 (see fig. 62b).
Preparation row K.
1st row (RS facing) * K1, insert needle into the stitch below the next stitch and knit letting the original stitch drop off the left needle, rep from * to end.
2nd row * K tog next stitch with the dropped thread of the previous row, K1, rep from * to end.
3rd row * insert needle into the stitch below the next stitch and knit letting the original stitch drop off the needle, K1, rep from * to end.
4th row * K1, K tog next stitch with the dropped thread of the previous row, from * to end.

Buttonholes

Buttonholes must be selected to suit the garment. Tiny buttonholes will not hold a thick chunky jacket closed, and large buttons on babies' wear look equally out of place.

Single decrease and increase buttonhole

The smallest buttonhole is made by working one increase followed by a decrease so that the number of stitches remains the same (see figs 219 and 220).
Work to the position for the buttonhole.
Put the yarn over the needle to make an extra strand between the last stitch and the following, then knit the next 2 stitches together.
On the following row work across all the stitches and the made strand, treating it as any other stitch.
The made stitch leaves a hole big enough for a small buttonhole.

Double decrease and increase buttonhole

The next size of buttonhole is made in a similar way but places a decrease at either side of the opening and keeps the number of stitches constant by working 2 increases between them (see figs 222 a b).
Work to 2 stitches before the buttonhole position.
Knit together the next 2 stitches, put the yarn round the needle twice then slip 1 stitch knitwise, knit the next stitch and pass the slipped stitch over the knitted stitch and work to the end of the row.
On the next row work to the strand over the needle, purl and knit into the strand over the needle and then complete the row.
The double increase leaves a hole between the 2 decreases.

Two row buttonhole

The two row buttonhole can be adapted to the required size by your altering the number of stitches cast on and off. You will find instructions for this in your printed pattern. The method can be untidy, however, if you cast on stitches incorrectly. Whenever possible use the one-row buttonhole, instead, which, although much neater, seldom appears in instructions.

To work the two row buttonhole
Work to the position where the buttonhole is required.

Cast off the required number of stitches then complete the row (see fig. 63a)

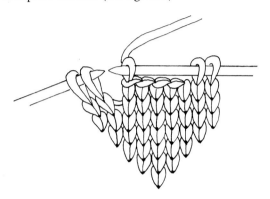

63a Cast off on right side

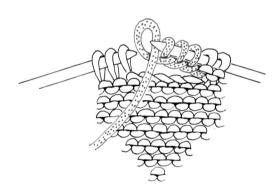

63b Cast on on wrong side

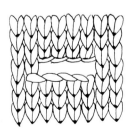

63c Completed two row buttonhole

On the next row, work to cast off stitches, form 1 loop for each stitch to be cast on (see fig. 63b). Draw the yarn firmly between last cast on stitch and 1st stitch to left of the cast on stitches and work to the end of the row (see fig. 63c).

One row buttonhole

This is worked with the right side facing.

Work to the buttonhole position, and leave the end of the yarn hanging at the right side of the buttonhole.

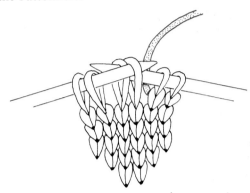

64 Cast off without yarn

Cast off the required number of stitches without knitting them first (see fig. 64). To do this slip 2 stitches on to right needle tip. Lift 1st stitch over 2nd and off right needle tip. Repeat this until the required number of stitches has been cast off (see fig. 65a).

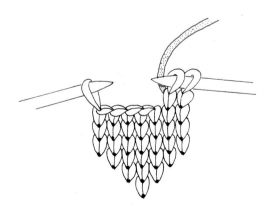

65a Completed cast-off edge

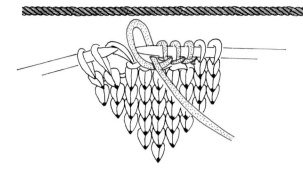

65b Cast on loops

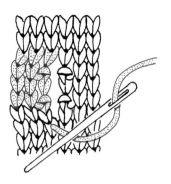

66b Work across both sides

Cast on the required number of stitches by forming loops on the yarn, left hanging at the right edge of the cast off stitches (see fig. 65b).

Complete the row by drawing the yarn firmly between the last cast-on stitch and the 1st stitch to the left, then complete the row.

Vertical buttonholes

Vertical buttonholes have to be worked in two stages but can be worth the extra time taken.

Work to the buttonhole position and leave the stitches to the left of this point on a spare needle.

Work the required number of rows on the stitches to the right for the length of the hole ending with the yarn at the opening edge. Do not break off the yarn. Slip the other stitches back on to the left needle, rejoin a new length of yarn and work this side until the same length as the first side, ending with yarn at the opening edge (see fig. 66a).

Use the yarn left at the right section opening edge to complete the row (see fig. 66b).

Double buttonholes

Where buttonholes are placed on a double band they can be worked as for the two or one row buttonhole and joined during making up when they can be strengthed with both edges touching.

They can also be worked as for a held opening, *see* **Openings**. When making up of seams is complete, withdraw the holding yarns and graft both edges of each buttonhole, (*see* **Grafting**, or join the loops by oversewing and strengthen.

Strengthening buttonholes

All buttonholes, small or large, should be strengthened during making up. Use a thinner matching yarn to the garment yarn or buttonhole twist.

Work buttonhole stitch along straight edges (see fig. 67a). Corners or small round buttonholes are best worked with straight

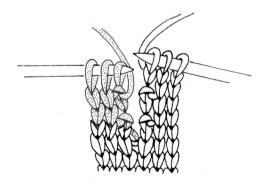

66a Work right side then left side

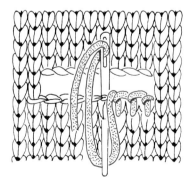

67a Buttonhole stitch along straight edges

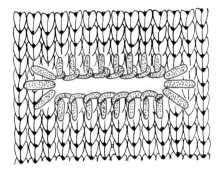

67b Work round corners with straight stitches

stitches. For neatness, work by the horizontal and vertical lines of the knitting (see fig. 67b).

Facing buttonholes

One method of strengthening buttonholes and front edges is to line the edge with a firm ribbon or petersham.

Pin the ribbon in place on the wrong side. Tack so that there is no chance of its slipping and to check that it is the correct length. Hem or oversew the ribbon edge to the garment and buttonhole stitch round the buttonholes (see fig. 68).

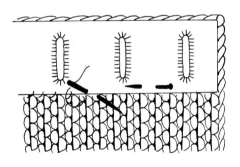

68 Ribbon facing for buttonhole strengthening

Buttons

All but the smallest buttons on babies' wear or very fine yarn should be sewn on so that they have room to lie evenly on top of the knitted thickness when they are in place through the buttonhole. One method of holding them above the wool surface as they are sewn on is to place a match stick or knitting needle at either side beneath the button. This holds the buttons in place as the first few stitches are made. To complete, remove the match sticks once the centre threads are in place and wind the yarn several times round this shank before finishing off (see fig. 69).

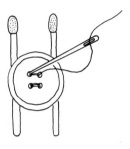

69a Hold button over matchstitcks

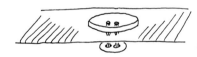

69b Sew directly through button holes to disc holes

Strengthening buttons

All buttons are better sewn on through other small flat buttons or through plastic discs that can be purchased in haberdashery departments.

Hold the flat button or disc on the wrong side immediately under the button on the right side and sew through both rather than just into the knitting. This avoids the drag against the button being taken by the soft fabric as it pulls against the disc instead.

Covered buttons

Button moulds or discarded buttons can be covered with tiny scraps of knitting.

Work on finer needles than usual for the yarn that is being used. Work a circle from the edge inwards or the centre outwards until the scrap is large enough to cover the base and tuck over the edges.

For a covered button draw the edges together behind and underneath the button and for a mould with a snap fastener, tuck in the ends and close.

Larger covered buttons make attractive ornaments and can be made to match a sweater, the button possibly using a finer pattern of the same design.

Cabled knitting

Cabled patterns, where stitches are crossed from one position to another, are worked with the help of a small double-pointed needle called a cable needle. They are a form of travelling stitch, although they travel only at certain points and seldom travel more than within the cable of which they are part (*see also* **Travelling stitches**). When they cross they are moved in front of or behind another group of stitches.

To work a front cable

Stitches crossed from right to left are held at the front of the fabric.

Work to the position of the four stitches to be cabled. Slip the next 2 stitches on to a cable needle and hold the cable needle at the *front* of the work. Knit the next 2 stitches in the usual way (see fig. 71a). The 2 stitches just knitted now take the place of the 2 stitches on the cable needle.

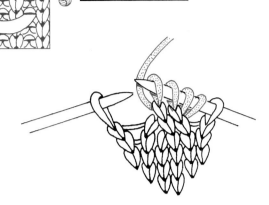

71b Knit stitches from cable needle

Knit the 2 stitches from the cable needle on to the right-hand needle to complete the changing of stitch positions (see fig. 71b). The abbreviation for this cable can be given as C4F, standing for cable 4 stitches to the front. The full explanation reading is: sl next 2 sts to CN, hold at front, K2, K2 sts from CN. This gives a cable as shown in fig. 72. The number may sometimes be given as C2F because only 2 stitches change place at one time; in this book, however, the number is always the same as the total number of stitches in the whole cable.

72 Stitches cabled to left

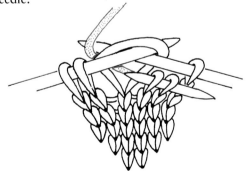

71a Hold stitches on cable needle at front

To work a back cable

To reverse the cable to crossing at the back, work to the stitches to be cabled. Slip the next 2 stitches on to a cable needle and hold them at the *back* of the other stitches (see fig. 73a).

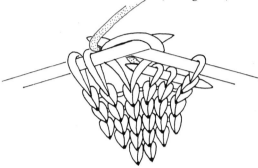

73a Hold stitches on cable needle at back

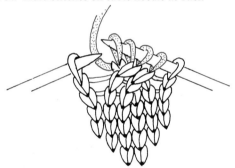

73b Knit stitches from cable needle

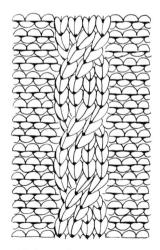

74 Stitches cabled to right

Knit the next 2 stitches on the left needle, then knit the 2 stitches from the cable needle (see fig. 73b). This forms the cable to the right and can be abbreviated to C4B, meaning cable 4 stitches holding needle at back. The explanation of the movement would read: sl, next 2 sts to CN, hold at back, K2, K2 from CN (see fig. 74).

All cable patterns are worked in this way, although the number of stitches may differ and the stitches may not always be knitted, some being purled. The instructions always carry an abbreviation's key.

Ribbon cable

When the C4F and C4B are worked alternately with several rows between each set of cabled stitches, the rope looks more like a ribbon, weaving back and forwards on the surface (see fig. 75a).

75a Ribbon cable

Double ribbon cable

Place 2 ribbon cables together, the first using C4B when the 2nd used C4F, and match C4F with C4B over the 2nd cable. When the next crossing is worked it gives a wide pattern with the lines forming rounds as the lines of cable meet and move away again (*see* **Aran stitch patterns**).

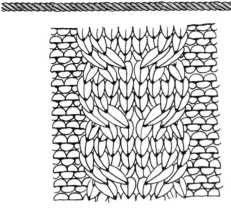

75b Horseshoe cable

Horseshoe cable

Many of the wide, more complex cable patterns are built up in just this way by your placing 2 patterns side by side. In the large cable pattern shown in fig. 75b, 2 cables, each 4 stitches wide, are worked with only C4B on the right side and C4F on the left side.

Using more than one cable needle

Some cable patterns require more than one cable needle if all the held stitches are not used before the needle is required again, or if some stitches are not to be cabled. This no more difficult than using one needle, and instructions always give details, as in intertwined cable in **Cable stitch patterns**.

Continental cable needles

Continental cable needles, which are not flat, can be useful as they hang away from the actual knitting needles and are less inclined to become entangled with the immediate stitches being worked.

76 (*Left*) Gull stitch cable. (*Centre*) Staghorn cable. (*Right*) Lobster claw cable

Coloured cables

Working cables in more than one colour can be a most effective way of adding to a simple cable pattern. Panels worked in this way can edge centre openings or be used as attractive cuffs (see detailed instructions for two-coloured cable in **Cable stitch patterns**).

Cable stitch patterns

Cable patterns are not difficult to knit, but you need a small cable needle to move stitches from one position to another.

Gull stitch cable

The rows 1 to 4, when repeated, give a true gull stitch cable, but this variation shows how a simple pattern can be extended to give a new or original look (see fig. 76a).
Worked over 10 sts.
1st row (WS facing) K2, P6, K2.
2nd row P2, K2, sl2 with yarn back, K2, P2.
3rd row K2, P2, sl2 with yarn forward, P2, K2.
4th row P2, sl next 2 sts to CN, hold at back, K1, K2 from CN, sl next st to CN, hold at front, K2, K1 from CN, P2.
5th–8th rows As 1st–4th rows.
9th row As 1st row.
10th row As 2nd row.
11th–14th rows As 1st and 2nd rows, twice.
Rep 1st–14th rows as required.

Staghorn cable

This shows another possible variation because the cable is not worked in just 2 positions, but moves from centre to outside in 3 stages (see fig. 76b).

Special abbreviations
C4B – sl 2 sts to CN, hold at back, K2, K2 from CN.
C4F – sl next 2 sts to CN, hold at front, K2, K2 from CN.
Worked over 20 stitches.
1st, 3rd and 5th rows (WS facing), K2, P16, K2.
2nd row P2, K4, C4B, C4F, K4, P2.

4th row P2, K2, C4B, K4, C4F, K2, P2.
6th row P2, C4B, K8, C4F, P2.
Rep 1st–6th rows as required.

Lobster claw cable

Many cables can be used for pattern making by very small variations of basic cables (see fig. 76c).
Worked over 12 sts.
1st row (WS facing) K.
2nd row P2, K1, P6, K1, P2.
3rd row K2, P2, K4, P2, K2.
4th row P2, K2, P4, K2, P2.
5th and 6th rows As 3rd and 4th rows.
7th row As 5th row.
8th row P2, sl next 2 sts to CN, hold in front, P2, yon, from CN K2 tog tbl, sl next 2 sts to CN, hold at back, K2 tog, yon, P2 from CN, P2.
Rep 1st–8th rows as required.

Tyrolean cable

The Tyrolean cable is often used as the base for brightly coloured wool embroidery and can be worked without the popcorns if preferred. Traditionally, every knit stitch is worked through the back of the loop on every row, but the instructions have been given for the plain knitted version.

Special abbreviations
C6B – slip 3 sts to CN, hold at back, K3, K3 from CN
C6F – slip next 3 sts to CN, hold at front, K3, K3 from CN.
MB – into next st work K1, yon, K1, yon, K1, turn, K5, turn P5, turn K5, turn, Psl2, K3 tog, p2sso.
Worked over a panel of 23 stitches.
1st row (WS facing) K4, P15, K4.
2nd row P4, C6F, K3, C6B, P4.
3rd row As 1st row.
4th row P4, K15, P4.
5th–8th rows Rep 3rd and 4th rows twice.
9th row As 3rd row.
10th row P4, C6B, K3, C6F, P4.
11th and 12th rows As 3rd and 4th rows.
13th row As 3rd row.
14th row P4, K7, MB, K7, P4.
15th row As 3rd row.
16th row P4, K6, MB, K1, MB, K6, P4.

17th row As 3rd row.
18th row As 14th row.
19th and 20th rows As 3rd and 4th rows.
Rep 1st–20th rows as required.
See **Embroidery** for stitch working instructions.

Two-coloured cable

You can use different colours for any cable pattern where the different lines or ropes of stitches are to cross. Use a separate small ball or bobbin of yarn for each vertical line, even when the colour is to be used twice on adjoining areas.

Twist one yarn over the other on the wrong side at every colour change so that no holes occur.
Worked over a number of stitches divisible by 12 using a background colour and 2 contrasting colours.
1st row (RS facing) * With A P3, ybk, with B twisted under A K3, with C twisted under B K3, with 2nd ball of A twisted under C and fwd P3, rep from * to end.

2nd row * With A K3, yfwd, with C twisted under A P3, with B twisted under C P3, with A twisted under B and bk K3, rep from * to end.
3rd and 4th rows As 1st and 2nd rows.
5th row With A P3, ybk, slip next 3 sts to CN, hold at front for left cross or back for right cross, twist C under A and K next 3 sts, twist B under C and K 3 sts from CN, twist A under B and P3, rep from * to end.
6th row * With A K3, yfwd, twist B under A P3, twist C under B P3, twist A under C K3, rep from * to end.
7th row * With A P3, ybk, twist C under A K3, twist B under C K3, twist A under B and P3, rep from * to end.
8th–9th rows As 6th and 7th rows.
10th row As 6th row.
11th row With A P3, ybk, slip 3 C sts to CN, hold at back or front of work in same way as previous cable row, twist B under A and K next 3 sts, twist C under B and K 3 sts from CN, twist A under C and P3, rep from * to end.
12th row As second row.
Rep 1st–12th rows as required.

77 (*Left*) Intertwined cable. (*Right*) Scots lace cable

Intertwined cables

This cable twists the outside stitches under the centre stitches, and, therefore, you will need two cable needles for it. The cable can be reversed alternately so that the upper central stitches pass under the next cross-over if preferred. All stitches can also be worked in stocking stitch, giving a round-edged cable (see fig. 77a).
Worked over a panel of 12 stitches.
1st row (RS facing) P3, K6, P3.
2nd row K3, P6, K3.
3rd row P3, K2, P2, K2, P3.
4th row K3, P2, K2, P2, K3.
5th and 6th rows Rep 3rd and 4th rows.
7th row P3, sl next 2 sts to 1st CN, hold at back, slip next 2 sts to 2nd CN and hold at front, K next 2 sts, P 2 sts from 2nd CN, K2 sts from 1st CN, P3.
8th, 9th and 10th rows As 4th, 3rd and 4th rows.
11th and 12th rows As 1st and 2nd rows.
Rep 1st-12th rows as required.

Scottish open cable

Cable patterns need not always be heavy and rope-like as this pattern shows. Worked in fine yarn it repeats well to give an openwork fabric or can be used to form panels (see fig. 77b).
Worked over a number of stitches divisible by 12 stitches.
1st row (RS facing) * P1, K1, P2, [yon, K2 tog] twice, P2, K1, P1, rep from * to end.
2nd row * K1, P1, K2, P2, yon, P2 tog, K2, P1, K1, rep from * to end.
3rd and 4th rows As 1st and 2nd rows.
5th row * P1, K1, P2, sl next 2 sts to CN, hold at front, K2, K2 from CN, P2, K1, P1, rep from * to end.
6th row As 2nd row.
7th–14th rows Rep 1st and 2nd rows.
Rep 1st–14th rows as required.

78 Tilting openwork cable pattern

Tilting openwork cable pattern

Cables are usually vertical or horizontal if worked from side to side of the garment, but this design tilts them from side to side. The openwork bias is used to draw the cabled stitches first in one direction and then in the other (see fig. 78).

Special abbreviations

C4B – sl 2 sts to CN, hold at back, K2, K2 from CN.
C4F – sl 2 sts to CN, hold at front, K2, K2 from CN.
Worked over a number of stitches divisible by 13, plus 2.
1st row (WS facing), K2, * P5, K1, P5, K2, rep from * to end.
2nd row P2, * K1, [yon, K2 tog] twice, P1, K5, P2, rep from * to end.
3rd row K2, * P4, K2, P5, K2, rep from * to end.
4th row P2, * K1, [yon, K2 tog] twice, P2, K4, P2, rep from * to end.
5th row As 3rd row.
6th row P2, * K1, [yon, K2 tog] twice, P2, C4B, P2, rep from * to end.
7th–12th rows Work 3rd, 4th, 5th, 6th, 3rd and 4th rows.
13th row As 1st row.
14th row P2, * K5, P1, [SSK, yon] twice, K1, P2, rep from * to end.
15th and 17th rows K2, * P5, K2, P4, K2, rep from * to end.
16th row P2, * K4, P2, [SSK, yon] twice, K1, P2, rep from * to end.
18th row P2, * C4F, P2, [SSK, yon] twice, K1, P2, rep from * to end.
19th–24th rows Work 15th, 16th, 17th, 18th, 15th and 16th rows.
Rep 1st–24th rows as required.

Casting on and off

Casting on is the method of placing the loops or stitches on to the needle in readiness for working. There are many different ways of casting on, and, although two methods are used most often, each has its own purpose. Some methods are useful, some decorative and some strong.

The two most used methods are the thumb and the two-needle method. Both give elastic, strong, general purpose edges.

The thumb method

Worked with one ball of yarn and one needle.

Make a slip knot some distance along the yarn towards the ball and place the knot on the needle. The short end from the needle to the yarn end must be at least 4 times the length of the edge to be cast on (see fig. 79).

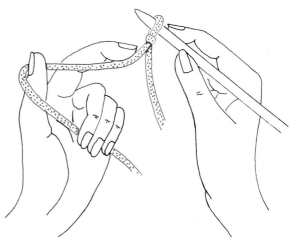

79 Place slip knot on needle

Hold the needle in the right hand with the yarn to the ball over the right forefinger, under the 3rd finger, over the 4th finger and round the little finger (see fig. 80a).

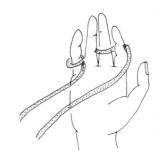

80a Wind yarn round right-hand fingers

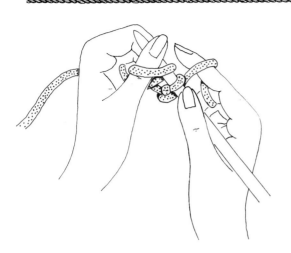

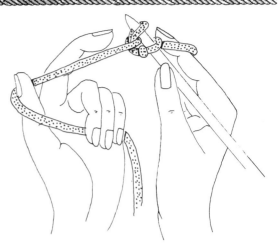

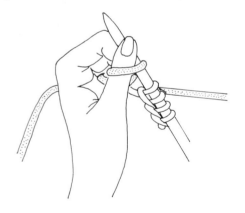

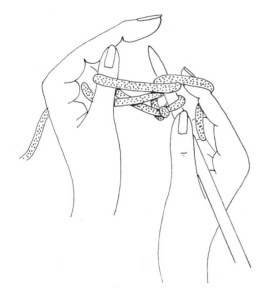

81b Draw through a new loop

Draw the yarn through the thumb loop to form a new loop on the needle, making two loops or stitches (see fig. 81b).

Rearrange the yarn on both right and left hands as before and make another new loop in the same way. Repeat this until there are the required number of stitches (see fig. 82).

80b Wind short end round thumb

Hold the short end under the last 3 fingers of the left hand and lift the yarn close to the needle in a loop across the front of the thumb from right to left and round behind it (see fig. 80b).

Insert the tip of the needle through the thumb loop and with the right forefinger bring the yarn from the ball round the tip of the needle from back to front, close to the thumb loop (see fig. 81a).

82a Make more stitches in the same way

81a Put needle tip into thumb loop

82b The finished edge

The two-needle cable edge method

Worked with two needles and one ball of yarn.

Work a slip knot not less than 10cm (4in.) from end of yarn and place on one needle in the left hand (see fig. 83).

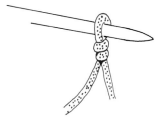

83 Place slip knot on left needle

Take the other needle in the right hand and insert the tip of it through the loop on the left needle, with the yarn to the ball over the right forefinger (see fig. 84).

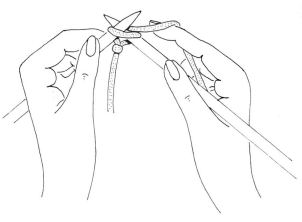

84 Put right needle into loop and yarn round needle

Draw the strand between the needles through the original loop with the right needle and slip it on to the left needle so that there are two loops or stitches.

* Insert the tip of the right needle between the 2 loops and draw a new loop through as before * (see fig. 85a). Repeat from * to * until the required number of stitches are on the left hand needle (see fig. 85b).

85a Put right needle between two stitches

85b Draw through a new stitch

The reverse side of this cable edge is sometimes used as the right side of the garment because of its neat appearance.

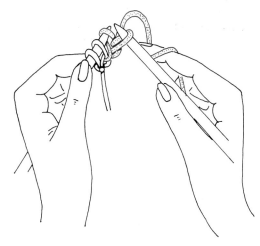

86 Put needle into loop and draw through a new stitch

The two-needle chain edge method

Ideal when working lace patterns or when stitches are to be picked up from the cast-on edge. The chain edge method is worked in a similar way to the cable edge but is worked into the stitch instead of between the stitches.

Place a slip knot on the left needle and work the first new loop as given for the cable cast on.

Insert the tip of the right needle into the new loop from front to back and draw through another new loop and place it on the tip of the left needle (see fig. 86).

Continue making new stitches in this way, working through the loop of the previous stitch until sufficient stitches have been made.

Continental casting on methods

Although the previous three methods are enough for everyday use there are several continental, decorative and invisible methods which give neater edges, particularly where the edge is to remain unseamed.

Italian casting on method

The finished edge is not unlike the thumb method already given, but the edge is not bulky and is particularly useful where the cast-on edge is to become part of a seam, or when stitches are to be picked up from it. Make a slip knot about 4 times the length of the cast-on edge in from the end of the yarn (see fig. 87a).

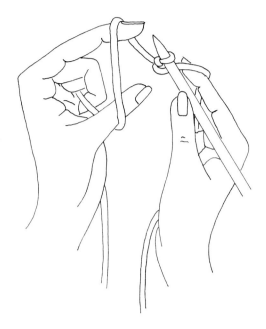

87b Hold short end between finger and thumb

87a Place slip knot on needle

* Place the needle in the right hand with the yarn to the ball round the right fingers as given for the thumb method and pass the short end over the forefinger of the left hand from back to front and down under the front of the thumb. The end of yarn is held against the palm of the left hand by the last three fingers (see fig. 87b).

Draw the tip of the left forefinger sharply back so that the yarn from the ball forms a loop, crossing with the yarn to the thumb (see fig. 88).

88 Draw finger back to form to loop

89 Put needle tip under crossed yarn

91 Draw loop up to needle

90 Draw through new loop

Insert the tip of the needle under the crossed yarn on the forefinger (see fig. 89).

With the right forefinger bring the yarn round under the tip of the needle and draw a new loop through under both yarn to forefinger and yarn to thumb (see fig. 90).

Draw up the yarn so that the new loop fits on to the needle (see fig. 91).

Work other stitches in the same way, repeating from * to * until the required number has been made.

German casting on method

This method is another way, and can be a very quick way when practised, of working the thumb method.

Place the yarn over the left fingers about 4 times the length of the cast-on edge in from the start of the yarn. Pass the short end round and under the thumb and the yarn to the ball over and round the forefinger. Hold both ends of yarn against the palm of the left hand with the unused fingers (see fig. 92).

With a needle in the right hand insert the needle tip through the thumb loop from the back and under the strand of yarn to the forefinger

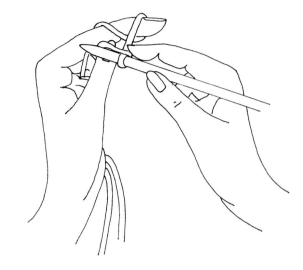

92 Hold both ends of yarn in left palm

94 Draw through new loop

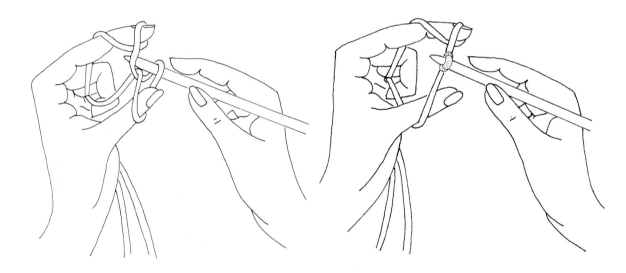

93 Insert needle through loop and under yarn

95 Draw stitch up on needle

(see fig. 93). Draw the tip of the needle back and through the thumb loop or help the thumb loop to slip over the needle tip so that a loop is formed (see fig. 94).

Draw the thumb back against the yarn between thumb and loop on the needle to take away any slackness and leave the loop fitting the needle (see fig. 95).

Two-needle method for ribbing

Where ribbing is to be worked immediately after casting on, the edge can be given a rolled or machine knit type of edge by working a different version of the two needle cable cast on.

Place a slip knot and one stitch on the left hand needle just as for the cable method.

* Insert the tip of the right needle between the

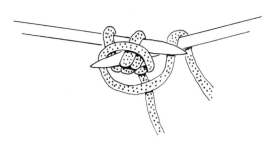

96a Insert needle between stitches from back to front

stitches on the left needle from back to front and bring the yarn over the right needle tip, then under the tip and use the right needle to draw a new loop through to place on the left needle (see fig. 96a).

Insert the right needle between the last 2 stitches on the left needle from front to back, bring the yarn under the right needle tip and draw through a new loop to place on the left needle * (see fig. 96b).

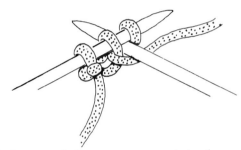

96b Insert needle between next two stitches from front to back

Repeat from * to * working through between the loops for every new stitch but alternating between knitting and purling them.

End with a knit stitch and then work the first row thus, * K1 through back of loop, P1 through back of loop, rep from * to end. Continue with K1, P1 rib for the required depth.

Invisible casting on

Edges which will show in the finished garment, collars, cuffs, welts and pockets, can all be given a finish of their own if you cast on with an invisible edge. The finished result is a neat rolled edge with the stitches rolling round the edge and no harsh line of the 1st row loops in sight.

Rolled edge casting on

Using a contrast yarn of similar thickness to the actual garment yarn cast on by any method half the total number of stitches required. The contrast yarn is removed once the edge is completed.

Using the actual garment yarn P 1 row and K 1 row, then rep these 2 rows once more.

5th row (P side facing) * P 1st st on left needle, with right needle tip lift the loop from back to front directly under the next st that shows against the contrast yarn 4 rows below, put the yarn round the needle tip as for a purl st and draw through a new loop on to the right needle, P the next st on the left needle and P up a st from the next loop showing on the contrast (see fig. 97a).

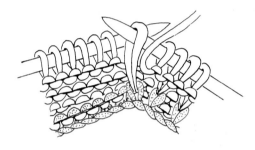

97a Purl stitch then purl up stitch on contrast

Continue in this way, alternately purling a stitch and picking up a stitch purlwise until all the cast-on stitches have been worked. The number of stitches on the needle will have doubled and the contrast yarn can be removed. This completes the edge and the garment can be continued. Where the welt is to be ribbed set the

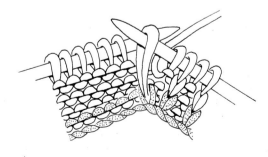

97b Purl stitch then knit up stitch on contrast

ribbing pattern on the 5th row by working the 1st and alternate stitches purl but knit up each loop shown on the contrast yarn (see fig. 97b).

Ribbed invisible cast-on method

For a single ribbed welt an invisible cast on can be worked so that the edge also looks like ribbing.

Using a contrast yarn of similar thickness to the actual garment yarn, cast on half the total number of stitches required. This yarn is removed once the edge is complete. Using the correct garment yarn work thus:
1st row K1, * yon, K1, rep from * to end (see fig. 98a).

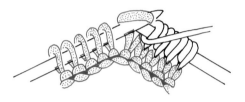

98a Yarn over needle, knit next stitch on contrast

2nd row K1, * yarn to front, sl1 purlwise, yarn to back, K1, rep from * to end.
3rd row Sl1 purlwise, * yarn to back, K1, yarn to front, sl1 purlwise, rep from * to end.
Rep 2nd and 3rd rows once more.
Continue in ribbing thus:
Next row K1, * P1, K1, rep from * to end.

98b Work in single rib

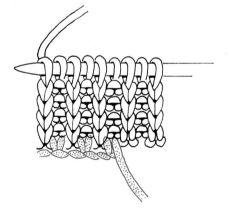

Next row P1, * K1, P1, rep from * to end.
Continue until rib is required length. Remove contrast yarn (fig. 98b).

Decorative casting on methods

The invisible cast-on methods give a perfect edge for tailored and sports garments but both a knotted edge and a picot edge can give the garment 'finish' right from the start.

Knotted edge cast on

This method of strengthening and decorating the edge was often used on fishermen's guernseys as it showed up well on the dark wool.
    Use the thumb method of casting on.
    Place a slip knot and one stitch on the right needle (see fig. 99a).

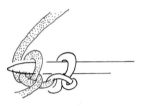

99a Two stitches on needle

    Take a needle in the left hand and with the tip lift the 1st loop over the 2nd and off the needle, leaving 1 stitch on the right needle (see fig. 99b).

99b Lift first over second to leave one completed knot stitch

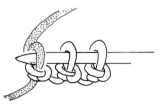

99c Three completed knot stitches

Make 2 stitches more and again lift 1st over 2nd with left needle tip. There are now 2 sts on right needle. Continue in this way casting on 2 sts for every 1 finished st required (see fig. 99c).

Channel Island casting on method

Strength as well as decoration is provided by this method; you use two strands for the left-hand loops but only one strand of yarn for the right-hand loops.

Double back one end of the yarn for at least 4 times the length of the edge to be cast on, plus an extra 10cm (4in.). Make the slip knot using one strand of the double yarn only, about 10cm back along the double strand, and place it on the right-hand needle. This leaves a single strand for use with the right hand and leads back to the ball, while there is a double thread to twist round the left thumb. Leave about 10cm of the double yarn hanging down by the slip knot which can be darned in once the edge is complete.

* Take the single yarn over and round the needle before working a stitch from the thumb loop (see fig. 100a).

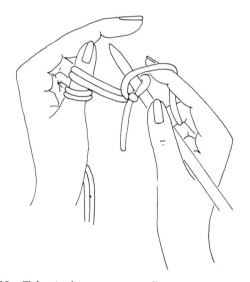

100a Take single yarn over needle

Wind the doubled yarn round the thumb, insert the right needle tip, draw a loop through and place it on the needle. This holds the yarn put over the needle in place and gives 3 stitches on the needle (see fig. 100b).

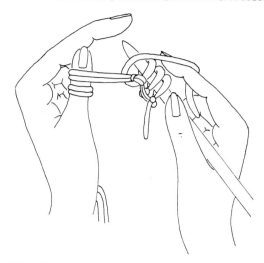

100b Wrap double yarn round thumb

Rep from * until the required number of stitches are obtained, noting that each movement places 2 stitches on the right needle.

Picot casting on method

The picot edge is made by first making a braid with loops at each side. From one edge a loop is picked up for every stitch required at the base of the garment or on a sleeve or collar edge. It is worked with 2 needles and 1 ball of yarn.

Place a slip knot on the left needle and make 1 new loop out of it as for two-needle casting on. Keep both loops on the left needle.

* Insert the right needle tip into the 1st st from back to front as if to purl. Keeping the yarn at the front, sl the st to the right needle and take the yarn over the top of the needle to the back so that there are 2 strands on the right needle. If necessary hold the yarn over the needle with a finger tip to keep it from slipping, then K the last st (see fig. 101a).

101a Yarn over needle, slip one, knit one

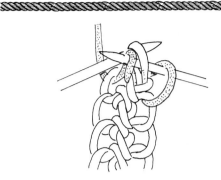

101b Lift slipped stitch over knitted stitch

With the left needle tip lift the middle st (the slipped st) over the last st and off the needle, leaving 2 sts on the needle. Turn (see fig. 101b).

Rep from * until there are enough loops on one side of the braid to allow 1 loop to be used for each st required.

Place the braid lengthwise and K up 1st from each loop.

Open edge casting on method

There are times when an open edge is useful. When stitches are to be picked up from the original edge or when stitches are required to be knitted in both directions such as from a centre back cast-on edge.

Work over 2 needles held together using one ball of yarn and a length of contrast yarn, which is later withdrawn.

Place a slip knot over both needles, leaving an end of yarn not less than 10cm (4in.) (see fig. 102a).

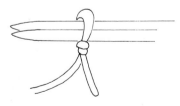

102a Place slip knot over two needles

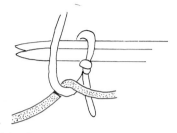

102b Joining in contrast

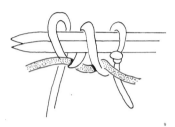

102c Working in front of first stitch

Hold the yarn upwards and place the contrast yarn over the loop (see fig. 102b).

Twist the contrast yarn along beneath the needle, winding the yarn alternately behind and in front of it thus – * Take the yarn up over the needles and down behind them and up under the contrast yarn, then up over the top of the needle (see fig. 102c). Carry the yarn on down behind the needle and take the contrast yarn to the left across the main yarn. Rep from * until the required number of sts are on the needle (see fig. 103a).

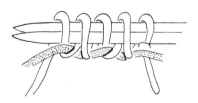

103a Work alternately in front of, then behind, contrast

Leave the contrast yarn in place and knit the 1st row, taking care that the 1st st does not unwind before it is knitted (see fig. 103b). The contrast yarn should be kept in place until the loops are ready to be knitted up.

Draw the yarn out and slip the loops on to the needle as the yarn is removed.

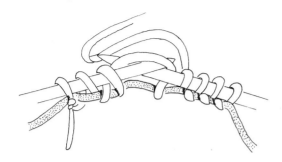

103b Knit next row

Casting on during knitting

Casting on during knitting can pose problems and leave gaps if the wrong method is used. On stocking stitch, stitches to be cast on at the right edge are placed at the beginning of the row on knit rows and for the left edge at the beginning of the row on purl rows.

On knit rows make a loop in the yarn and place it on the needle so that it cannot unwind (see fig. 104a). Work each required loop in the same way then continue to knit in the usual way (see fig. 104b).

On purl rows cast on the required stitches in exactly the same way and, when the correct number are on the needle, purl across the row as usual.

Any number of stitches can be cast on in this way.

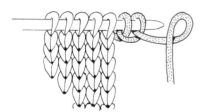

104a Place turned loop on needle

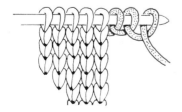

104b Continue in same way

Casting on for round knitting

Any method of casting on can be used for round knitting whether worked on a set of double pointed needles or on a circular needle.

Sets of needles can twist as the stitches are cast on particularly at the end of one needle and the beginning of the next. To avoid this, cast on all the stitches on to one long needle and, only when the total number have been cast on and checked, slip the required number on to each needle, then join into a circle immediately with as little movement as possible (see fig. 105a & b).

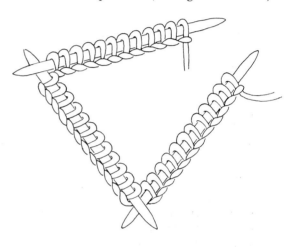

105a Stitches divided on to three needles

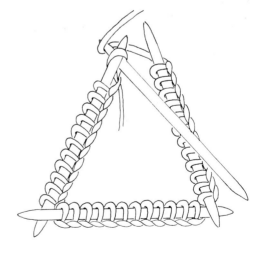

105b Carrying yarn across join of circle firmly

Casting on with a circular needle avoids this problem but take care that none of the stitches are twisted before they are joined into a circle.

Casting off

Stitches can be finished off in several ways, the simplest of which is to cast them off.

On knit stitches cast off on the right side, beginning with the yarn at the needle tip.

Knit the 1st and 2nd stitches in the usual way, then with the left needle tip lift the 1st stitch worked over the 2nd stitch and off the needle (see fig. 106a). This leaves the piece with 1 stitch cast off.

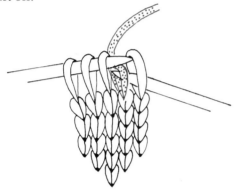

106a Lift first stitch over second

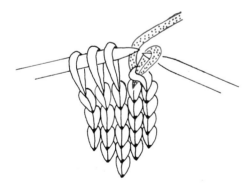

106b One stitch cast off

* Knit the next st, giving 2 loops again on the right needle then with the tip of the left needle lift the 1st stitch over the 2nd and off the needle (see fig. 106b). Rep from * until only 1 stitch remains on the right needle.

Break off the yarn, leaving an end long enough to darn in and pull the end through the last loop.

On purl stitches cast off with the yarn at the right tip and the purl side of the stitches (ridged side) facing.

Purl 2 stitches and with the left needle tip lift the 1st stitch over the 2nd and off the needle tip (see fig. 107a).

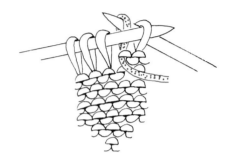

107a Lift first stitch over second

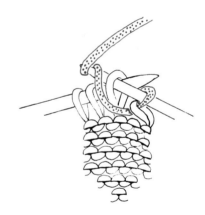

107b One stitch cast off, purl next stitch

* Purl the next stitch so that there are again 2 loops on the right hand needle, then lift the 1st loop over the 2nd and off the needle tip (see fig. 107b).

Rep from * until 1 stitch remains on the right needle. Break off the yarn, leaving sufficient to darn in and draw the tail of yarn through the last stitch.

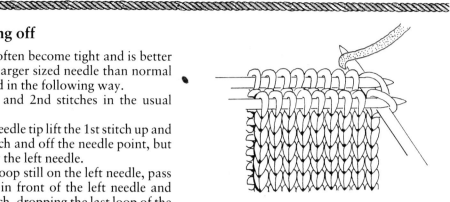

Delayed casting off

Casting off can often become tight and is better worked using a larger sized needle than normal or can be worked in the following way.

Work the 1st and 2nd stitches in the usual way.

With the left needle tip lift the 1st stitch up and over the 2nd stitch and off the needle point, but do not withdraw the left needle.

With the last loop still on the left needle, pass the right needle in front of the left needle and knit the next stitch, dropping the last loop of the 1st stitch lifted over at the same time (see fig. 108).

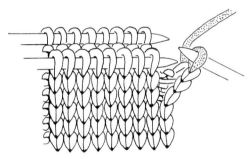

109a Knit together first stitch on both needles

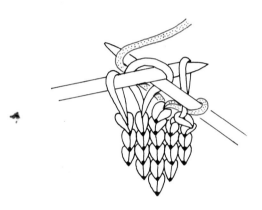

108 With last loop on left needle knit next stitch

* With 2 loops on the right needle use the left needle tip to lift the 1st loop over the 2nd and off the needle tip, but do not slip the loop off the left needle. Take the right needle tip in front of the last loop, knit the next stitch and pass it to the right needle, dropping the held loop at the same time. Repeat from * until all the stitches are cast off.

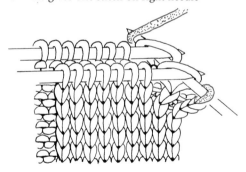

109b This gives one stitch on right needle

109c Knit next two stitches together in same way

Casting off two edges together

For a visible finish place the stitches to be cast off with wrong sides touching and work the cast off on the right side, starting with yarn at the right edge along with both needle points.

Insert the right needle tip through the 1st stitches on both back and front needles. Bring the yarn round and draw a new loop through

both stitches just as if they were knitted together (see fig. 109a).

Place this stitch on the right needle (see fig. 109b). Work the next 2 stitches in the same way (see fig. 109c). There will now be 2 stitches on the right needle (see fig. 110a).

With the left needle tip lift the 1st stitch on the right needle over the 2nd stitch and pass the loop off the right needle. This casts off 1 stitch (see fig. 110b).

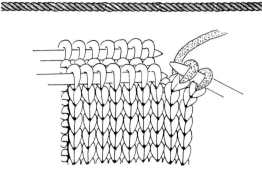

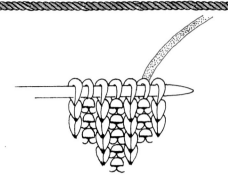

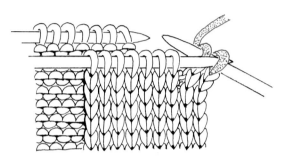

110a Two stitches on right needle

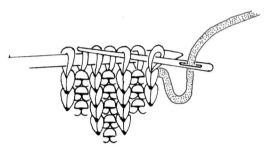

111 Thread and needle point at right

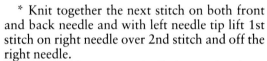

110b Lift first stitch over second

* Knit together the next stitch on both front and back needle and with left needle tip lift 1st stitch on right needle over 2nd stitch and off the right needle.

Continue from * until all the stitches have been cast off.

For an invisible finish place both right sides together and work along the stitches in the same way, purling both stitches together instead of knitting them together.

Rolled edge casting off

This edge matches the twisted stitch cast on, and the two needle ribbing cast on.

Thread the remaining yarn into a wool needle and, with both thread and needle point at the right, work the stitches as follows (see fig. 111a).

* Insert the threaded wool needle into the 1st knit stitch knitwise, and slip it off the knitting needle.

Miss the next stitch, a purl stitch, and insert the wool needle purlwise through the next knit stitch (see fig. 111b).

Insert wool needle through the 1st purl stitch purlwise and slip the stitch off the knitting needle (see fig. 112a).

112a Insert the wool needle through the next purl stitch knitwise

Miss the next knit stitch and insert the wool needle knitwise through the next purl stitch.

Rep from * until all the stitches have been worked through twice (see fig. 112b).

After working once through each of the first 2 stitches each pair is worked through twice.

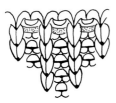

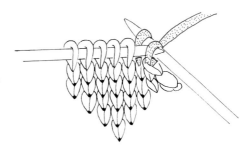

112b Completed edge

The first time it is left on the knitting needle and is worked the opposite way to the type of stitch – i.e. knitwise for a purl stitch and purlwise for a knit stitch. The second time it is worked in the same way as the stitch, knitwise for a knit stitch and purlwise for a purl stitch, and is slipped off the knitting needle. It is in fact a type of grafting, although grafting is usually worked where two edges are being placed together. Other ribs can be worked in a similar way including garter stitch, and moss stitch, following the same principle.

Picot edge casting off

This method of casting off decorates the edge at the same time as the stitches are worked off the needle. Work normally until the last row has been completed. Take the finished knitting in left hand with point of needle and yarn at right edge.

 * Insert the right needle tip into the 1st stitch on the left needle and work a new loop out of it as for two needle lace casting on. Work another new loop out of the 1st stitch (see fig. 113).

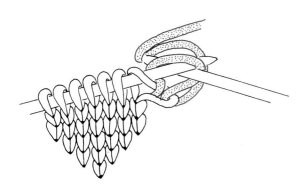

113 Draw new loop through first stitch

114a Cast off three stitches

Without turning the needle cast off these 2 cast on stitches and then cast off 1 more stitch, leaving 1 stitch remaining on right needle. Slip this stitch back to the left needle (see fig. 114a).

Repeat from * until all the stitches are cast off (see fig. 114b).

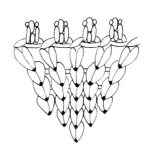

114b Finished edge

Charts

Charts are used whenever it is possible to make a pattern simpler by showing shaping, coloured or textured patterns, motifs or repeats, more easily than by printing words. A chart shows at a glance the position of one row to the next or where a section fits into the whole; words, although helpful, do not give as clear a picture until they have all been read and worked.

Colour or motif charts

A chart may be shown in different ways.

It may be shown with one symbol or sign depicting the stitches which are to be worked in

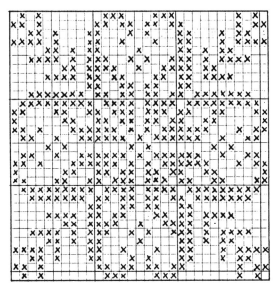

115   One colour chart

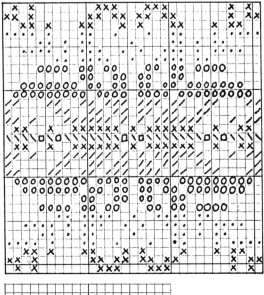

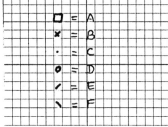

116   Multicoloured chart and key

colour or added to the garment after knitting by Swiss darning (see fig. 115). This chart can be worked in a contrast against the main colour background or it may be left to the knitter to use colours as preferred.

The same motif can also be shown with several different symbols showing where each different colour is to be worked (see fig. 116). A key along with the symbol shows exactly which colour is which and would relate to the instructions, where the specific colours would be given against the letters shown on the chart.

Pattern charts

A pattern, lace or textured, can also be shown in chart form. It is quicker to read than words and shows instantly the depth of a repeat and the width of the motif (see fig. 117). Again, symbols explain exactly what the chart shows. The chart in fig. 117 shows a lace pattern where the number of stitches remains constant, decreases being matched on the same row with increases.

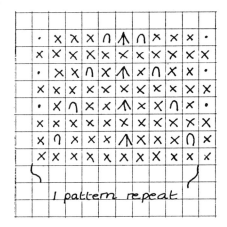

117   Lace pattern chart: x = K1; • = P1; $\cap$ = yon; $\uparrow$ = SK2togPO.

Lace patterns are not always worked in this way, and altering numbers of stitches may need to be shown (see fig. 118). The addition of spaces does not make the chart more difficult to see when knitting, but the finished shape is less clear except for experienced knitters.

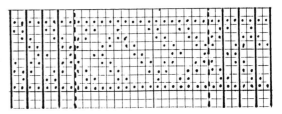

118 Spaces on lace chart

119 Pattern repeat and different row endings for more than one size

Repeat charts

Charts may also be used to show not only the colour or pattern repeat but how this repeat fits into several different sizes. This avoids complicated instructions for the beginning and ending of rows, which alter for every size given (see fig. 119).

Garment charts

A chart can also be used to show every detail of a garment section: the number of rows, the position and amount of shaping, an all-over coloured pattern and the number of sizes that it can be worked in (see fig. 120).

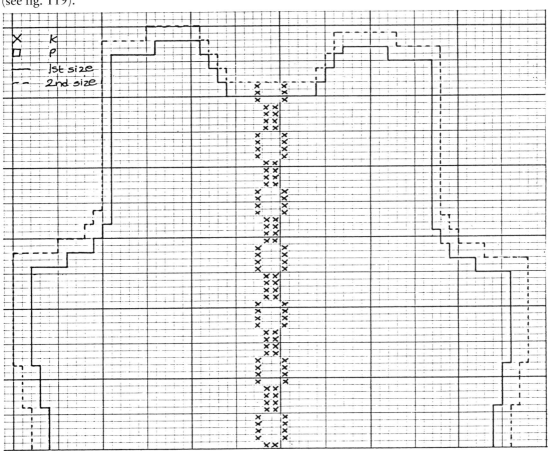

120 Front and back garment chart

Reading charts

Instructions usually add in words anything that is not shown on the chart, particularly if there is any point that is not straightforward.

Most charts are read from right to left for right side rows and left to right for wrong side rows. Colour work, very often on stocking stitch, usually carries a note that right side rows are knitted and wrong side rows are purled. Lace or textured pattern charts may show the pattern as seen from the right side, which means that a knit stitch symbol may have to be worked purlwise on the wrong side.

The alternative on a lace pattern may be to show the right side rows only on the chart with an additional note that each wrong side row is to be purled. When the chart shows the row numbers it is immediately obvious whether all rows are shown or only alternative rows.

A chart like fig. 119 where several sizes are shown will give further explanation in words

indicating exactly how to proceed. For this chart it could read:

1st row Work from A(B; C; D) to X, rep from X to Y until 2(4: 6: 8) sts rem, work from Y to Q(R; S; T).

Alteration charts

Charts should also be used when making alterations or adapting existing designs (*see* **Alterations**).

Chevron stitch patterns

Chevron patterns can be made with only knit and purl stitches; you either alter the positions to form the chevrons, or make the actual stitches follow the chevron movement by, for example, working with decreases and increases.

121 Knit and purl chevron pattern

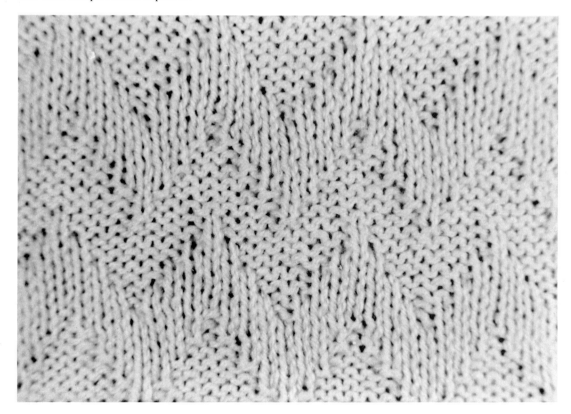

Knit purl chevron

In this pattern the chevron is formed by knit and purl stitches. It is their formation that gives the chevron appearance (see fig. 121).

Worked over a number of stitches divisible by 8, plus 1.

1st row (RS facing) K1, * P7, K1, rep from * to end.

2nd row P1, * K7, P1, rep from * to end.

3rd row K2, * P5, K3, rep from * to last 7 sts, P5, K2.

4rd row P2, * K5, P3, rep from * to last 7 sts, K5, P2.

5th row K3, * P3, K5, rep from * to last 6 sts, P3, K3.

6th row P3, * K3, P5, rep from * to last 6 sts, K3, P3.

7th row K4, * P1, K7, rep from * to last 5 sts, P1, K4.

8th row P4, * K1, P7, rep from * to last 5 sts, K1, P4.

9th–16th rows As 2nd, then 1st, 4th, 3rd, 6th, 5th, 8th and 7th rows.

Rep these 16 rows as required.

Lace chevron pattern

This dainty lace is a basic lace pattern. Repeats can be separated by more rows in stocking stitch or can be grouped in several repeats before a wider area of stocking stitch is worked (see fig. 122).

Worked over a number of stitches divisible by 10, plus 1.

1st and every alt row P.

2nd row * K5, yon, SSK, K3, rep from * to last st, K1.

4th row * K3, K2 tog, yon, K1, yon, SSK, K2, rep from * to last st, K1.

6th row * K2, K2 tog, yon, K3, yon, SSK, K1, rep from * to last st, K1.

8th row * K1, K2 tog, yon, K5, yon, SSK, rep from * to last st, K1.

10th row K2 tog, yon, K7, * yon, sl1, K2 tog, psso, yon, K7, rep from * to last 2 sts, yon, SSK.

Rep 1st–10th rows as required.

122 Lace chevron pattern

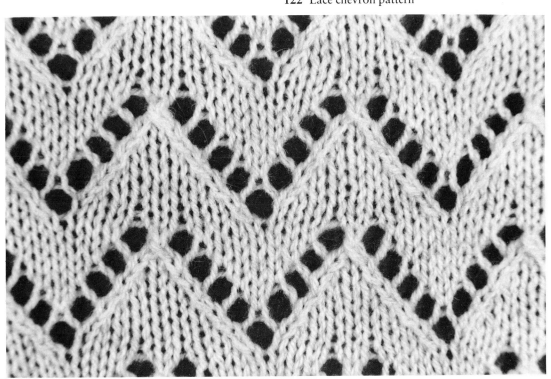

Chevron-striped pattern

A pattern which can be worked in stocking stitch or in garter stitch, this chevron stripe forms its own lines by the placing of the increase and decrease.

Worked over a number of stitches divisible by 12, plus 3 (see fig. 123).

1st row (RS facing) With A, K1, SSK, * K9, sl2, K1, p2sso, rep from * to last 12 sts, K9, K2 tog, K1.

2nd row With B, K1, * P1, K4, [K1, yon, K1] all in next st, K4, rep from * to last 2 sts, P1, K1.

3rd and 4th rows As 1st and 2nd rows using B.

Rep 1st–4th rows as required.

Additional colours may be added making the colour repeat random or over more than 4 rows.

To work in stocking stitch, work 2nd row with all sts purled.

Circular knitting

Circular knitting is worked in rounds instead of rows and uses sets of three, four or five double-pointed needles or, for larger items, circular needles. It has many advantages, especially because it needs little making up.

Most folk knitting is worked 'in the round' and although seamless is not shapeless; the shaping is worked in as required. Pattern in colour, as in self colour, is much easier on round knitting with the patterned right side always facing the knitter and therefore in view, with no blind wrong side rows to deal with when the pattern is not seen as it is worked.

Small items

Small items and garments such as socks, stockings, gloves, mittens and caps need to be worked on sets of needles but have not sufficient stitches over all to work on circular needles (see fig. 124).

123 Striped chevron pattern

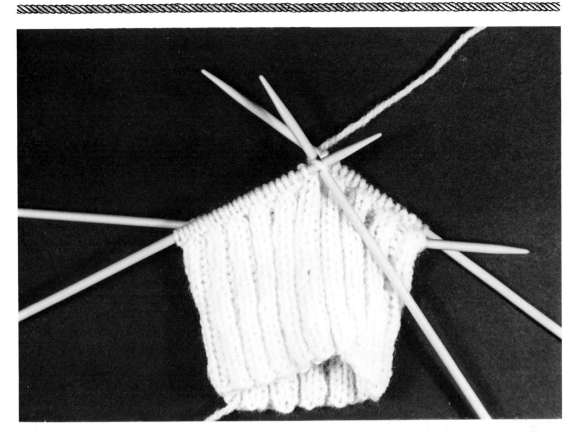

124 Stitches arranged on three needles, using the fourth to work with

Garments and larger items

An adult sweater can be worked on a set of 3 long double-pointed needles, as used in Shetland, or on four or more shorter double-pointed needles or it can be worked on a circular needle. The circular needle requires sufficient stitches at its narrowest point to reach round the circular needle from one point to the other without straining the stitches apart (see fig. 125).
For sizes of needles *see* **Equipment**.

Patterns

Patterns, both textured and coloured, have more possibilities in round knitting than in flat knitting (knitting worked in rows). Pattern can be worked on right side rows on every round, but in flat knitting right side rows are only on alternate rows. Stitches that are forming travelling stitch patterns, particularly one that moves on every row, become easier to read because they require none of the wrong side row abbreviations, possibly reducing the number of abbreviations by half.

Pattern changes

It is necessary to understand how fabrics are formed when changing to round knitting.
Stocking stitch becomes every round knit.
Reverse stocking stitch becomes every round purled.
Garter stitch becomes 1 round knit and 1 round purl, alternately.

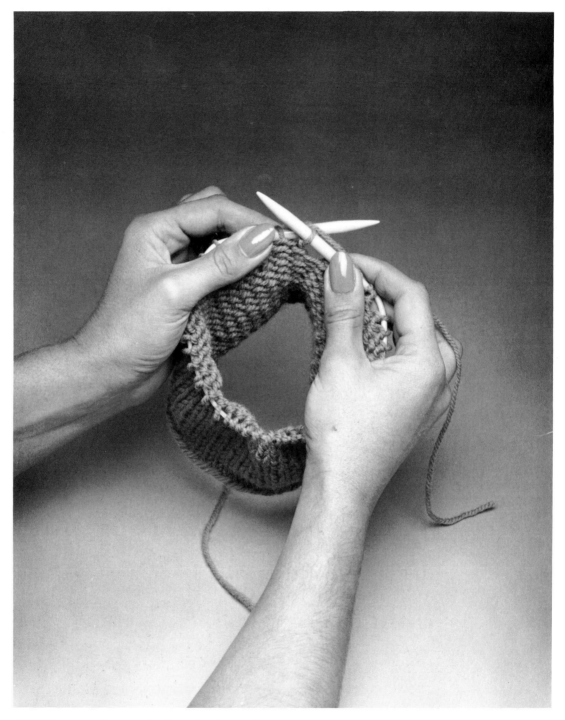

125 Stitches worked round using a circular needle

Coloured knitting

Coloured knitting covers more than one technique of carrying the yarn from one colour point to the next, and includes Fair Isle (Shetland) knitting, jaquard knitting, picture knitting and the knitting of large geometric patterns. All the various techniques may be required to get the best results, as in picture knitting, or a pattern may be from the folk range of designs and will then probably only use one technique, which was used originally by the area where the knitting evolved (see fig. 126).

Stranding

Stranding is the name given to patterns which have the yarns carried loosely across the back of the fabric when they are not in use. Fair Isle patterns are always worked in this way, the strands evened out after the garment is finished by being placed, wet, on a drying frame. This allows the strands and stitches to dry out; both the strands and the stitches are then pulled slightly to become smooth.

Stranding leaves no sign of the carried colours on the right side of the work, except when they are in use for one or more stitches. The patterns do have to be suitable because the strands become untidy when they are carried over more than five stitches.

Many designs, as long as the groups of colour are close together, are suitable for stranding although many so-called Fair Isle designs such as rows of carrots or rabbits, quite suitable for stranding, are not true Fair Isle designs.

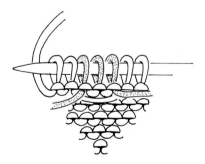

126 The wrong side of a stranded pattern

Method of stranding

Stranding is easiest if both right and left forefingers are used to carry the yarn round the needle tips, the background colour in the right hand and the contrast in the left hand. As the yarn not working the stitch is carried along the wrong side of the fabric, take great care never to catch it in with the colour being used and draw it through to the right side where it can be seen.

Knit rows

The left hand keeps the contrast below the needle tip while the right hand brings the background colour round the needle tip to knit the stitch. This is repeated until the colours change (see fig. 127a).

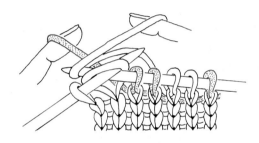

127a Right hand knits with left carrying contrast

The left forefinger then brings the yarn round the needle, and the tip is used to draw through the new stitch while the right hand keeps the background colour away from the needle tip and above the other stitches (see fig. 127b). Always consider the tension: if the work is dragged tightly it will distort the stitches; if it is too slack the stitches will hang between the colour groups.

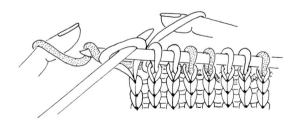

127b Right finger keeps yarn above contrast . . .

Purl rows

The purl row, although a little more difficult to learn, is worked in the same way. The left hand keeps the contrast below the right-hand purled stitches until the contrast is in use (see fig. 127c).

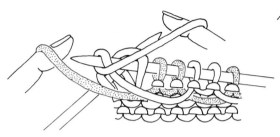

127c left hand carries contrast yarn under on purl side . . .

Then the right hand holds the background colour up and away from the needle tips (see fig. 127d).

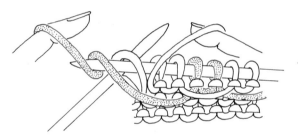

127d the left finger passes the contrast round the needle point

Weaving colours

The alternative to stranding is to weave the colours not in use alternately over and under the stitches being worked. It is essential that this is worked in the correct way so that the woven colour is hidden by the stitch being worked. Worked in the wrong way the colour on the wrong side will be dragged into a position that will show on the right side, even if it is not pulled through to the front of the work.

Knit rows

To weave B, shown in red, over A, shown in black, B is placed over the right needle tip from

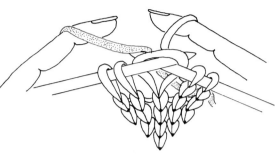

128a Place B above needle as A is used to knit

back to front and A knits the stitch, drawing the new loop to the front beneath B. When you do this, ensure that B, although caught in, does not show on the right side but is above the A stitch (see fig. 128a).

To weave B under A it is simply held below the stitch as it is worked in A (see fig. 128b).

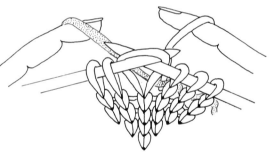

128b Hold B beneath stitch to be worked with A

When colours change A is held above B as it knits the stitch to weave it over (see fig. 129a).

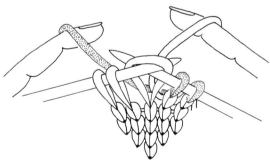

129a Take A round right needle tip before knitting stitch with B

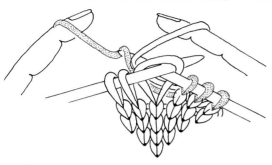

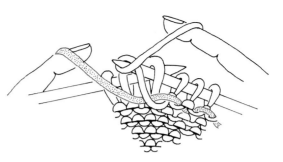

129b Before knitting stitch take A back round under needle point

To weave A under B it is brought under the right needle tip and close into the stitch between the needles while B is placed round the needle tip ready to work the stitch (see fig. 129b). A is then passed back under the right needle tip so that it crosses in front of B and is held in this position as B is used to draw through the new loop to the right side (see fig. 129c).

130b Weave A below B purlwise

To weave A above B, hold A above and away from the needle tip as the B stitch is purled (see fig. 130b).

To weave A under B, first hook A round in front of B. Take A round under the right needle tip and then up to behind the needles (see fig. 131a).

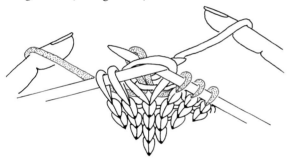

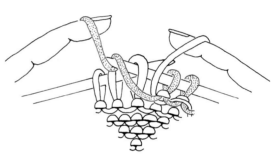

129c Complete knitting of B stitch

Purl rows

To weave B above A, B is placed close to the stitch being purled so that A passes round the needle to purl the stitch below B; the new stitch is then drawn through (see fig. 130a).

130a Weave A above B purlwise

131a Weave A over B

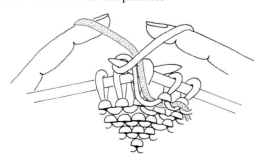

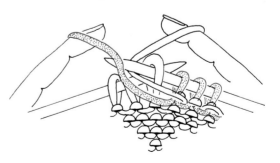

131b Take A between needles under left then right needle tips

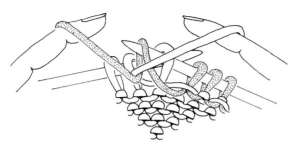

131c

Take B over the needle tip ready to purl the stitch and bring A back down and under the right needle tip back to the right of the stitch being worked. This crosses it over B, and the B stitch can then be purled by drawing the A yarn to the front (see fig. 131c).

Method of working colour blocks

Blocks of different colours, whether geometric or not, can be worked with small balls of the colour, wound on to bobbins, and twisted over the next colour at every colour join to avoid holes forming. Small areas, which seem not to be large enough to require a bobbin, can be worked with a length of yarn from the ball. This can be withdrawn easily from other ends and will not tangle as readily as a ball.

Work to the colour change, then pass the colour that has been in use over the colour to be used and bring the next colour up so that the yarns link or are twisted over the joining point (see fig. 132).

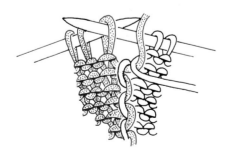

132 Twist one yarn over the other on the wrong side

Picture knitting

Where irregular shapes, large and small, are worked in the same design, all the methods must be combined. Strand yarns over small patterns where they need not be carried over more than 5 stitches. Where the colour has to be carried over many stitches, consider whether it can be woven along the back or if it is better to use a separate thread. For areas of some size use the separate small ball or bobbin, twisting one yarn over at colour changes.

For small areas that have irregular sides take special care. Yarn carried from one stitch to a stitch on the next row which is before the positon of the yarn will drag the stitch sideways and spoil the finished design.

On knit rows, if the yarn is to be used again on the next purl row before the point at which the yarn has been left hanging, it must be woven along the wrong side until it is level with the stitch it will be required for or 1 stitch to the left of this point. It must be woven to a point at which it must be drawn to the stitch. This means that on the following row it must be to the right of the 1st stitch it is to work (see fig. 133a).

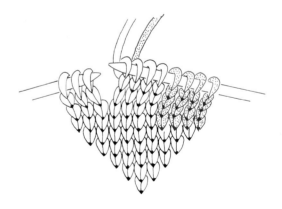

133a Weave yarn on back to its new position

On purl rows the same must be remembered. If it is to be used on the next knit row before the point at which it has been left hanging, it must be woven in along the purl row, so that it is ready to use (see fig. 133b).

When looking at a chart for picture knitting, always read 2 rows at once, so that the yarn can

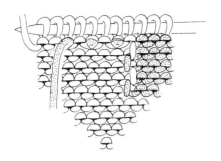

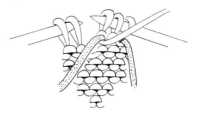

134b Weave alternatley over and under stitches

133b Weave alternately over and under stitches

be correctly placed. This applies to the end of each colour area, not just at the end of the last colour section.

Joining in yarn

Yarns should never be knotted into place. Join at the start of a row, when the end of the yarn just used and the end of the new colour can both be left at the side edge, to be darned in when the garment is complete.

Joining in a new colour for a block or area which is not at the side edge should be carried out before the area is reached. Joined at that point a hole will be left unless the ends are very carefully darned in and twisted in opposite directions.

Work to several stitches before the colour change. Loop the next colour over the one in use (see fig. 134a). Weave in the next colour, alternately over and under the next stitches as they are made (see fig. 134b).

When the change point is reached leave the completed colour and pick up the next colour (see fig. 135a). When the work is complete the end of yarn, where it begins to be woven in, can be cut off. The other end of yarn, if not carried to a new position, can be darned in (see fig. 135b).

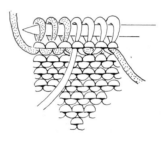

135a Change to next colour leaving previous yarn on wrong side

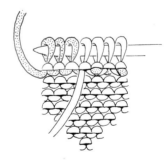

135b Trim off excess yarn

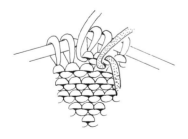

134a Loop new colour over colour in use

Conversion charts

Centimetres/inches chart

These figures are given to the nearest quarter of an inch.

cm	1	2	3	4	5	6	7	8	9	10	11	12	13	14	15
in.	½	¾	1¼	1½	2	2¼	2¾	3¼	3½	4	4¼	4¾	5¼	5½	6
cm	16	17	18	19	20	21	22	23	24	25	26	27	28	29	30
in.	6¼	6¾	7	7½	7¾	8¼	8¾	9	9½	9¾	10¼	10½	11	11½	11¾
cm	31	32	33	34	35	36	37	38	39	40	41	42	43	44	45
in.	12¼	12½	13	13½	13¾	14¼	14½	15	15¼	15¾	16¼	16½	17	17¼	17¾
cm	46	47	48	49	50	51	52	53	54	55	56	57	58	59	60
in.	18	18½	19	19¼	19¾	20	20¼	20¾	21¼	21¾	22	22½	22¾	23¼	23½

136 Centimetre/inches conversion chart. Please note that these conversions are *approximate* to the nearest quarter inch.

Measurements chart

These are the approximate measurements used by manufacturers for the various size and age ranges.

age	3m	6m	9m	12m	18m	2yr	3yr	4yr	6yr	8yr	10yr	12yr	14yr
chest (cm)	45	46	48	51	52	53	55	57	61	66	71	76	86
chest (in.)	17½	18	19	20	20½	21	21½	22	24	26	28	30	34

137 Children's size chart

bust/chest cm	76	81	86	91	97	102	107	112	117	122	127
bust/chest in.	30	32	34	36	38	40	42	44	46	48	50

138 Adult size chart

Needle size chart

This chart shows the relation between European metric needle sizes, the original English numbering and the numbering used in the United States of America.

metric	2	2¼	2½	2¾	3	3¼	3½	3¾	4	4½	5	5½	6	6½	7	7½	8	9	10
British	14	13	–	12	11	10	–	9	8	7	6	5	4	3	2	1	0	00	000
American	0	1	–	2	–	3	4	5	6	7	8	9	10	10½	–	–	11	13	15

139 Needle size conversion chart

Ounce to gramme chart

Old designs often pose a problem for today's knitter if the original yarn stated is given in ounces. The chart shows the conversion from ounces to grams. This will only serve as a guide if the original ply and type of yarn is used. If a man-made yarn is substituted for a 100 per cent wool, even if it is the same ply, it is likely to weigh less than the original.

oz	1	2	3	4	5	6	7	8	9	10	11	12	13	14	15	16
gm	28	57	85	113	142	170	198	227	255	283	312	340	369	397	425	454

140 Ounces/grammes conversion chart

Ounce balls to gramme balls

This chart gives a guide to the number of balls required in 25g, 50g or 100g balls to substitute for the number of balls given in ounces, provided the yarn is of the same type.

oz balls	1	2	3	4	5	6	7	8	9	10	11	12	13	14	15	16
25gm balls	2	3	4	5	6	7	8	9	10	11	12	13	14	15	16	17
40gm balls	1	2	3	3	4	5	5	6	7	8	8	9	10	10	11	12
50gm balls	1	2	2	3	3	4	4	5	6	6	7	7	8	8	9	10
100gm balls	1	1	1	1	2	2	2	3	3	3	4	4	4	4	5	5

141 Ounce balls/gramme balls conversion chart

Cords

Cords for lacing, tying and decoration can be made in many different ways, with fingers, Knitting Nancy, knitting needles or crochet hook.

Finger cords

Thick yarn is easier to use for a sample but strands of any type of yarn can be used.

Take 2 lengths of yarn. Work a slip knot at the base of one and immediately below this slip knot, knot both ends together. Place the slip knot on the right forefinger with the end from it held against the right-hand palm and thumb and finger holding the base knot. Take the other end in the left hand and hold it against the palm of the hand with the last three fingers.

* Insert the left forefinger through the right hand loop and under the left hand strand (see fig. 142a). Draw up a new loop on the left finger tip (see fig. 142b). Drop the right finger tip loop and gently draw back on the right strand until the loop is firmly against the slip knot (see fig. 143).

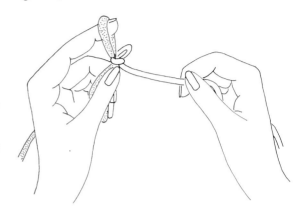

143 Slip loop from right finger and draw up right strand

142a Lift strand in loop with left finger

142b Draw loop up on left finger

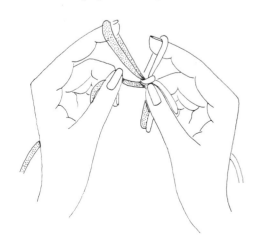

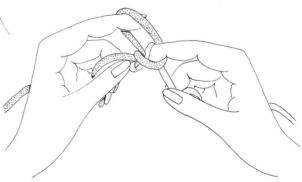

144 Bend right finger under strand through loop

Bend the right forefinger under the right strand through the loop on the left forefinger (see fig. 144).

Draw up the new loop on the right finger (see fig. 145a). Drop the loop off the left finger and draw up on the left strand until the loop is close to the knot before it (see fig. 145b).

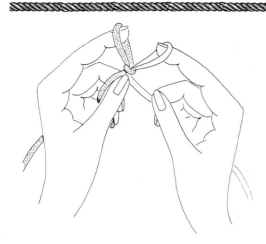

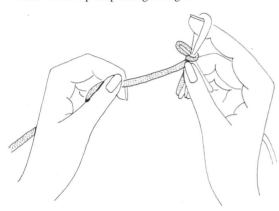

145a Draw up loop on right finger

145b Drop left loop and draw back on left strand

Repeat from * lifting new loops with alternate fingers and drawing back with alternate strands until the cord is the desired length (see fig. 146).

146 Finished cord

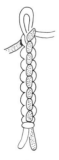

Colour variations

Colour can be added by using one dark strand and one light or one metallic and one wool. Thicker cords can carry more colour if both strands are double thickness. Each strand can be two-coloured.

Knitting Nancy braid *see* **French knitting**

Knitting needle cord

Using 2 double-pointed needles cast on 3 stitches.
    * Take the needle with the stitches in the left hand and the other needle in the right hand. Knit all 3 stitches.
    Do not turn but slip the stitches back to the right end of the same needle.
    Repeat this row from * to end until the length of cord required is made. Cast off.
    This forms a narrow tubular cord and can be used to form toggle-type button loops, braid edging or for lacing (see fig. 147).

147 Three stitch braid

Crochet cords

The simplest crochet cord is made by starting with a slip knot in the end of a length of yarn.
    Insert the crochet hook through the loop and pull the yarn back through the loop with the hook, forming a new loop on the crochet hook.
    Repeat this, drawing through new loops until the required length has been worked. Break off the yarn and draw through the last loop (see fig. 148).

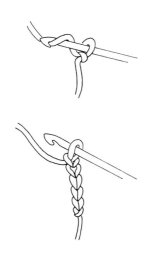

148 Draw single loop through to form chain

Courtelle
See **Yarns.**

Cotton
See **Yarns**

Crochet hooks
See **Equipment**

Crochet stitches

Simple crochet stitches can be useful on edges and are often used as a method of trimming continentally-designed garments. All instructions are given for working directly on to a knitted edge.

Slip stitch

A slip stitch is the stitch with the least height and is seldom used all along a row. It is used during a row, particularly on an edge like shell edge where a very low stitch is placed between the shells for greater separation.

Insert hook through right corner of knitted edge.

Loop the yarn over the hook and draw through to right side. Leave the short end at the side to darn in later. This leaves 1 loop on hook.

* Insert the hook through the knitted edge, put the yarn round the hook and draw the new loop through both knitted edge and loop on hook.

To work more slip stitches rep from * to end of knitted edge (see fig. 149).

149 Single loop slip stitch

Break off yarn and draw end through last loop.

Double crochet

Join into right corner of knitted edge as for slip stitch, then work 1 ch.

* Insert hook through edge, put yarn round hook and draw loop through to right side. There will be 2 loops on the hook.

Put yarn round hook again and draw new loop through both loops, leaving 1 loop on hook. This completes 1 dc. To work more dc rep from * to end of edge. To finish, break off yarn and draw end through last loop or, if a 2nd row is to be worked, work 1 ch and turn the work. Work the 2nd row by repeating from * until the end of the row working 1 dc into the 2 strands at the top of each dc on the previous row (see fig. 150).

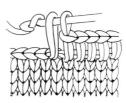

150 Double crochet

Treble crochet

Join in to right corner of knitted edge as for slip stitch. Work 2 ch. Put yarn round hook.

* Insert hook about 1 stitch along knitted edge, yarn round hook again (see fig. 151 *Top*) and draw loop through to right side so that there are now 3 loops on hook. Put yarn round hook (see fig. 151 *Centre*) and draw through 2 loops, then put yarn round hook again and draw through both remaining loops, leaving 1 loop on hook (see fig. 151 *Bottom*).

To work more stitches rep from * ending by breaking off yarn and pulling through last loop or working 2 ch and turning ready for 2nd row which is worked by repeating from *, lifting the 2 strands at the top of each treble worked on the previous row.

152 (*Top*) Picot edge. (*Centre*) Shell edge. (*Bottom*) Crab stitch edge

Crochet edgings

These simple edgings are worked on to 1 or 2 base rows of dc. The number of base rows is decided by the required depth of the finished edge.

Picot edging

1st row * 1 ss into 1st st, 3 ch, 1 ss into same st, 1 ss into each of next 2 sts, rep from * to end of row (see fig. 152a).

Shell edging

1st row 1 ss into 1st st, * 3 tr into next st, 1 ss into each of next 2 sts, rep from * to end of row (see fig. 152b).

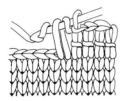

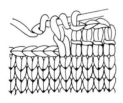

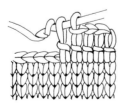

151 (*Top*) Yarn round hook, draw through a new loop, yarn round hook again. (*Centre*) Yarn round hook and draw through two loops. (*Bottom*) Yarn round hook and draw through last two loops

Crab stitch edging

Work 1 base row of dc, 1 ch, do not turn.
2nd row Work 1 row dc back along edge just worked. This draws each loop towards right forming a corded or twisted edge (see fig. 152c).

Crossed stitches

See Twisted stitches under **Basic stitches** and **Continental stocking stitch**.

Cut and sew knitting

In many countries, knitters prefer to make garments such as coats, jackets and cardigans in the round, even if they are to have front openings. For the opening the knitting is marked at the opening line, stitched neatly with a double row of stitching about 1cm to either side of the opening line, and then cut.

Toys and smaller articles can be made in the same way where a rectangle of knitted fabric is made without any shaping, then stitched securely where required and cut out before being seamed. The stitching can be worked by hand but is most successful where it can be done with a sewing machine.

Dale knitting

See **English knitting**

Danish knitting

By the eighteenth century the knitters of Denmark were supplying an item for the women's traditional costume. Above the full skirt a knitted blouse was worn beneath a tight-fitting short jacket. The blouse, often ribbon trimmed or bound, was worked in fine wool, sometimes black, often madder or occasionally a dark green.

The pattern was self-coloured and usually had star and diamond brocade-type patterns, with the exception of blouses found on the most southerly island. Here, now in the care of Falster Minders, a museum in Nykøbing, lies a store of blouses. Like Austrian patterns, many of the travelling stitch designs are twisted and in the fine wool seem to be moulded or chiselled into the fabric, often felted with much washing through the years.

Not as heavy or all-over like Aran patterns, each, if it uses more than one pattern, seems to have an immense sense of relation between stitches. A wide front panel in a travelling and ribbed diamond lattice will have a much smaller pattern, different but similar in some way on the sleeves.

Darts

It is possible to shape knitting much as a dart is used to shape woven fabric. This is worked by making short rows, or rows which are turned before they reach the normal row end, thus making one side longer than the other. They can

be worked on leggings and skirts where the centre back is longer than the side seams, on collars where the centre back needs to be deeper than the sides, or on an outsize blouse where the centre would sit without wrinkles when longer than the front. Darts can be used to form rounds for cushions, rugs or place mats that are worked from side to side with wedge-shaped sections of turned rows. Also, on collars and cuffs that are knitted sideways, darts can be used to give greater fullness above the wrist or on the outer edge of the collar. They have many uses and are simple to work.

Working short rows

Where short rows are turned without being worked in the following way they leave holes but this can easily be avoided.

Work to the turning point. Bring the yarn to the front and slip the next stitch, take the yarn across the front of the slipped stitch and back to WS between the needles (see fig. 154a).

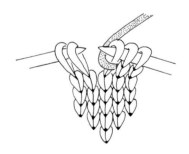

154a Yarn in front of slipped stitch

Pass the slipped stitch back to the left needle (see fig. 154b) and turn the work with wrong side facing. The yarn is now ready to purl the next stitch and on to row end or next turning point; the slipped stitch is to the right of the 1st stitch worked on this row (see fig. 155a).

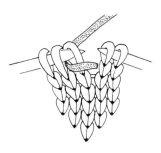

154b Slipped stitch returned to left needle

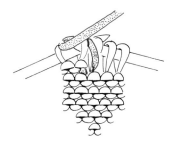

155a Purl stitch to left of yarn

Continue to work rows gradually shorter than the one before turning in the same way, until the number of rows required has been reached (see fig. 155b).

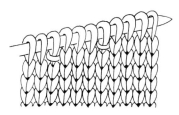

155b Wedge effect of short rows

Finishing off

Once the dart is fully worked, the holes made by turning need to be closed. This is carried out on the 1st row worked across all the stitches when the shaping is complete. Work to the first turning point and work the stitch that has the strand of yarn carried across the front of it. With the left needle tip lift the strand from across the

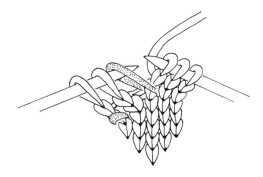

156 Lifting strand at turning point to knit together with next stitch

stitch on to the needle tip, then knit or purl it together with the stitch to the left of it. This closes the gap (see fig. 156).

Placing darts

The dart can be placed exactly where it is needed. Darts worked from the centre of the row outwards will make the side edges longer than the centre. Leaving stitches gradually at the side edges will lengthen the centre. On a button band the band can be shaped to turn to right, as required by a V-shaped neckline, by leaving unworked stitches at the right edge or to the left by leaving unworked stitches at the left edge. Collars can be turned in this way at the neck edge and again in the centre back so that the back depth is greater than the side depth.

Decreases

Decreases are the means used to reduce the number of stitches in a row so that the row becomes smaller. They may be used for several reasons:

- to shape at row ends or at any point along a row
- as a design feature as well as shaping
- in stitch pattern made usually with an increase to keep stitch count constant, although the increase may not be worked on the same row
- all of these reasons simultaneously

Types of decreases

There are three different categories of decreases:
- single decreases, where two stitches become one
- double decreases, where three stitches become one
- multiple decreases, where more than three stitches become one

Single decreases

There are three ways of decreasing one stitch:
- simple decrease, knitwise and purlwise
- twisted decrease, knitwise and purlwise
- slipped decrease, knitwise and purlwise

Simple decreases

The most used decrease is worked by knitting or purling two stitches together and can be placed anywhere on the row, singly or across all the stitches.

K2 tog decrease

Insert the right needle through the front of both of the next two stitches from left to right and put the yarn round under the right needle tip (see fig. 157a).

Use the right needle to draw a new loop through both stitches, turning two stitches into one and forming a stitch below the new stitch which leans towards the right (see fig. 157b).

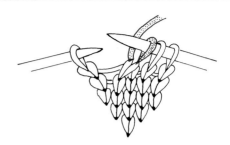

157b Knit both stitches together

P2 tog decrease

Insert the right needle tip through the front of both of the next two stitches from right to left. Put the yarn over and round the right needle tip (see fig. 158a).

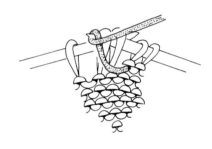

158a Insert needle through both loops purlwise

Use the right needle to draw a new loop through both stitches, making one stitch from two (see fig. 158b).

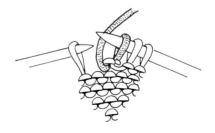

158b Completed K2 tog tbl

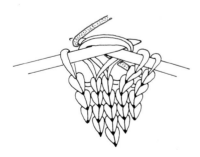

157a Insert needle through both loops knitwise

Twisted decreases

When stitches are being worked through the backs of the loops the decrease must be made in the same way. The K2 tog decrease also slopes to the right and a decrease is often required for design purposes to slope left, which is achieved by working through the back of the loops.

K2 tog tbl decrease

Insert the right needle tip through the next two stitches together, passing the needle through the back of both stitches from right to left and put the yarn under the right needle tip (see fig. 159a).

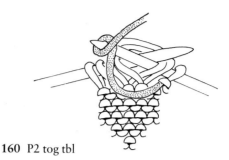

160 P2 tog tbl

both loops together. Purl the stitch in this position drawing through one stitch where there have been two (see fig. 160).

Slipped decreases

Slipped decreases are used because the slipped stitch lifted over the other stitch gives a prominent slope to the left. It can be worked in two ways. One is the standard method and is abbreviated to sl1, K1, psso or more briefly SKPO. The newer method is just as simple and gives a much neater, clearer line, particularly when worked two or more rows apart. It is abbreviated to SSK and can be used in place of an SKPO in any instructions.

SKPO decrease knitwise

Slip the next stitch knitwise to the right needle (see fig. 161a).

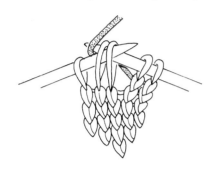

159a Insert needle through back of both loops

Use the right needle to draw a new loop through both stitches, leaving one stitch where there had been two (see fig. 159b). The stitches taken together lie with a slope to the left.

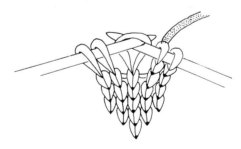

161a Slip one stitch knitwise

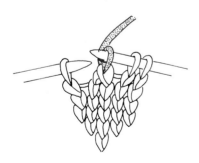

159b K2 tog, leaving one stitch

P2 tog tbl decrease

Insert the right needle tip through the next two stitches from left to right through the backs of

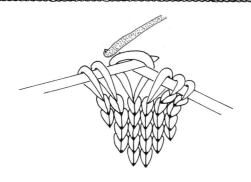

161b Knit next stitch

Knit the following stitch (see fig. 161b). Use the left needle to lift the slipped stitch over the knitted stitch (see fig. 162a) and off the right needle tip (see fig. 162b).

This reduces two stitches to one and leaves a stitch beneath the new stitch that slopes to the left.

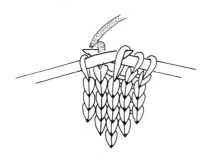

162a Lift slipped stitch over knitted stitch

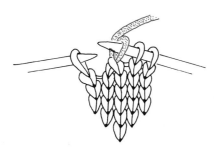

162b Completed decrease

SSK decrease
Insert the right needle tip in the next stitch knitwise and slip it to the right needle (see fig. 163a).

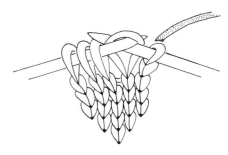

163a Slip one stitch knitwise

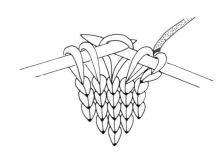

163b Slip next stitch knitwise

Slip the next stitch knitwise also. They must be slipped singly (see fig. 163b).

Insert the left needle tip from left to right through the front of both slipped stitches together.

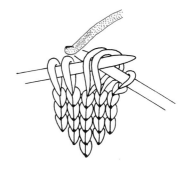

164 Insert left needle through both stitches and knit together

Knit together in this position, making one stitch out of two and leaving a decrease which slopes to the left (see fig. 164).

Slipped decrease purlwise

A slipped purled decrease is seldom given in printed instructions as it is usually replaced by a P2 tog tbl. There is a better way of working this which more closely matches the slipped knitted decrease.

Purl the first of the two stitches which are to form the decrease, then slip it back on to the left needle. Lift the stitch beyond it to the left over the purled stitch and off the left needle tip, then slip the stitch back on to the right needle and continue to the row end.

Paired decreases

When decreases are used on opposite sides of a stitch or stitches, or at opposite ends of the needle, the decreases must be paired. This means that you must work a decrease to slope in the opposite directions.

On raglan shaping decreases are usually paired to slope in the same direction as the slope of the edge but they can also be paired in the reverse way to slope away from the edge. They may be used in this way to form a decrease but also to form a decoration, standing out against the vertical and horizontal lines of the surrounding stitches. Purled decreases are paired by the way their slope shows not on the purled side but on the knit side of the work. To slope the same way as the decreased edge they must be paired thus:

Left side	*Right side*
K2 tog	SSK or SKPO or K2 tog tbl
P2 tog	P2 tog tbl or P1, sl1, psso.

Paired to slope with the slant of the decreased edges the pairing is said to be 'smooth'.

When the decrease is reversed and slopes in opposition or conflict to the slant of the edge it is said to be rough or reversed. The decreases placed in patterns where they are opposed to the slant or are reverse paired are feathered; in this case the pattern is called feather and fan.

To slope in the reverseway to the edge:

Left side	*Right side*
SSK, SKPO or K2 tog tbl	K2 tog
P2 tog tbl or P1, sl1, psso.	P2 tog

The pairing of K2 tog at the left and SKPO at the right can be seen in fig. 165a while fig. 165b shows how much better the left slope at the right edge looks when worked with the SSK decrease.

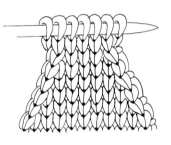

165a SKPO at right, K2 tog at left

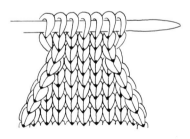

165b Neater line using SSK at right

Double decreases

Double decreases, where three stitches become one, only appear to slope, depending on how they are made because with three stitches forming only one there is in fact a centre stitch.

There are again three ways of working double decreases
- simple double decreases
- twisted double decreases
- slipped double decreases

Simple double decreases

The simple double decrease takes three stitches together knitwise or purlwise and leaves one stitch uppermost that slopes to the right on the right side of the work.

K3 tog decrease
Insert the right needle tip through the front of the next three stitches together from left to right (see fig. 166a).

167a Insert needle purlwise through three stitches

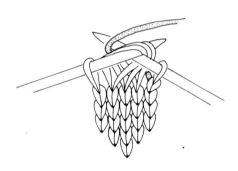

166a Insert needle knitwise through three stitches

Bring the yarn under the right needle tip and knit together, using the right needle to draw through one new loop where there were three stitches previously (see fig. 166b).

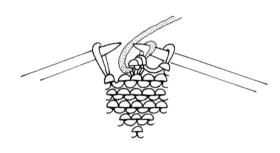

167b Purl together

P3 tog decrease
Insert the right needle tip through the next three stitches from right to left (see fig. 167a).

Put the yarn over and round the needle tip and use the right needle to draw through one stitch where previously there were three stitches (see fig. 167b).

Twisted double decreases

The twisted double decreases are worked in the same way as the single twisted decreases but over three stitches instead of two.

K3 tog tbl decrease
Insert the right needle tip through the back of the loops of the next three stitches together from right to left and knit in this position, using the right needle to draw through the new stitch (see fig. 168a).

This stitch appears to slope to the left on the right side as does the purled version.

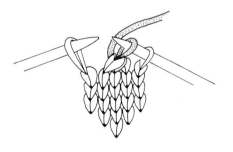

166b Knit together to leave one stitch

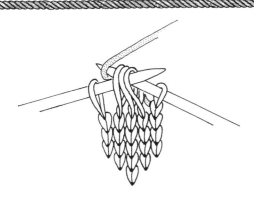

168a K3 tog tbl

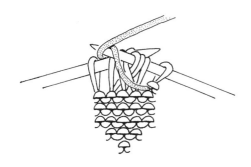

168b P3 tog tbl

P3tog tbl decrease
Insert the right needle tip through the backs of the next three stitches together from left to right and purl them in this position (see fig. 168b).

Slipped decreases

With three stitches to use for the decrease there are four different ways of working, all four of which have matching wrong side decreases, giving the same slant and appearance from the right side. The abbreviations for these decreases are less well known because only one, SK2togPO, is in constant use.

These methods are:
- SK2togPO or Sl1, K2 tog, psso decrease which slopes left (see fig. 169)
- SKORO decrease, the reverse of the 1st decrease with the main stitch sloping right (see fig. 170)
- S2KPO decrease which slopes to the left (see fig. 171). This is similar to a reversed K3 tog decrease

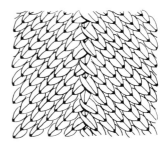

169 SK2togPO decrease

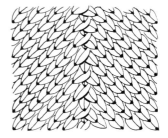

170 SKORO decrease

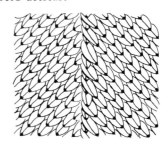

171 S2KPO decrease

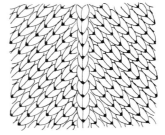

172 S2togKO decrease

- S2togKO decrease which leaves a central stitch dominant and which has a vast design potential almost completely overlooked (see fig. 172)

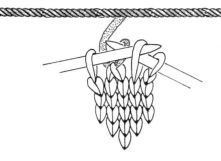

173 SK2togPO decrease

SK2togPO decrease

Slip the first of the three stitches to be used knitwise to the right needle.

Knit the next two stitches together and, with the left needle tip, lift the slipped stitch over the two stitches knitted together and off the right needle point (see fig. 173).

Purlwise

The matching wrong side double decrease can be abbreviated to SPSRORO for slip, purl, slip, return, over, return and over.

Slip one stitch to right needle, purl one and slip next stitch purlwise also to right needle, return the last two stitches to the left needle and lift the slipped or second stitch over the purled or 1st stitch and off the left needle tip (see fig. 174a).

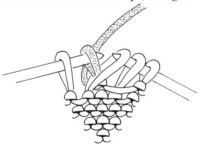

174a Slip one, purl one and slip one purlwise, return to left needle and lift second stitch over first

174b Return stitch from left to right needle and lift first stitch now to right of it over it and off needle

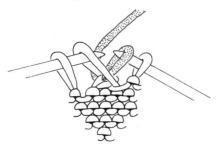

Return the purled stitch to the right needle and with the left needle tip lift the first slipped stitch over the purled stitch and off the needle (see fig. 174b).

SKORO decrease

The abbreviation is for slip, knit, pass slipped stitch over, return to left needle and pass next stitch over.

Slip one stitch knitwise to right needle, knit one, with left needle tip lift the slipped stitch over the knitted stitch and off the right needle tip (see fig. 175a).

175a Lift slipped stitch over knitted stitch

Slip the knitted stitch back to the left needle and with the right needle tip lift the stitch beyond it over the knitted stitch and off the left needle tip (see fig. 175b).

Return the knitted stitch to the right needle to complete the decrease.

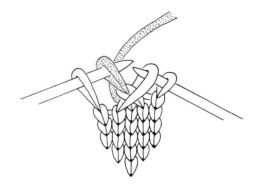

175b With right needle tip lift stitch to left of returned stitch over it and off the needle

Purlwise

The abbreviation for this double decrease is P2togRPO for purl two tog, return, pass over.

Purl next two stitches together and return to left needle. With right needle tip lift stitch beyond the returned stitch over it and off the left needle tip then slip the purled stitch back to the right needle and complete the row (see fig. 176).

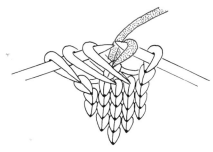

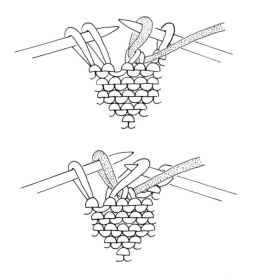

176 Completed P2togRPO decrease

S2KPO decrease

Slip the next two stitches knitwise and singly from left to right needle.

Knit next stitch and with left needle tip lift both slipped stitches over the knitted stitch and off the right needle tip (see fig. 177).

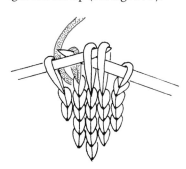

177 Slip next two stitches knitwise and singly, to right needle, knit next stitch and lift both slipped stitches over it

Purlwise

The wrong side decrease which gives the same appearance on the right side is abbreviated to PR2PO for purl, return, pass next 2 stitches over.

Purl one stitch and return to left needle. Use right needle tip to lift the stitch beyond over the purled stitch and off the left needle point.

Again use the right needle point to repeat this and lift the next stitch over the purled stitch and off the left needle point (see 178).

Return the purled stitch to the right needle to complete the decrease.

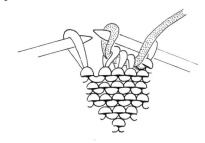

178 Completed PRS2PO decrease

S2togKO decrease

Insert the right needle from left to right through the front of the next two stitches together and slip them on to the right needle (see fig. 179a).

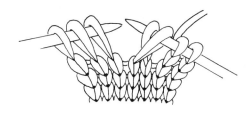

179a Insert needle through both of next two stitches and pass to right needle

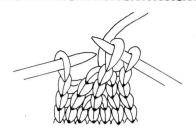

179b Knit next stitch and lift both slipped stitches over

Knit the next stitch and use the left needle point to lift both slipped stitches over the knitted stitch and off the right needle point to complete the decrease (see fig. 179b).

Purlwise

This can be abbreviated to PS2RPO and stands for purl, slip two, return and pass over.

Purl one stitch and slip next two stitches knitwise and together to right needle, return both slipped stitches which are now twisted and the purled stitch to the left needle (see fig. 180a).

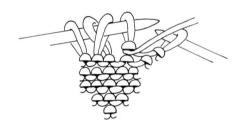

180a Purl one then slip next two stitches together to right then pass all three stitches back to left

With the right needle tip lift both the slipped stitches over the purled stitch and off the left needle point (see fig. 180b).

Return the purled stitch to the right needle to complete the decrease.

180b Lift both slipped stitches over purled stitch

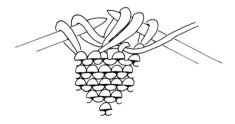

Paired double decreases

When double decreases are placed close together or on opposite sides of rows or groups of stitches they must be paired. This, as for single decreases, is to make matching slants one left with one right. When the slants echo the slope caused by the decrease they are said to be regular or smooth, and when they are the reverse way to the slant they are reversed or rough.

The pairing of double decreases is as follows:

Left side	*Right side*
K3 tog	K3 tog tbl
K3 tog	S2KPO
SKORO	SK2togPO
P3 tog	P3 tog tbl
P3 tog	PR2PO
P2togRPO	SPSRORO

Reverse these reading left for right and right for left for the reverse or rough pairing.

The S2togKO and PS2RPO do not require to be paired because of their central vertical stitch.

Designing

Designing knitted garments brings together all aspects of knitting. Once inspired by an idea, you must then set about realizing it. In many cases this first step may be reversed – that is, a knitting pattern or technique may spark off the idea. Whichever way a thought begins, it is essential to good design that the technique must fit the style. Bad design is often a result of a good idea that is forced into an unsuitable form, be it of shape, texture, tension or all three at once.

The best of folk knitting provides perfect examples of the knitter's skill and the complete understanding of what can be achieved with yarn, colour and stitches. Austrian stockings show the precision of pattern fitting shaping, colour symbols in pattern show in Estonian socks; similarly, the knitters of Shetland and Iceland create designs suited to the exact characteristics of the yarns.

To transform the idea to reality you must choose your yarn and stitch pattern or patterns and then make a tension square.

Tension

When you are designing it is essential that you are in complete control of what the stitches do and what shape is made, and know the number of stitches to give the required measurement. *Nearly* the correct measurements will not do.

The tension square should be as large as possible and is only of use if the garment is to be made with the same needles and yarn. This provides the important information of how many stitches and rows there are to one inch or one centimetre.

For more information *see* **Tension.**

Shape

Planning the shape comes next. It is a good idea to plan this on a diagram which can gradually be filled in with the information required and should show half the body (see fig. 181).

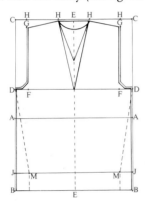

181 Designer's chart

Line AA
Line AA = ¹/₂ total bust/chest measurement plus ¹/₂ total tolerance to be added.

The diagram shows half the complete garment and may show back with any alteration for front superimposed upon it (*see* **Tolerance**).

Lines CB
Lines CB are total length from shoulder (or centre back neck) to lower edge.

Line EE
This line can be dotted as it shows centre line and may not be a line required other than for placing centre of neckline and shoulders.

Line DD
Line DD gives the armhole line; you can place this by measuring up from the lower edge the side seam measurement or down from the shoulder line the depth required for the armhole.

Point FF
On line DD mark the amount of indentation to be allowed for the armhole.

Point GG
Place points GG inside CC on shoulder line and join with FF.

Points HH
Mark straight shoulders by measuring from GG towards centre line and marking points HH. The distance between HH must also equal the width across centre back neck.

Where shoulder lines are to be sloped the position of GG must be dropped from its present position by the amount of slope required.

The correct amount for an individual measurement is found by subtracting the waist to tip of shoulder measurement from the waist to centre back neck measurement. A standard allowance is about 2.5cm or 1in.

Adding row and stitch numbers
As tension is already known it is possible to add to the diagram the number of stitches required at the widest point AA and the number of rows between CB.

Lines DG
Lines D and G can be joined to give the armhole line once you have decided on the method of shaping the armhole curve. This may be a curve from D to join the dotted line from F to G or it may be a sloping straight line from D to the dotted line from F to G. Where a sleeve is indented but has no armhole shaping you will simply have to draw in a line from F to G.

Line JJ
Where a ribbed welt is to be added, you must mark on line JJ the required distance above BB. For a straight-sided sweater the next stage (MM) can be omitted.

Points MM

For a shaped side place points MM on line JJ after the amount of shaping has been decided on. New lines can then be drawn to both D points from the M points.

Confirming stitch numbers

The addition of shaping or the welt or both means adjusting the number of stitches for the width.

Placing neck

The depth of the neckline can be marked on line EE and can then be marked in and any shaping calculated.

Any other alterations for a specific design can be added in the same way so that the diagram or map can be put to use and both front and back knitted.

Charting

Also see **Charts**

Coloured patterns may need additional planning and it may be necessary to turn the diagram into a chart for every stitch to be worked, or for the addition of further, more complex alterations.

Diagonal knitting

A bias to knitting is added by placing a decrease to one side of the fabric and an increase to the opposite side. This can be worked on narrow stripes used for bias trims and bindings, on stitch patterns and for complete garment sections.

To work bias braid

Cast on a small number of stitches.
1st row K2 tog, K to last st, M1, K1.
2nd row P.
Rep these 2 rows as required.

This gives a left bias or slope towards the left, shown by the direction the stitches take between the increase and decrease when the sides are held vertically (see fig. 182).

The reverse slope can be worked by altering the decrease to the end of the row and placing the increase at the beginning.
Cast on a small number of stitches.

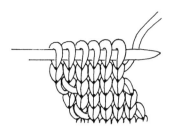

182 Diagonal braid

1st row K1, M1, K to last 2 sts, K2 tog.
2nd row P.
Rep 1st and 2nd rows.

Pattern making

To form patterns which slope alternately left and right the increases must always be placed directly above each other and the decreases above the decreases. The stitches in between will slope towards the decrease and away from the increase (see figs 122 and 123).

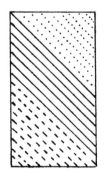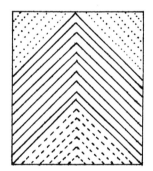

183a Diagonal rectangle   **183b** Creating a chevron

183c Reversed chevron

Garment design

A garment may be designed with all the stitches sloping in one direction by your working a large rectangle in the same way that the bias braid was made.

For a rectangle, starting from one corner, work increases at both ends of the right side rows until the edge of the fabric is the correct length to form the width of the lower edge.

This number of stitches is then retained by working as for the braid decreasing at one end and increasing at the other, until one side is the correct length for the garment. The top edge is then formed by decreasing at both edges until the corner opposite to the cast-on corner is completed (see fig. 183a).

Variation comes with the position of the diagonal lines. A chevron can be created by working decreases in the centre of the garment with increases at either side. This chevron has diagonal lines running from sides to centre (see fig. 183b). Reversed chevrons, with lines from centre out to the sides and upwards, are made by placing paired increases or a double increase in the centre of the garment section with decreases at the side edges (see fig. 183c).

Double knitting

Double knitting, or the knitting of two separate layers of fabric, both sides of which show stocking stitch, can be worked with a special combination of slipped stitches and yarn held to the front.

To work double fabric

Cast on a number of sts divisible by 2.
1st row (RS Facing) K1, * K1, sl1 purlwise with yarn in front, rep from * to last st, K1.

Rep this row as required.

Owing to the large number of slipped stitches this is best worked on larger needles than usual for the yarn used (see fig. 184a).

When using as the section of a self-lined garment cast off in the usual way for a closed edge. For an open edge cast off, slip all the sts for one 'side' on to a spare needle and cast off normally one side and then the other.

184 (*Left*) Double knitting, reversible.
(*Right*) Two-coloured double knitting, reversible

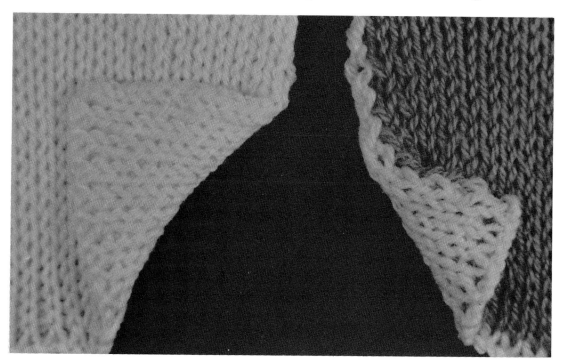

Two-coloured double fabric

As a change from knitting pins, which can only be used for rows, a pair of double-pointed needles or a circular needle make it possible to work a double fabric with one colour used for one side and another colour used for the other side or lining. Although both sides are quite separate, the ends are joined. With a pair of double-pointed needles or circular needle cast on an even number of stitches with A (see fig. 184b).

1st row With B, * K1, yarn to front, sl1 purlwise, rep from * to end. Do not turn.

2nd row Slip sts back to right end of needle and pick up A from under B so that the yarns are twisted, with A, * with yarn back sl1, P1, rep from * to end. Turn and take up B from under A.

3rd row With B, * sl1 with yarn back, P1, rep from * to end. Do not turn.

4th row Slip sts back to right end of needle and pick up A from under B, with A, * K1, with yarn to front sl1 purlwise, rep from * to end. Turn.

Rep 1st–4th rows until required length.

Cast off using one colour only for a closed edge.

For an open edge slip all B sts on to one needle and cast off A sts with A, then B sts with B.

Double-pointed needle stitch patterns

Many patterns, suitable for working round, present problems for the knitter used to working rows.

In round knitting, particularly where more than one colour is involved, if only one round is worked, a colour used for the previous round and the changed colour for the round just completed both finish at the same point. It is easy to work the next round with either A or B. In flat knitting one row in A and one row in B leaves A at the wrong end of the needle if it is required for the next row.

This can be overcome if you use either a pair of double-pointed needles or a circular needle. In both cases the work can be slipped back to the right end of the needle and another row worked in the same direction as the first.

Striped rib pattern

Although this is a 14 row repeat all A rows are worked as either knit or purl rows and the pattern is worked on the remaining rows.

Worked over a number of stitches divisible by 4, plus 3.

Cast on using A and a pair of double-pointed needles or a circular needle (see fig. 185a).

185 (*Top*) Striped rib pattern.
(*Bottom*) Two-coloured moss stitch

1st row (RS facing) With A, K. Do not turn.

2nd row Slip sts back to right end of needle and with B, (RS facing) K1, * sl1 with yarn at back, K3, rep from * to last 2 sts, sl1, K1. Turn.

3rd row With A, (WS facing) P. Do not turn.

4th row Slip sts back to right end of needle and with B, (WS facing) P1, sl1 with yarn forward, P3, rep from * to last 2 sts, sl1, P1. Turn.

5th–8th rows Work rows 1, 2, 3, and 1 again.

9th row With B, (WS facing) P1, * sl1 with yarn forward, P3, rep from * to last 2 sts, sl1, P1. Do not turn.

10th row Slip sts back to right end of needle and with A. (WS facing), P. Turn.

11th row With B, (RS facing) K1, * sl1 with yarn back, K3, rep from * to last 2 sts, sl1, K1. Do not turn.

12th row Slip sts back to right end of needle and with A, (RS facing), K.

13th and 14th rows Rep 9th and 10th rows.

Rep from 1st–14th rows as required.

Two-colour moss stitch

Worked in toning shades this pattern gives a subtle tweed effect.

Worked over an odd number of stitches.

Cast on with A, using two double-pointed needles or a circular needle (see fig. 185b).

1st row With B (RS facing) P1, * K1, P1, rep from * to end. Do not turn.

2nd row (RS facing) Slip sts back to right end of needle. With A K1, * P1, K1, rep from * to end. Turn.

3rd row With B (WS facing), K1, * P1, K1, rep from * to end. Do not turn.

4th row (WS facing) Slip sts back to right end of needle. With A P1, * K1, P1, rep from * to end. Turn.

Rep 1st–4th rows as required.

Two-colour fisherman's rib

This gives a reversible fabric and a fascinating colour change between one side and the other.

Worked over an odd number of stitches (see colour plate 5(a)).

Cast on with A using two double-pointed needles or a circular needle.

Preparation row With A, K1, * P1, K1, rep from * to end. Do not turn.

1st row Slip sts back to right end of needle and with B, (RS facing), K1, * P into st below next st on needle, K1, rep from * to end. Turn.

2nd row With A, (WS facing), K1, * K1, P into st below next st on needle, rep from * to last 2 sts, K2. Do not turn.

3rd row Slip sts back to right end of needle and with B, (WS facing) P1, * K into st below next st on needle, P1, rep from * to end. Turn.

4th row With A, (RS facing), K1, * P1, K into st below next st on needle, rep from * to last 2 sts, P1, K1.

Rep 1st–4th rows as required.

For method of knitting below a stitch see **Knitting below stitches.**

Double check fabric

Completely reversible, this check makes a striking pattern for jackets and matching scarves (see colour plate 5(b)).

Worked over a number of stitches divisible by 16, plus 8.

Cast on using A and double-pointed needles.

1st row With A, (RS facing), [ybk, K1, yf, sl1] 4 times, * [ybk, sl1, yf, P1] 4 times, [ybk, K1, yf, sl1] 4 times, rep from * to end. Do not turn.

2nd row Slip sts back to right end, with B, (RS facing), [ybk, sl1, yf, P1] 4 times, * [ybk, K1, yf, sl1] 4 times, [ybk, sl1, yf, P1] 4 times, rep from * to end. Turn.

3rd row With B, (WS facing), work as for 1st row. Do not turn.

4th row Slip sts back to right end of needle, with A, (WS facing), work as for 2nd row. Turn.

5th row With A, (RS facing), work as for 1st row. Do not turn.

6th row Slip sts back to right end of needle, with B, (RS facing), work as for 2nd row. Turn.

7th row With B (WS facing), work as for 1st row. Do not turn.

8th row Slip sts back to right end of needle, (WS facing), work as for 2nd row. Turn.

9th row With B, (RS facing), work as for 1st row. Do not turn.

10th row Slip sts back to right end of needle, with A, (RS facing), work as for 1st row. Turn.

11th row With A, (WS facing) work as for 1st row. Do not turn.

12th row Slip sts to right end of needle, with B, (WS facing), work as for 2nd row. Turn.

13th row With B, (RS facing), work as for 1st row. Do not turn.

14th row Slip sts back to right end of needle, with A, (RS facing), work as for 2nd row. Turn.

15th row With A, (WS facing), work as for 1st row. Do not turn.

16th row Slip sts back to right end of needle, with B, (WS facing), work as for 2nd row.

Rep 1st–16th rows as required.

Cast off using 1 colour only.

Dropped stitches

Intentionally dropped stitches are made in three different ways.

- dropped and unravelled for several rows before being picked up again
- dropped to a pre-formed platform so that it can unravel no further
- made with more than one twist of yarn round the needle so that the extra loops round the needle can be dropped and can lengthen the stitch

Dropped and picked up stitches

The depth of the dropped stitch can be varied by your making the number of strands above it and the curve of the sides greater or smaller.

Work six rows in stocking stitch, ending with a purl row. Knit to the position for the first dropped stitch.

Drop the next stitch off the left needle and unravel it until the required number of strands is seen above it; then pick up the loop of the dropped stitch with the left needle tip. (See fig. 186a)

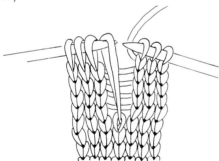

186a Lifting dropped stitch

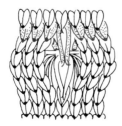

186b Knitted stitch holds the strands

Insert the right needle into the picked up stitch and lift the four strands above it also on the right needle and knit the dropped stitch, catching in the strands at the same time (see fig. 186b).

Stitches dropped to a platform

For this type of dropped stitch an increased stitch at the base of the ladder to be left must be made. This must be worked in the number of rows below the dropped stitch equal to the number of strands which are to show, plus the row on which the increase is to be made.

Work to the point at which the base of the ladder is to be. Lift the thread before the next stitch on to the left needle tip and knit a stitch out of this loop in the usual way (*see* **Increases**).

Work five rows more and then knit to the made stitch on the next row. Drop the next stitch and continue to work the remainder of the row (see fig. 187a).

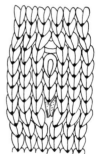

187a Dropping the made stitch

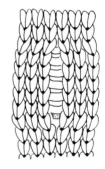

187b Unravelling the stitch to its platform

The dropped stitch will unravel or can be unravelled only as far as the stitch it was made from six rows below (see fig. 187b).

Lengthened stitches

The length of the stitch can be altered by the number of times the yarn is thrown or wound round the needle tip before the stitch is knitted. The diagram shows the yarn being put twice round the needle tip but this can be three or four times as stated in the instructions.

After winding the yarn round the tip, knit the stitch in the usual way (see fig. 188a).

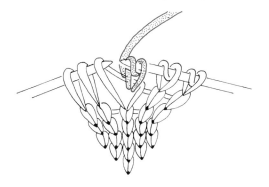

188a Wind yarn twice round needle

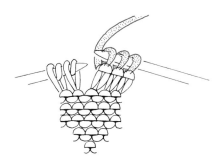

188b Drop extra loops as stitch is purled

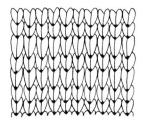

189 Alternately lengthened rows

On the next row the extra loops are dropped, lengthening the stitch, and the remaining loop is worked in the usual way, knitted or purled (see fig. 188b).

This gives a deeper row between ordinary rows (see fig. 189).

Yarn wound three times round the needle tip on every stitch would increase the size of the loops for that row (see fig 190a).

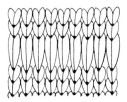

190a Deeper lengthened rows

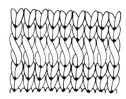

190b Single twisted rows

The lengthened stitches can also be twisted by winding the yarn round the needle tip in a more complex way (see fig. 190b).

Two twisted rows, worked together, appear even more complex (see fig. 190c).

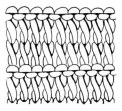

190c Double twisted rows

To twist a dropped stitch

Once practised, this method of winding the yarn round both needle tips can be worked quickly and makes a fabric that grows equally quickly. Suitable for many yarns, it is also effective worked in knitting ribbon.

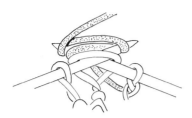

191a Twist yarn right, left then right round needle tips

Insert the needle knitwise into the stitch and take the yarn up and over the right needle tip, under and over the left needle tip and back under the right needle tip (see fig. 191a).

Do not hold the needles tightly together but use the right needle tip to draw through one stitch on the needle in the usual way. The new stitch is drawn through only the actual stitch on the needle and not through any of the twists on the needle tips (see fig. 191b).

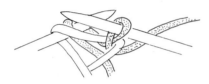

191b Draw loop through single strand on needle

Lengthened dropped stitches

Lengthened stitches can also become dropped stitches and are usually dropped in order to alter their position on the finished fabric.

Lengthen the stitch in the usual way by winding the yarn several times round the right needle tip before knitting the stitch (see fig. 192a).

192a Twist yarn twice round needle

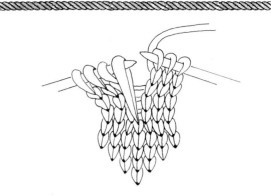

192b Lengthened stitch

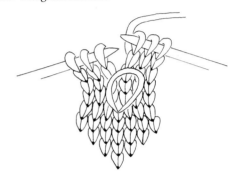

192c Drop lengthened stitch

Several rows are then worked, dropping the extra loops and slipping the stitch without working it until the background is the same length as the stitch (see fig. 192b). It is then dropped off the needle (see fig. 192c).

Drop stitches moved to left

Once it is dropped several more stitches must be worked before the dropped stitch can be knitted

193a Several stitches must be worked before the dropped stitch can be knitted up

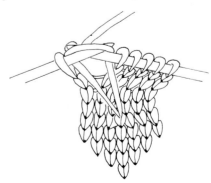

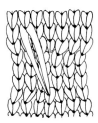

193b Dropped stitch in new position

into its new position if it is then to be moved to the left (see fig. 193a b).

Drop stitches moved to right

After dropping the stitch several stitches must be slipped to the left needle before the dropped stitch can be knitted up. The instructions usually give warning of this; work them as slipped stitches only knitting them after the dropped stitch is in place (see fig. 194a b). *See* Gull check in **Dropped and lengthened stitch patterns.**

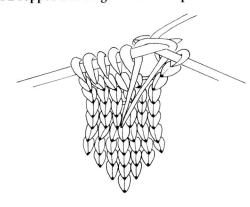

194a Stitches slipped back to left needle to move dropped stitch to new position

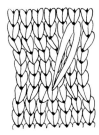

194b Dropped stitch knitted up to the right of its old position

Drop stitch patterns

Drop stitch patterns give a new dimension to lace knitting. They can often seem very different if worked in chunky yarns instead of the fine yarn usually associated with lace patterns.

Vertical drop stitch pattern

This is something of a ghost stitch as it is the invisible stitch that forms the pattern (see fig. 195a).
Worked over a number of stitches divisible by 8, plus 4.

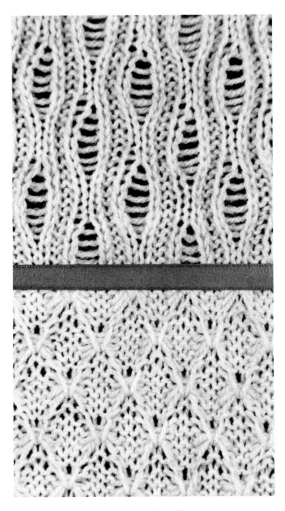

195 (*Top*) Vertical dropped stitch.
(*Bottom*) Dropped stitch honeycomb

Preparation row (RS facing) K1, * P2, K1, yon, K1, P2, K2, rep from * to last 3 sts, P2, K1.

1st, 3rd and 5th rows P1, * K2, P2, K2, P3, rep from * to last 3 sts, K2, P1.

2nd and 4th rows K1, * P2, K3, P2, K2, rep from * to last 3 sts, P2, K1.

6th row K1, * P2, K1, drop next st off needle and let it unravel 6 rows down where the yon will stop it, K1, P2, K1, yon, K1, rep from * to last 3 sts, P2, K1.

7th, 9th and 11th rows P1 * K2, P3, K2, P2, rep from * to last 3 sts, K2, P1.

8th and 10th rows K1, * P2, K2, P2, K3, rep from * to last 3 sts, P2, K1.

12th row K1, * P2, K1, yon, K1, P2, K1, drop next st off needle and unravel 6 rows down, K1, rep from * to last 3 sts, P2, K1.

Rep 1st–12th rows as required.

Drop stitch honeycomb

Giving this ruched effect, the dropped stitch gathers together the strands above (see fig. 195b).

Worked over a number of stitches divisible by 4, plus 3.

Preparation row P.

1st row (WS facing) K.

2nd row P.

3rd and 4th rows As 1st and 2nd rows.

5th row As 1st row.

6th row P3, drop next st off left needle and let it unravel until there are 5 loose strands above it, insert the right needle tip into the dropped st from behind and P it and the 5 loose strands above it together, P3, rep from * to end.

7th, 9th and 11th rows K.

8th and 10th rows P.

12th row P1, * drop next st and unravel until there are 5 loose strands, pick up loop from behind and P tog with 5 loose strands, P3, rep from * to last 2 sts, work 1 dropped st as before, P1.

Rep 1st–12th rows as required.

Blister stitch

Worked in contrasting colours the blisters can be repeated in the same contrast or can use any number of colours to build up a colour sequence (see colour plate 6(a)).

Worked over a number of stitches divisible by 4, plus 3.

Preparation row With B, P.

1st and 3rd rows (RS facing) With A, K.

2nd and 4th rows With A, P.

5th row With B, K3, drop next st off needle and unravel 4 rows down, insert right needle into front of B st in row below unravelled sts and K it catching in the loose strands above it, K3, rep from * to end.

6th row With B, P.

7th–10th rows With A, as 1st–4th rows.

11th row With B, K1, * drop st as on 5th row and K up B st 5 rows below catching in loose strands above it, K3, rep from * to last 2 sts, work drop st, K1.

12th row With B, P.

Rep 1st–12th rows as required.

Gull check

Dropped stitches need not be picked up immediately above their dropping point. The stitches in this pattern are picked up to either side of the dropping position (see colour plate 6(b)).

Worked over a number of stitches divisible by 7, plus 1.

Cast on using A.

1st row (WS facing) With A, K3, * P2, K5, rep from * to last 5 sts, P2, K3.

2nd and 4th rows With B, K3, * sl2 with yarn back, K5, rep from * to last 5 sts, sl2 K3.

3rd and 5th rows With B, P3, * sl2 with yarn forward, P5, rep from * to last 5 sts, sl2, P3.

6th row With A, * K1, sl2 with yarn back, drop next A sl st off needle to front of work, sl same 2 sts back to left needle, pick up dropped st and K it, K2, drop next st off needle to front, K2, pick up dropped st and K it, rep from * to last st, K1.

Rep 1st–6th rows as required.

Duplicate stitch

See **Swiss Darning**

Dye numbers

Most balls of yarn carry two numbers. One is the dye shade number and the other the dye lot number. The dye shade number gives the number of the particular colour but the dye lot number is the number of the actual dye bath. Balls from a different dye bath may vary in shade but carry the same dye numbers. This variance, although slight, may show when knitted. It is to avoid this that instructions advise you to buy all the yarn required at one time and check that it has not only the shade number but also the same dye lot number.

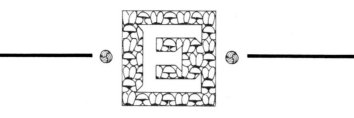

Edges

Edges which are neither cast on or off are just as important, whether they are to be seamed or not.

Edges to be seamed

Edges which retain a straight line are the easiest to seam. Uneven edges and the 'serrated' edge, formed by increasing on the edge stitch, make it difficult to sew straight seams when it is time to make up.

Increases and decreases
The best placing for shaping, which allows seams to be worked immediately within an unbroken line, is to place them inside one or more edge stitches.

Unseamed edges
Edges which are to show on the finished garment can be worked so that they appear to best advantage. The type of edge used will depend on the finished appearance.

A firm edge, suitable for all edges to be seamed, is made by slipping the first stitch and knitting the last stitch on every row irrespective of whether the fabric is stocking stitch, garter stitch, reversed stocking stitch or a patterned fabric.

On shaped edges, where increases are to be worked, it is possible to place decreases or increases inside this edge, retaining the single stitch edge which, when seamed, will give an unbroken line (see fig. 197a).

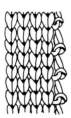

197a Seam edge

Chain edge
On items where the edge is to stand free, as on a single thickness scarf, a chain edge leaves one stitch for every two rows (see fig. 197b).

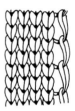

197b Chain edge

On stocking stitch
The chain edge is worked on stocking stitch by slipping both the first and last stitches on every knit row. These stitches must be slipped knitwise. On purl rows every stitch along the row is purled.

On garter stitch
A chain edge on garter stitch is worked only on the first stitch of every row. Slip the first stitch purlwise with the yarn forward, take the yarn back and knit to the end of the row. Repeat this on every row to be worked.

Picot edging
A picot edging is decorative on lace fabric and is also useful where stitches are to be picked up from that edge. It is worked by placing a yon loop before the first stitch of every row. Worked in this way it also acts as an increase, gradually widening the work by two stitches every two rows. Where the number of stitches is required to remain constant and it is being made only to give the picot edge it must be worked as follows:
1st row (RS facing) Insert needle knitwise into 1st and 2nd sts, as if to K tog, bring the yarn up and over the front of the right hand needle,

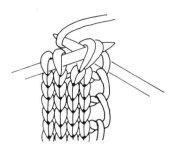

198 Picot edge

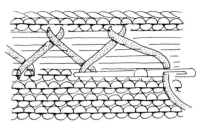

199a Herringbone casing

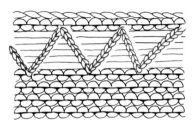

199b Chain stitch casing

under the right needle tip and draw through the new stitch with the right needle tip in the usual way. (See fig. 198)

The similar yon placed at the other edge is worked on the purl row thus:

2nd row Insert needle purlwise through 1st and 2nd sts, take the yarn behind the right needle over the top of the 2 loops on the needle points and under the right needle point, then purl the stitch in the usual way using the right needle to draw the new stitch through. The yon and the loop from the 2 sts worked together leaves 2 stitches on the right needle.

Elastic

Elastic can be used with knitted garments to hold edges more firmly in place.

Added to ribbing

Shirring elastic either worked on alternate rows along with the stitches over the first inch of rib or threaded, darning fashion, through the rows after they are worked will give ribbing extra strength.

Elastic can also be threaded through hems and secured either to side seams or, as for waists, with the ends sewn together.

Single fabric elastic casing

For a less bulky casing for elastic than found with a double hem, work on the wrong side of the fabric using herringbone stitch to hold the elastic against the wrong side of the garment (see fig. 199a). A stronger edge can be worked as in

fig. 199b by working a chain of crochet alternately anchored to the knitting above and below the elastic.

Embossed stitch patterns

Stitches which seem to be raised above the surrounding fabric require no unusual technique, even when one edge is open.

Embossed bell motifs

This is an old pattern which can be combined with other patterns to create a novel pattern. The bells can be repeated to form flower heads, the stalks continued upwards into ribbing. To cast on during working *see* **Casting on and off** (see fig. 200a).

Worked over a number of stitches divisible by 8, plus 4.

1st row (RS facing) P.
2nd row K.
3rd row P4, * cast on 8 sts, P4, rep from * to end.
4th row K4, * P8, K4, rep from * to end.
5th row P4, * K8, P4, rep from * to end.
6th row K4, * P8, K4, rep from * to end.

200 (*Top*) Embossed bell pattern.
(*Bottom*) Embossed puff stitch

7th row P4, * SSK, K4, K2 tog, P4, rep from * to end.
8th row K4, * P6, K4, rep from * to end.
9th row P4, * SSK, K2, K2 tog, P4, rep from * to end.
10th row K4, * P4, K4, rep from * to end.
11th row P4, * SSK, K2 tog, P4, rep from * to end.
12th row K4, * P2, K4, rep from * to end.
13th row P4, * K2 tog, P4, rep from * to end.
14th row K4, * P1, K4, rep from * to end.
15th row * P3, K2 tog, rep from * to end, P1.
16th row K.
Rep 1st–16th rows as required.

Embossed puff stitch

This embossed stitch raises the puff by lifting the thread between one stitch and the next and working a stitch into this thread (see fig. 200b). Worked over a number of stitches divisible by 10, plus 2.
1st row (WS facing) K2, * P5, K2, P1, K2, rep from * to end.
2nd row P2, * lift thread before next st on to left needle and K it, called M1, K1, M1, P2, SSK, K1, K2 tog, P2, rep from * to end.
3rd row K2, * P3, K2, rep from * to end.
4th row P2, * M1, K3, M1, P2, sl2 knitwise, K1, p2sso, P2, rep from * to end.
5th row K2, * P1, K2, P5, K2, rep from * to end.
6th row P2, * SSK, K1, K2 tog, P2, M1, K1, M1, P2, rep from * to end.
7th row Work as for 3rd row.
8th row P2, * sl2 knitwise, K1, p2sso, P2, M1, K3, M1, P2, rep from * to end.
Rep 1st–8th rows as required.

Embroidery

Knitting is an ideal base for embroidery, the vertical and horizontal lines acting as a guide for added decoration. The stitches can be
* similar to the knitting as in Swiss darning
* contrasting lines, diagonal, curved or knotted, using the complete range of embroidery stitches

The base knitting can be used in three different ways:
* as a background with the embroidery added
* as part of the final pattern, the embroidery being added to highlight, or make use of, part of the knitted in pattern, as in Tyrolean cable patterns
* with another decorative technique such as appliqué or ribbon slotting

Swiss darning

One stitch in Swiss darning copies the exact outline of the knitted stitch beneath it and can be used for the addition of motifs that were intended to be knitted in. Use yarn of equal thickness to the knitted yarn – thinner yarn will not cover the stitches beneath and thicker yarn will buckle the surrounding knitting.

Thread the yarn into a blunt-tipped wool needle and run in the end on the wrong side. If an end of yarn is left on the wrong side it can be darned into the back of the fabric or a nearby seam once the motif is complete.

Bring the needle through to the right side at the base of a stitch (see fig. 201a).

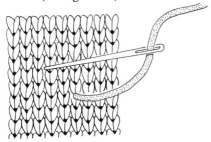

201a Draw needle out on right side

Pass the needle under both threads at the base of the next stitch immediately above (see fig. 201b).

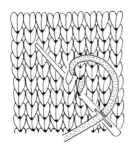

201b Under both threads on stitch above

Take the needle through to the wrong side at the base of the first stitch and out at the base of the next stitch to be worked (see fig. 202a).

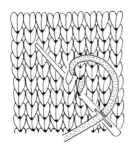

202a Take yarn to back at base of stitch

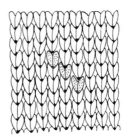

202b Work other stitches as required

Work other stitches in the same way, working along one row then reversing back along the next row and so on until the motif is completed (see fig. 202b).

Embroidery stitches

In using any of the usual embroidery stitches best results are obtained by working through the holes between or in stitches rather than splitting the yarn. This is one reason for using a blunt-pointed wool needle rather than an embroidery needle.

Cross stitch

Like Swiss darning, cross stitch can be used for a small highlight stitch or for working a complete motif (see fig. 203a).

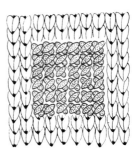

203a Completed stitches

Use the lines of the knitted stitches as a guide working over one, two or more stitches and rows. On some tensions this will not produce a truly square stitch which in working picture motifs particularly must be remembered. Work all the stitches in one direction first (see

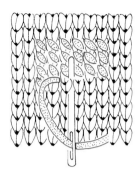

203b   Work half stitch in one direction

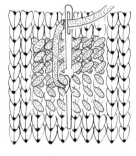

203c   Work second half of stitch in other direction

fig. 203b) then work the second stitch in the opposite direction (see fig. 203c). When the stitches are worked in any direction the finished effect is much less satisfactory as the texture looks uneven.

Straight stitches

Straight stitches in any direction, vertical, horizontal or diagonal can be worked and built up into interesting patterns or small shapes (see fig. 204).

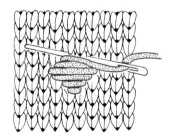

204   Straight stitches can be used to form small shapes

Chain stitch

Chain stitch is useful as an outline stitch, or, worked between leaf motifs, to act as a stem.

Insert the needle from back to front of work, coming out at the starting point of the first stitch.

Insert the needle into the same point again but with a loop of yarn beneath the point. Bring the point out to the right side at the length of the first stitch (see fig. 205a).

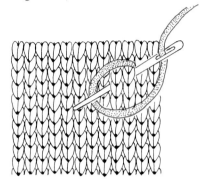

205a   Lift length of first stitch with yarn under needle tip

Draw the first loop up to be held in position by the strand at its end. Put the loop under the needle tip and again bring out the needle tip at the length of the second stitch (see fig. 205b).

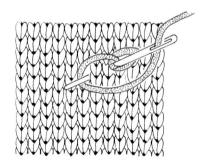

205b   Insert needle into first stitch

Continue to work loops in this way until the chain is the required length (see fig. 206a).

Finish by taking the last stitch over the last chain and finishing it off on the wrong side (see fig. 206b).

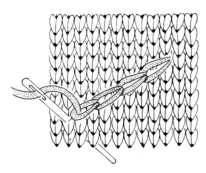

206a Work chains in this way

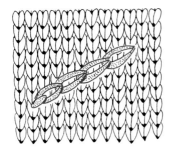

206b End with small stitch over last

Lazy daisy stitch

This stitch is also known as link stitch and is essential to the bright coloured flowers that decorate Ṭyrolean cable patterns.

Work each petal as for a final chain stitch.

Bring the needle out to the right side of the work at the start of a petal. Loop the yarn under the needle, which enters the base of the stitch at the same point again and comes out at the opposite end of the petal (see fig. 207).

207 Single chain stitches form petals

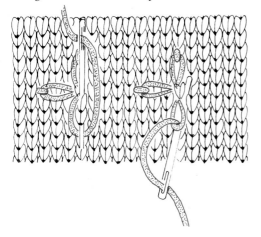

Draw up the yarn so that the thread coming out on the right side at the petal tip holds the petal loop in place.

Complete the petal before moving to the next position by inserting the needle to the wrong side with a straight stitch that holds the petal end in place.

French knots

Knots, if not knitted in, can be used in outline, to emphasize a colour change or appliquéd edge or as flower centres.

Bring the yarn out on the right side. Wind the yarn round the needle twice, or more times for larger knots (see fig. 208a).

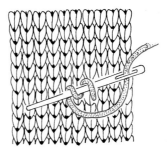

208a Wind yarn twice round needle

Keeping the wound threads close to the knitting, draw the needle and thread through and return the needle into the same space, back on to the wrong side (see fig. 208b).

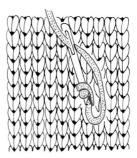

208b Push twist close to background

Work as many knots as required and finish off the yarn on the wrong side (see fig. 208c).

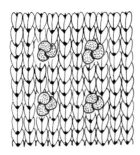

208c Yarn through to back holds knot in place

Tambour stitch

Tambour stitch, which looks like chain stitch, is worked with the use of a crochet hook to draw the loops through to the right side.

Secure the yarn on the wrong side. Insert the hook through the knitted fabric and with the hook catch the yarn from the wrong side and draw it through. Insert the hook through the next space one or two stitches up from the 1st stitch. Draw through another loop from the wrong side, at the same time drawing the first loop up against the fabric. Do not drag the stitches too tightly or the base knitting will be distorted (see fig. 209a).

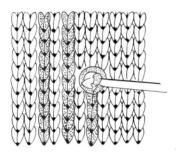

209a Vertical tambour stitch

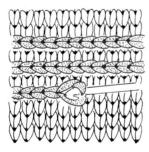

209b Horizontal tambour stitch

Tambour stitch can be used vertically or horizontally and can be used to add lines of stitches which echo the knitted stitches and can quickly turn a plain section of stocking stitch into a checked pattern or tartan-like fabric (see fig. 209b).

Diagonal lines can be worked similarly but must lie across the knitting stitches (see fig. 209c).

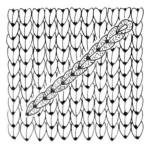

209c Diagonal tambour stitch

Blanket stitch

Blanket stitch in one or more colours makes a bold line. Worked closely together it can be used in appliqué work, holding the outside edge of the shape closely against the knitted base fabric.

Secure the end on the wrong side and bring the needle out on to the right side at the correct depth for the stitch. Work between the knit stitches or through the centre using the row lines as a guide. Take the yarn round to the right and insert the needle directly through the knitting 2 or more rows down, bringing the tip out in line with the first stitch. Draw the yarn up before making the next stitch in the same way. The straight stitch holds the loop in place (see fig. 210a).

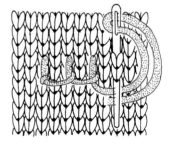

210a Insert the needle vertically

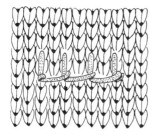

210b Finished blanket stitch

Work along the row as required (see fig. 210b).

Blanket stitch can be made row on row, by your placing the straight stitches between the previous straight stitches (*see* **Tyrolean cable**).

Mock smocking

Straight stitches can be used to draw ribbing together to form smocking but this can be bulky and cause distortion on thick yarns (see fig. 211a).

It does prove a way of decorating travelling stitches, and you can add colour to a base pattern by working straight stitches, lazy daisy stitches or cross stitches over stitch crossing points (see fig. 211b).

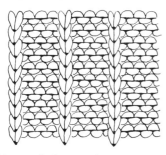

211a Ribbing ready for smocking

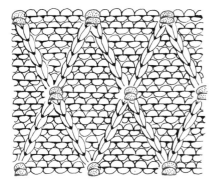

211b Drawn together with small stitches

English knitting

Knitting came to England from Europe many hundreds of years ago and by the sixteenth century was a craft worthy of its own guild, providing incomes for many families.

Although eventually machines were to cause the end of organized commercial hand knitting, in 1589 Queen Elizabeth I refused to grant a patent monopoly for the first stocking loom invented by William Lee of Nottingham, saying 'I have too much love for my poor people who obtain their bread by the employment of knitting, to give my money to forward an invention that will tend to their ruin'. In fact their ruin was long postponed and during the following years knitting grew and expanded to cover the production of stockings, gloves, petticoats, cavalry hose, and many other items.

New yarns were added to wool with the arrival of silk and cotton, and changes were made according to the fashions. Silk workers made shirts in brocade patterns of knit and purl stitches and garments of many sorts, vests, underwear and sleeves were made from cotton.

Schools were promoted for the teaching of children and apprentices, and knitting areas could be found in Dorset, Hampshire, Leicester, Nottinghamshire and in Yorkshire.

Speed was essential to knitters who worked in a way forgotten today. It may have been that much of the work was made on round needles or sets of needles, making for speed, with the right side always facing the knitter. Unsuitable for two needle knitting, this method is still used in Shetland where fast knitting is still imperative and an understood skill.

The industrial revolution saw the change of knitting from an income-earning skill to a domestic hobby, promoted vastly by the upspring of women's magazines.

Before knitting ceased to be practised by professional knitters, gloves had become a famous export of the Dales. Made in fine wool, usually in two contrasting colours, these gloves were often intricately and individually designed; names and initials or dates were knitted into the welt for special orders. Patterns ingeniously fitted around hand and palm and the fingers often carried a different pattern to the hand back or cuff.

With the growth of magazines and published books the information for home knitters has grown from those days, bringing many new techniques and stitch patterns, if no return to the speed used by knitters from the past.

English knitting terms

See **Abbreviations**

Entrelacs

The knitting of entrelacs can be called patchwork knitting. It is the working of rectangles, usually in alternating or varied colours, which are worked in rows, not individually. Each area, however, is worked on its own but it is knitted from the previous row and becomes the base for the following row. It comes from the French *entrelacer* meaning to interlace.

To work entrelacs

The rectangles require a base row of triangles so that they start from a straight edge. The number of stitches of each triangle will determine the size of the rectangles. Stocking tops may have only six or eight stitches, or a sweater may have ten or twelve stitches for each triangle. This sample is worked with six stitches for each base triangle and four triangles are sufficient for an experiment.

Cast on 24 sts with A, and use A for the 4 base triangles.

1st and 2nd rows * P2, turn, K2, turn (see fig. 212a).

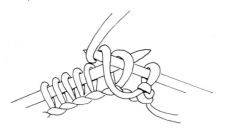

212a Purl two stitches

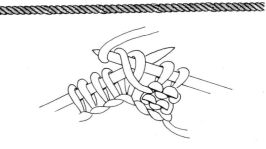

212b Purl three stitches

3rd and 4th rows P3, turn, K3, turn (see fig. 212b).
5th and 6th rows P4, turn, K4, turn.
7th and 8th rows P5, turn, K5, turn.
9th row P6, do not turn or break yarn. This completes the 1st triangle, which can be left on the right needle as the next is worked.

Work the 2nd triangle from * until there are 6 sts on right needle. Do not turn or break off yarn (see fig. 213a).

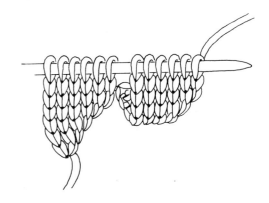

213a Completed triangles

Work 3rd and 4th triangles as for 2nd.

When the right (knit) side is facing there will be 4 triangles on one needle, similar to the 2 shown in fig. 213a.

Begin 1st row of rectangles which has a half rectangle at each end. Break off A and leave length at end of row for darning in when complete.

1st and 2nd rows ** With B and RS facing, K2, turn, P2, turn.

3rd and 4th rows K into front and back of 1st st to inc, sl next st knitwise, K next st, pass slipped st over and off needle tip, turn, P3 (see fig. 213b), turn.

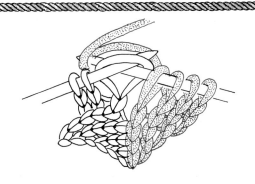

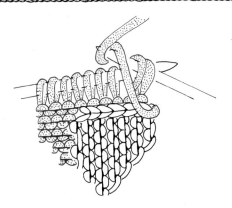

213b SKPO across colour change

5th and 6th rows Inc in 1st st, K1, SKPO, turn, P4, turn.
7th and 8th rows Inc in 1st st, K2, SKPO, turn, P5, turn.
9th row Inc in 1st st, K3, SKPO, do not turn. This completes the half rectangle at the side. Continue to work the complete rectangles thus *** With RS facing and B, K up 6 sts along left side of triangle, turn (see fig. 214).

215a P2 tog at beginning of row

This completes 1st row of half and full rectangles.
Turn work so that wrong side is facing.
1st and 2nd rows **** With A and WS facing, P up 6 sts along side of rectangle, turn, K6, turn.
3rd and 4th rows P5, P tog last A st and next B st, turn, K6, turn (see fig. 215b).

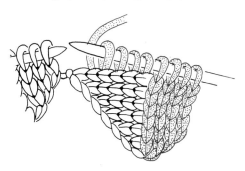

214 Knit up stitches along side of triangle

1st and 2nd rows P6, turn, K5, SKPO, (sl last B st and K next A st), turn.
Rep 1st and 2nd rows 5 times.
This completes 1st whole rectangle. Rep from ** * until 2 more full rectangles are worked.
Work last half rectangle thus
1st and 2nd rows With B and RS facing, K up 6 sts along side of last triangle, turn, P2 tog, P4, turn (see fig. 215a).
3rd and 4th rows K5, turn, P2 tog, P3, turn.
5th and 6th rows K4, turn, P2 tog, P2, turn.
7th and 8th rows K3, turn, P2 tog, P1, turn.
9th and 10th rows K2, turn, P2 tog, break off B and draw through last st, leaving end to darn in.

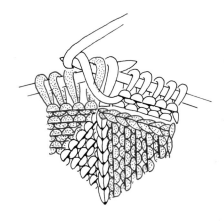

215b P2 tog over colour change

Rep 3rd and 4th rows 4 times.
Last row P5, P2 tog. Do not turn. ***** Rep from **** until 3 more rectangles are worked. Turn.
Continue in this way working alternate lines in B and A, rep from ** to ***** until the required length is reached. To obtain the right length it may be necessary to end with either a row of A or a row of B rectangles. To give a straight top edge the last row must be filled in

with triangles. The instructions for triangles in A to follow the last line of B rectangles and in B to follow a last line of A rectangles are given.
For a line of triangles needed to follow a line of A rectangles work in B with RS facing.
1st and 2nd rows K2, turn, P2, turn.
3rd and 4th rows Inc in 1st st, SKPO, turn, P3, turn.
5th and 6th rows K2, SKPO, turn, P3, turn.
7th and 8th rows K2 tog, SKPO, turn, P2, turn.
9th row Sl1, K2 tog, psso. Do not turn but cont along row by knitting up 6 sts from next rectangle, working the rectangles as on previous rows but dec 1 st at beg of every right side row until all sts are worked off.
For a line of triangles needed to foll a line of B rectangles retain the last st of the final B rectangle but work in A with WS facing.
1st and 2nd rows P up 5 sts, turn, K6, turn.
3rd and 4th rows P5, P2 tog, turn, K6, turn.
5th and 6th rows P2 tog, P3, P2 tog, turn, K5, turn.
7th and 8th rows P2 tog, P2, P2 tog, turn, K4; turn.
9th and 10th rows P2 tog, P1, P2 tog, turn, K3, turn.
11th and 12th row (P2 tog) twice, turn, K2, turn.
13th row P3 tog.
Cont by repeating these 13 rows until all sts are worked off.

Designing with entrelacs

It is essential to try out a large swatch of pattern before calculating the number of stitches required. The pattern spreads considerably and if worked immediately after a ribbed welt, you will need to reduce the number of stitches from the welt by between a quarter and a third.

Refinements of stocking stitch entrelacs

Scottish sock knitters have used this design in round knitting for sock tops, working rectangles alternately on right and wrong side of rounds. The shape of the rectangles is improved by working the colour joins differently and slipping the first stitch of every row, on triangles, half rectangles and rectangles (see fig. 378). On knit rows slip the first stitch purlwise and on purl rows slip the first stitch knitwise.

For every SKPO substitute an SSK and for every P2 tog work sl1, P1, psso.

Fashion uses

Although the stocking stitch side has been used as the right side, the purl side shows a more interestingly shaped pattern and can be varied by using more than two colours. Texture and pattern added to the various patches are only a small evolvement and emphasize the pattern when openwork is used for the lines in one direction and solid stitches or texture are used for the other line.

Estonian knitting

People on remote islands or in areas far from towns seem to be far more skilful knitters than the people who might be thought of as luckier inhabitants of more lively areas. Fishermen's guernseys are at their most decorative in the Outer Hebrides or the extreme north of Caithness; Fair Isle and Shetland lead the world in patterned work and in fine shawls, and the islands that made up Estonian pattern repeat the story, giving the design of knitting yet another facet. From the islands of Mohn and Runo come two very different types of knitting, both decorative and outstanding. Dark stockings are highly patterned from above the ankle, often separating on either side of the foot shaping. This pattern, so cleverly placed, is not knitted in but is worked in a contrast yarn that is woven between the knitting stitches, giving a brighter, almost padded, look to the designs (see fig. 216).
Life was hard in the islands where the inhabitants had to live off the land and the sea, where homes and their trappings were made by themselves and where the insides of the houses were sombre with only natural earthen colours for decoration. Yet against this muted background were the lively stockings of Mohn (see colour plate 4), scattered with flower shapes and hearts, small birds and other banded symbols. The sparkling colours came from their own dyes – magenta and firey red, orange of the brightest marigold and deep gold, blue of the clear sky and darkest violet – and were put all together on one stocking pattern.

216 Estonian woven patterned stockings

Equipment

Knitting is not an expensive craft to start. Needles come in many sizes, lengths and shapes, and your stock will grow as you become more experienced. Good quality needles are essential and those marketed by leading makers are worth any extra they may cost. Most sizes are made of anodized aluminium with plastic used for some of the larger thicknesses.

Knitting pins

Knitting pins with knobbed ends are made for flat knitting, knitting in rows, and are available in sizes from 1½–10mm and in different lengths.

- 1½–3mm available in 25, 30 and 35cm lengths.
- 3–7½mm available in 25, 30, 35cm and 40cm.
- 8, 9 and 10mm available in 30 and 35cm.
- 12 – 15mm available in 40cm only.

Knitting needles
(See page 79 for American needle sizes)

Double-pointed knitting needles in sets of four or five are available in sizes from 1½ – 10mm and also in different lengths.

- 1½–5mm available in 20 and 30cm lengths.
- 5½–7½mm available in 20, 30 and 35cm lengths.
- 8, 9 and 10mm available in 20, 30 and 35cm lengths.

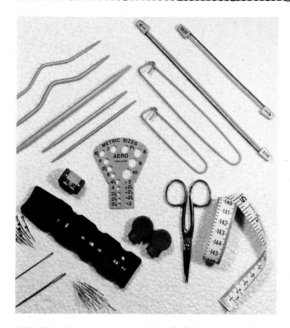

217 Knitting accessories: (*Top left*) Straight and cranked cable needles
(*Top right*) Two types of stitch holders
(*Centre*) Needle gauge, row counter, needle point protectors, scissors
(*Bottom left*) Pattern and row counter, pins, wool needles
Bottom right) Measuring tape

Different lengths

The length required may depend on the knitter's preference or the garment being knitted.

In knitting pins the length may be governed by area; people in the south tend to prefer short pins, whereas in the north people prefer longer pins that can be tucked under the arm when in use (see fig. 218).

Children's needles

Junior needles, which are shorter than adult needles, are also available in sizes from 2¼–4½mm and are made from the same material as adult needles. Plastic, bright-coloured needles are also sold for children but care should be made in purchasing these. Plastic that bends very readily is also inclined to snap equally readily, spoiling a piece of otherwise successful knitting.

Circular needles

Circular needles, Twin Pins when manufactured by Aero, are suitable for types of larger garments and can be used for working round on seamless garments or for working backwards and forwards in rows.

With anodized aluminium tips on a nylon cord they are made in sizes 2–7½mm and in several different lengths, 40, 60, 80 and 100cm.

The required length is usually stated in the pattern and is dependent on the fewest number of stitches required on a round-knitted garment. Sufficient stitches are necessary to reach from point to point. Each length of needle will then hold approximately three times the smallest number before a longer needle is requried. You should be able to shape most sweaters or skirts with all the required increases without having to alter the length of needle.

Accessories

Certain other accessories are useful and should be included in every work bag (see fig. 217).

Cable needles

Cable needles or short spare double-pointed needles are always useful for cable and travelling stitch patterns. They are sold in two sizes, one for use with 2¾–5mm needle sizes, the other for use with 5½–7½mm needle sizes.

Needle gauge

This is particularly useful when sets of unmarked double-pointed needles are separated and not returned to their holder.

Needle tip protectors

These are very useful for placing over needle tips when not in use.

Row counter and pattern counter

No knitter should be without a row counter, which should be constantly in use for checking that sleeves and half fronts are equal by being worked with the same number of rows, or for keeping check of shaping or pattern.

A pattern check can keep note of even more and has dials for noting numbers of pattern repeats worked, increases or decreases made as well as the number of rows worked.

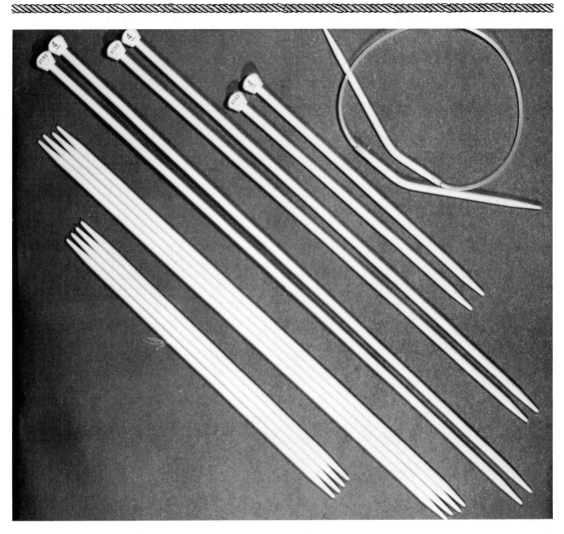

218 (*From top right*) Circular needle, junior needles, 30 and 35cm knitting pins, 20 and 30cm sets of double-pointed needles

Scissors
Small sharp-pointed scissors are needed for cutting all yarns and for the times when work has to be unpicked.

Stitch holders
Stitch holders are much safer to use than spare needles for holding stitches not in use during working or stitches held for a later section. They are made in various styles but have guards to avoid stitches falling off the ends or being pulled inadvertently out of the stitches.

Tape measure
A tape measure, preferably marked in inches and centimetres, is useful and should be of the best quality so that it does not easily become worn and stretched.

A firm rule
Essential for checking tension as a rule will remain flat, unlike a tape measure which is more suited to taking body measurements.

Wool needles
Wool needles are specially designed for sewing up and working with wool and have blunt tips which slip between the stitches without breaking and splitting the surface of the yarn. The are sold

in 2 sizes, both of which are useful – one for fine work and one for chunky garments.

Crochet hooks

These are not essential but for a more experienced knitter can be helpful. They are useful in working decorative edges and simple crochet decorative stitches and are always of use for picking up accidentally dropped stitches.

They are available in millimetre sizes 1.25, 1.50, 1.75, 2.00, 2.50, 3.00, 3.50, 4.00, 4.50, and 5.00 and are made in anodized aluminium. Larger hooks, suitable for thicker yarns, are also available in plastic in sizes 5.00, 6.00, 7.00, 8.00, 9.00, 10.00 and 12.00. Finer hooks, made in steel, are for use with finest cottons and are not likely to be of use for wool or with knitting. They are sizes 0.06, 0.75 and 1.00.

Eyelets

Eyelets have many uses, for buttonholes in fine yarn, as a means of working ribbon-slotting and in forming lace patterns. They can be worked as single holes, using either chain or open eyelets, double eyelets or picot eyelets or as a base for larger openings such as in bold eyelets, worked over four rows, and grand eyelets which are made by enlarging the 'yarn over needle' by passing the yarn twice or more round the needle.

Single eyelets

The first eyelet retains the lines of vertical stitches or chain of stitches and the other eyelet breaks the lines of stitches because of the slipped decrease.

Chain eyelet

The most used eyelet is a chain eyelet, worked by making an increase followed by a decrease; put a yarn over strand across the needle at the point where the eyelet is required; then take two stitches together (see fig. 219a b).

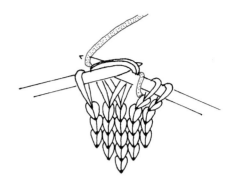

219a Yarn over needle, K2 together

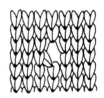

219b Chain eyelet

Open eyelet

The other single eyelet is slightly more open and is known as an open eyelet. It is made by placing a yarn over needle increase before a slipped decrease (which is worked with a slipped stitch knitwise as it is part of a decrease, if an SKPO decrease is used). The SSK can be placed in this position, its stitches already being turned into the correct position (see fig. 220).

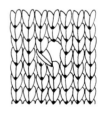

220 Open eyelet

Double eyelets

There are two types of double eyelets, embroidered eyelets and picot eyelets.

Embroidered eyelet

The embroidered eyelet gives a round hole and is formed between two paired decreases, one on each side of a single yarn over needle; a K2 tog can be used at the start paired with a K2togtbl, a SKPO or a SSK decrease at the end.

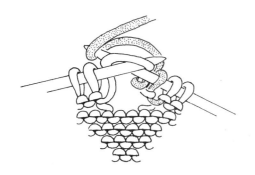

221 Purl into yarn over needle and then knit into same space

On the following row the yarn over is worked into twice, returning the number of stitches to the original number.

1st row K to eyelet position, K2 tog, yon, SSK, K to end.

2nd row P to yon made in previous row, P into this strand then knit into it also, replacing the decreased stitches, P to end of row (see fig. 221).

Picot eyelet

The picot eyelet is decorative and shows to its best advantage as a grouped pattern (see fig. 225b). The picot point in each hole is made by first purling, then knitting, the strands or loops made by yarn twice over the needle.

1st row Knit to the point for the eyelet, K2 tog, y2on, sl1 knitwise, K1, psso, work to end of row.

2nd row Work to y2on made on previous row, P the 1st loop of the y2on then K the 2nd loop and work to end of row (see fig. 222).

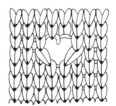

222 Finished eyelet

Multiple eyelets

Both bold and grand eyelets have variations. The bold eyelet, which takes four rows to make instead of two can also be used to make a twin eyelet. Twin eyelet is used in pattern building and eyelet motif forming because it leaves two smaller eyelets joined by a central strand, which is removed in the bold eyelet. The grand eyelet size is determined by the number of times the yarn is passed round the needle and how many stitches are made out of it.

Bold eyelet

Based on a double eyelet that is enlarged and worked over four rows, the bold eyelet is often to be found with smaller eyelets in lace patterns.

1st row K to eyelet position, K2 tog, y2on, SKPO, K to end.

2nd row P to 1 st before y2on made in previous row, P tog next st and 1st loop of y2on, K tog next loop of y2on and following st, P to end.

3rd row K to centre of eyelet, and work y2on between the 2 dec sts on last row, K to end.

4th row P to 1 st before y2on made in previous row, P tog next st with 1st loop of y2on including the strand across the hole, K1 and P1 both into 2nd loop of y2on and the strand below, leaving the hole clear, P to end.

Twin eyelet

Work 1st, 2nd and 3rd rows as for bold eyelet.

4th row P to st before y2on made on previous row, P tog next st and 1st loop of y2on, into 2nd loop of y2on K1, then P1, P to end.

Grand eyelet

The largest of all eyelets can be seen in fig. 225a. It is worked by making a large base strand by passing the yarn twice or three times over the needle, then working alternately knitted and purled stitches into the loops made by the multiple over. These stitches are placed so that the last loop is always worked with a knitted stitch on a purl row, and a purled stitch on a knit row.

For placing of eyelets and using them in pattern making, *see* **Lace holes**.

Eyelet stitch patterns

Eyelet patterns are very varied, from dainty broderie *anglais*-type patterns to 'grand' lace designs or multiple patterns using both large and small eyelets. *See also* **Lace holes** for the true character of eyelets as opposed to faggot patterns.

Rosebud pattern

This eyelet pattern uses an unusual method to place an eyelet on a small area worked on an odd number of stitches. It is suitable for all dainty garments (see fig. 224a).

Worked over a number of stitches divisible by 16, plus 9.

1st and every alternate row (WS facing) P.
2nd row K10, * K2 tog, yon, K1, yon, SSK, K11, rep from *, ending last rep K10 in place of K11.
4th row K9, * K2 tog, yon, K3, yon, SSK, K9, rep from * to end.
6th row K10, * yon, SSK, yon, K3 tog, yon, K11, rep from *, ending last rep K10 in place of K11.
8th row K11, * yon, SK2togPO, yon, K13, rep from *, ending last rep K11 in place of K13.
10th row K2, * K2 tog, yon, K1, yon, SSK, K11, rep from *, ending last rep K2 in place of K11.
12th row K1, * K2 tog, yon, K3, yon, SSK, K9, rep from * ending last rep K1 in place of K9.
14th row K2, * yon, SSK, yon, K3 tog, yon, K11, rep from * ending last rep K2 in place of K11.
16th row K3, * yon, SK2togP, yon, K13, rep from *, ending last rep K3 in place of K13.
Rep 1st–16th rows as required.

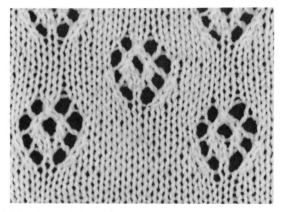

223   Rosebud pattern.

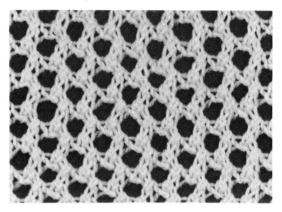

224   Cat's eye pattern

Cat's eye pattern

This Shetland lace pattern uses a picot eyelet, and the instructions are given in the traditional way, making two stitches out of a single 'yon'. The increases are not worked on the same row as the decreases, so count stitches only on even numbered rows (see fig. 224b).

Worked over a number of stitches divisible by 4.

1st row (RS facing), K4, * yon, K4, rep from * to end.
2nd row P2, * P2 tog, [P1, K1] into yon of previous row, P2 tog, rep from * to last 2 sts, P2.
3rd row K2, yon, * K4, yon, rep from * to last 6 sts, K4, yon, K2.
4th row P3, * [P2 tog] twice, [P1m K1] into yon of previous row, rep from * to last 7 sts, [P2 tog] twice, P3.
Rep 1st–4th rows as required.

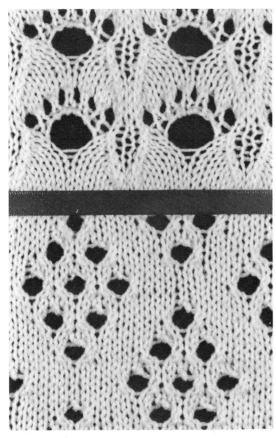

225 (*Top*) Crown of Glory pattern
(*Bottom*) Picot eyelet pattern

Crown of glory pattern

Again from Shetland, this pattern is also called cat's paw for obvious reasons. The large eyelet is made by winding the yarn three times round the needle. At its best is should be worked in fine yarn so that it retains its lacy quality (see fig. 225a).
Worked over a number of stitches divisible by 14, plus 5.
1st row (RS facing), K3, * SKPO, K9, K2 tog, K1, rep from * to last 2 sts, K2.
2nd row P2, * P1, P2 tog, P7, P2 tog tbl, rep from * to last 3 sts, P3.
3rd row K3, * SKPO, K2, y3on, K3, K2 tog, K1, rep from * to last 2 sts, K2.
4th row P2, * P1, P2 tog, P2, drop 3 loops of y3on made in previous row and into this large loop work K1, [P1, K1] twice, making 5 sts, P1, P2 tog tbl, rep from * to last 3 sts, P3.

5th row K3, * SKPO, K6, K2 tog, K1, rep from * to last 2 sts, K2.
6th row P2, * P1, P2 tog, P6, rep from * to last 3 sts, P3.
7th row K3, * K1, [yon, K1] 6 times, K1, rep from * to last 2 sts, K2.
8th row P.
9th row K.
10th and 11th rows As 8th and 9th rows.
12th row P.
Rep 1st–12th rows as required.
SSK can be substituted for SKPO to give a neater appearance but is not traditional.

Picot eyelet pattern

The eyelets form a diamond and the centre of each eyelet accentuates the diamond quality by its neat picot point (see fig. 225b).
Worked over a number of stitches divisible by 20, plus 8.
1st row (RS facing), K2 tog, y2on, SSK, * [K2 tog, y2on, SSK, K4] twice, K2 tog, y2on, SSK, rep from * to last 4 sts, K2 tog, y2on, SSK.
2nd row P to y2on, P 1st st of y2on and K 2nd st, rep to end of row.
3rd row K.
4th row P.
5th row K2, K2 tog, * y2on, SSK, K4, [K2 tog, y2on, SSK] twice, K4, K2 tog, rep from * to last 4 sts, y2on SSK, K2.
6th, 7th and 8th rows As 2nd, 3rd and 4th rows.
9th row K4, * K4, [K2 tog, y2on, SSK] 3 times, K4, rep from * to last 4 sts, K4.
10th, 11th and 12th rows As 2nd, 3rd and 4th rows.
13th row K2, K2 tog, * y2on, SSK, K4, [K2 tog, y2on, SSK] twice, K4, K2 tog, rep from * to last 4 sts, y2on, K2 tog, K2.
14th, 15th and 16th rows As 2nd, 3rd and 4th rows.
17th row K2 tog, y2on, SSK, * [K2 tog, y2on, SSK, K4] twice, K2 tog, y2on, SSK, rep from * to last 4 sts, K2 tog, y2on, SSK.
18th, 19th and 20th rows As 2nd, 3rd and 4th rows.
21st row K2, K2 tog, * y2on, SSK, K2 tog, y2on, SSK, K8, K2 tog, y2on, SSK, K2 tog, rep from * to last 4 sts, y2on, SSK, K2.
22nd, 23rd and 24th rows As 2nd, 3rd and 4th rows.
Rep 1st–24th rows as required.

Diamond eyelet pattern (see fig. 304a)

This pattern shows the difference between the more usual lace outline of faggot stitches and this slightly less open diamond worked with eyelets.

Worked over a number of stitches divisible by 10, plus 4.

1st row (RS facing) K2, * yon, SKPO, K1, K2 tog, y2on, SKPO, K1, K2 tog, yon, rep from * to last 2 sts, K2.

2nd row Purl all the stitches, purling into the front then the back of y2on made in previous row.

3rd row K2, * K2 tog, yon, K6, yon, SKPO, rep from * to last 2 sts, K2.

4th, 6th and 8th rows P.

5th row K2, * K1, K2 tog, yon, K4, yon, SKPO, K1, rep from * to last 2 sts, K2.

7th row K2, * K2, K2 tog, yon, K2, yon, SKPO, K2, rep from * to last 2 sts, K2.

9th row and 10th rows As 1st and 2nd rows.

11th row K2, * K3, yon, SKPO, K2 tog, yon, K3, rep from * to last 2 sts, K2.

13th row K2, * K2, yon, SKPO, K2, K2 tog, yon, K2, rep from * to last 2 sts, K2.

15th row K2, * K1, yon, SKPO, K4, K2 tog, yon, K1, rep from * to last 2 sts, K2.

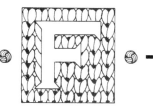

Faggot stitches

Faggot stitches are worked with an open increase and a decrease, as is an eyelet. They differ, however, in the way in which they are placed in design, *see* **Lace holes**. Faggot stitches are worked in two groups, over alternate rows, giving the strands between open work slender, twisted linking strands or lace faggot patterns where the increases and decreases are worked on both sides of the fabric on right and wrong sides and on every row. This produces interlaced strands of single thickness.

Basic faggot pattern

Like all faggot stitch patterns it consists of one row which is repeated throughout and is worked over an even number of stitches.
1st row K1, * yon, SSK, rep from * to last st, K1.

The yon or increase does little to affect the pattern but the decrease makes a great deal of difference (see fig. 228 *Top*). If, in this simple row, the decrease is altered from an SSK to a K2 tog the pattern also alters to the less open Turkish stitch, (see fig. 228 *Bottom*) (*see* **Faggot stitch patterns** for instructions).

Another simple change of decrease to a P2 tog and the result is purse stitch, named because it was the stitch used for the hand knitting of fine silk purses (see fig. 227). The row for this reads: * yon, P2 tog, rep from * to end. The placing of the yon at the beginning adds a lace edging at both sides.

227 Purse stitch

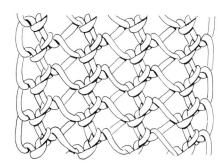

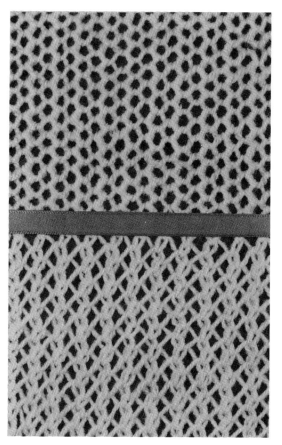

228 (*Top*) Basic faggot pattern
(*Bottom*) Turkish stitch

Faggot stitches are very often used for insertions and can give diagonal or straight interlaced stitches.

Purl beading ladder

Straight bars across the insertions are made by the first group of faggot stitches worked on alternate rows with a plain row between (see fig. 229a).

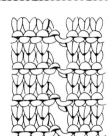

229a Pearl beading insertion

Worked over 5 stitches.
1st row Sl1 purlwise, K1, yon, K2 tog, K1.
2nd row Sl1 purlwise, K4.
Rep these 2 rows as required.

Double ladder insertion

The width of the strands in this version is made by using a double increase in place of a single increase (see fig. 229b).

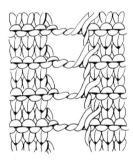

229b Double ladder insertion

Worked over 6 stitches.
1st row K1, K2 tog, y2on, K2 tog, K1.
2nd row K3, P into the 2nd of the loops made by the y2on, (the 1st loop has already been knitted), K2.
Rep these 2 rows as required.

Double herringbone lace faggot insertion

In this the straight ladder is altered to the diagonally linked strands of the true lace faggot (see fig. 230a).

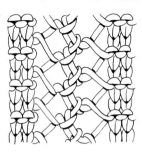

230a Double herringbone lace faggot insertion

Worked over 7 stitches.
1st row Sl1, K1, yon, K2 tog, yon, K2 tog, K1.
Rep this row as required.

Lace feather faggot insertion

At first glance this might be expected to show the diagonal linking strands like the previous pattern. It does not because it is feathered and so the decrease pulls against the slope of the increase, tilting the strands almost to a horizontal position (see fig. 230b).
Worked over 4 stitches.
1st row K1, yon, P2 tog, K1.
Rep this row as required.

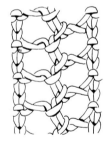

230b Lace feather faggot insertion

Bias

Lace faggot stitches can be worked with the yarn over needle before or after the decrease. When the decrease is worked on alternate rows, first at one side of the yarn over then at the other, a pattern which has no bias is created, as in Vandyke faggot stitch (see fig. 231) (for instructions *see* **Faggot stitch patterns**).

Many patterns combine altered decreases, either on the same row or after several rows, so

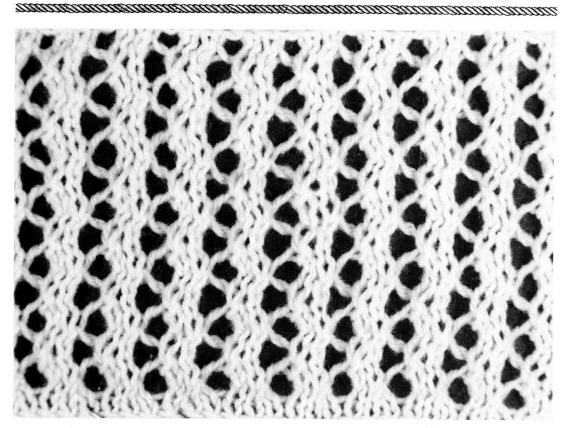

231 Vandyke faggot stitch

that the diagonal lines created can form a pattern, but a fabric which remains overall vertical is produced (see fig. 231b) (for instructions *see* **Lace stitch patterns**).

Faggot stitch patterns

Faggot stitches and lace faggot stitches are most often used as vertical insertion patterns to emphasize other vertical patterns, such as cables or lace insertions, but there are exceptions.

Vertical lace trellis pattern

A lace which is without bias, as many lace faggot stitch patterns are, is of great value. The bias in this pattern is avoided by the use of two decreases on alternating rows worked on opposite sides of the increase (see fig. 232a).

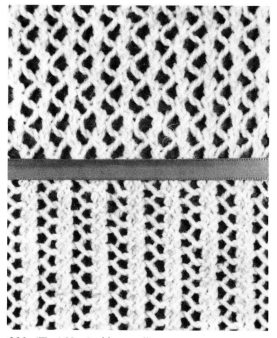

232 (*Top*) Vertical lace trellis pattern
(*Bottom*) Faggoting rib pattern

Worked over a number of stitches divisible by 2, plus 1.
1st and 3rd rows (WS facing) P.
2nd row K1, * yon, K2 tog, rep from * to end.
4th row * SSK, yon, rep from * to last st, K1.
Rep 1st–4th rows as required.

Turkish stitch pattern
(for illustration see fig. 227b)

One of the basic lace faggot stitch patterns, it creates a delightful lace fabric, less open than the SSK or the P2 tog basic versions.
Worked over an even number of stitches.
1st row K1, * yon, K2 tog, rep from * to last st, K1.
Rep this row as required.

Faggoting rib pattern

The addition of just one stitch changes the proportion of lace to solid (see fig. 232b).
Worked over a number of stitches divisible by 3.
1st row * K1, yon, K2 tog, rep from * to end.
Rep this row as required.

Vandyke faggot stitch
(for illustration see fig. 231a)

Lace and solid contrast, this stitch forms an unbiased fabric by the placing of the decreases on alternate rows.
Worked over a number of stitches divisible by 3.
1st row (RS facing), * K1, y2on, K2 tog, rep from * to end.
2nd row * P1, P into 1st loop of y2on and drop the 2nd loop P1, rep from * to end.
3rd row * K2 tog, y2on, K1, rep from * to end.
4th row Work as for 2nd row.
Rep 1st–4th rows as required.

Cable pattern

Simple, effective, useful, versatile and adaptable, this pattern is a springboard for variations as well as giving a beautiful use of faggoting (see fig. 233).
Worked over a number of stitches divisible by 10, plus 2.
1st row (RS facing) K4, * Tw2R, Tw2L, K1, SSK, yon, K3, rep from * to last 8 sts, Tw2R,

233 Cable pattern

Tw2L, K1, SSK, yon, K1.
2nd row P9, * P2 tog, yon, P8, rep from * to last 3 sts, P2 tog, yon, P1.
3rd row K3, * Tw2R, K2, Tw2L, K4, rep from * to last 9 sts, Tw2R, K2, Tw2L, K3.
4th row P.
5th row K2, * Tw2R, K4, Tw2L, K2, rep from * to end.
6th row P4, * P2 tog, yon, P8, rep from * to last 8 sts, P2 tog, yon, P6.
7th row K1 * Tw2R, K1, SSK, yon, K3, Tw2L, rep from * to last st, K1.
8th row K2, * P2, P2 tog, yon, P4, K2, rep from * to end.
9th row P2, * K2, SSK, yon, K4, P2, rep from * to end.
10th–13th rows Rep 8th and 9th rows twice.
14th row As 8th row.

15th row K1, * Tw2L, K1, SSK, yon, K3, Tw2R, rep from * to last st, K1.

16th row As 6th row.

17th row K2, * Tw2L, K4, Tw2R, K2, rep from * to end.

18th row As 4th row.

19th row K3, * Tw2L, K2, Tw2R, K4, rep from * to last 9 sts, Tw2L, K2, Tw2R, K3.

20th row As 2nd row.

21st row K4, * Tw2L, Tw2R, K1, SSK, yon, K3, rep from * to last 8 sts, Tw2L, Tw2R, K1, SSK, yon, K1.

22nd, 24th, 26th and 28th rows P5, * K2, P2, P2 tog, yon, P4, rep from * to last 7 sts, K2, P2, P2 tog, yon, P1.

23rd, 25th and 27th rows K5, * P2, K2, SSK, yon, K4, rep from * to last 7 sts, P2, K2, SSK, yon, K1.

Rep 1st–28th rows as required.

Fair Isle knitting

Legend attributes the start of Fair Isle knitting to the year 1588. It was then that the Spanish ship, the El Gran Griffon, was wrecked off Fair Isle, the most southerly island of the group known as Shetland. It was the crew survivors who, temporarily stranded on the island, are supposed to have inspired the islanders, already skilled stocking knitters, to make unusually patterned and coloured items.

Fair Isle and Lerwick, the main harbour on the Mainland island of Shetland, were both maritime cross-roads with Faroes and Iceland to the north, America to the west, Scotland and England to the south and to the east the Scandinavian countries, Denmark, Germany, Holland and beyond these again the East. At no time can the islands be considered cut off, remote or outlandish, for they were a seething trade centre, a place where textiles changed hands, where merchants came and went, where knitting as a means of earning was important and where the people had the skill to make the most of it. Whatever its start, it is perhaps the best known of all folk knitting traditions and, over the years, like all living traditions has grown and evolved into the patterns now known as Fair Isle.

Today, the traditional and gradually evolving patterns can be seen at a permanent exhibition in the National Trust bird observatory on Fair Isle. The shades of natural wool are immense, but it was the dyed wool that gave Fair Isle knitting its popularity. Colours were made from the natural island substances – lichens that gave soft madder and yellow, blue, brown and the creamy white of the natural fleece. By the beginning of the twentieth century the patterns were being copied by other Shetland knitters, the patterns being evolved, growing in number and reaching fashionable acclaim when the then Prince of Wales wore a Shetland pullover while visiting St Andrews.

Further growth has continued with new shapes, based on Norwegian motifs; these have taken on new meaning with the subtle method of adding colour, so characteristic of the Fair Isle knitting known today.

The yarn used has much to do with the appearance of patterns, for never could similar shapes in Norwegian or Swedish knitting, worked in heavier wools or differently spun wools, look like the Fair Isle knitting. Patterns suitable for textiles have, throughout the world, many similar characteristics and the star so often found in the knitting of Norway exists in brocade and damask, bead work and woven textiles, carpets and embroidery.

In knitting, particularly round knitting when the right side is facing at all times, similar characteristics are to found. Upright long vertical lines are avoided, diagonal lines are favoured, geometric lines and shapes abound and are symmetrical in both directions. They are symmetrical in repeating to the sides, and in having a middle line or round so that the second half of the pattern is the reverse of the first half. Long before the intricate instructions of today, patterns only lived on if they were capable of being remembered. So the simple O and X shapes used in Fair Isle are still popular because they can be knitted with ease and because they are suitable for stranding, the simplest method of working coloured knitting at speed (see fig. 372).

For further working instructions on stranding *see* Stranding in **Coloured knitting**.

Fair Isle knitting patterns

Traditional Fair Isle knitting patterns are worked by stranding the yarn across the wrong side of the work. For working method *see* Stranding in **Coloured knitting**.

Banded pattern

The basic banded pattern is often repeated vertically with different centres to the central motif, or the motif position is alternated to come above the double lines on the next band, reverting to the original for the following band (see fig. 234).

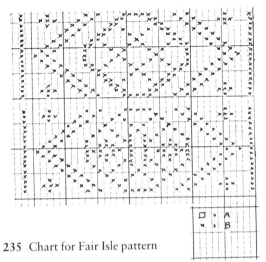

235 Chart for Fair Isle pattern

Faroese knitting

Less well known than Fair Isle knitting, the patterns of the Faroe islands are quite distinct. Here, too, wool was an important commodity and, as in Iceland, was at one time a legal currency.

236 Patterns from the Faroe Islands

234 Traditional Fair Isle pattern

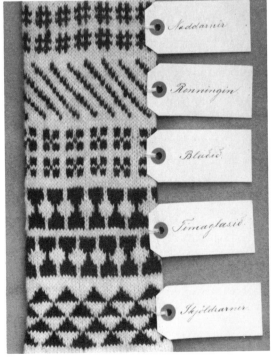

The chart, as is usual in Shetland knitters' own notebooks, is only to show the pattern; the colouring is left to the knitter. Work in shades of fawn and grey on cream, or shade both background and pattern changing only 1 colour on any 1 row (see fig. 235). It is worked over 38 sts.

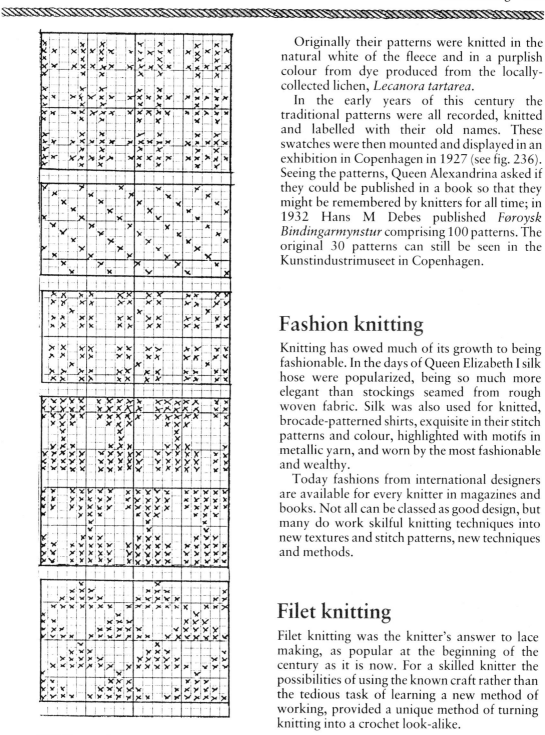

237 Pattern charts

Originally their patterns were knitted in the natural white of the fleece and in a purplish colour from dye produced from the locally-collected lichen, *Lecanora tartarea*.

In the early years of this century the traditional patterns were all recorded, knitted and labelled with their old names. These swatches were then mounted and displayed in an exhibition in Copenhagen in 1927 (see fig. 236). Seeing the patterns, Queen Alexandrina asked if they could be published in a book so that they might be remembered by knitters for all time; in 1932 Hans M Debes published *Føroysk Bindingarmynstur* comprising 100 patterns. The original 30 patterns can still be seen in the Kunstindustrimuseet in Copenhagen.

Fashion knitting

Knitting has owed much of its growth to being fashionable. In the days of Queen Elizabeth I silk hose were popularized, being so much more elegant than stockings seamed from rough woven fabric. Silk was also used for knitted, brocade-patterned shirts, exquisite in their stitch patterns and colour, highlighted with motifs in metallic yarn, and worn by the most fashionable and wealthy.

Today fashions from international designers are available for every knitter in magazines and books. Not all can be classed as good design, but many do work skilful knitting techniques into new textures and stitch patterns, new techniques and methods.

Filet knitting

Filet knitting was the knitter's answer to lace making, as popular at the beginning of the century as it is now. For a skilled knitter the possibilities of using the known craft rather than the tedious task of learning a new method of working, provided a unique method of turning knitting into a crochet look-alike.

Blocks and spaces

Just as in filet crochet or darning on to filet net, the patterns consist of openwork squares contrasted against solid squares, patterns being built up easily on squared paper.

Working spaces

Work to the position where the space is required, put the yarn twice over the needle then slip the next two stitches singly and knitwise. With the left needle tip, lift the first slipped stitch over the second and off the needle point (see fig. 238a), slip another stitch knitwise (238b), again take the slipped stitch over the third slipped stitch and off the needle point, and knit the last stitch on the right needle which is in fact the third slipped stitch (see fig. 238c).

The single space or open square on the chart represents the three stitches on the right needle that have made the space, two loops made by the y2on and one knitted stitch; it also includes the following row on which the stitch is knitted. The first of the two y2on loops are knitted and the second loop is purled.

Working blocks

Each block is made by knitting three stitches over four rows (see fig. 239).

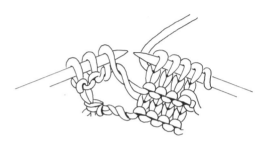

239 Three knitted stitches on two rows count as one block

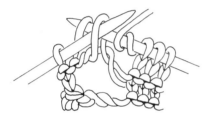

238a Cast off one stitch without using yarn

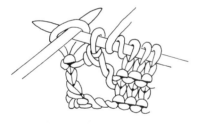

238b Cast off second stitch in the same way

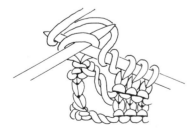

238c Knit the next stitch to complete one space

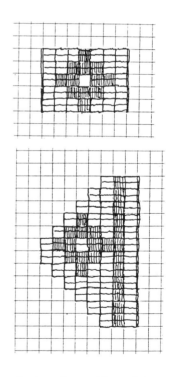

240 Charts for insertion and lace edging

Using squared paper

When a pattern is charted it is made of blocks and spaces. As the block uses four rows to be made square and the space only requires two, two spaces are made to every block.

For a design where the blocks are intended to be square and worked over four rows it is necessary to show two spaces by drawing a line across one square. If unsquared blocks of three stitches and two rows are to be teamed with spaces the pattern can use one square of graph paper for a block and one square for a space. Remember that whichever is used it will give a perfect way of planning and mapping out what is to be worked but will not show the pattern to scale (see fig. 240a).

Casting on

The chart, whichever version is being used, shows a number of squares and spaces. You must multiply this number by three to find how many to cast on and must then have edge stitches added. The number of edge stitches will depend on whether you are knitting a single item or making a panel that will have knitting on either side of it, or adding lace.

For lace, only one edge stitch at the start is required as the final stitch can be used as the other edge. For panels, you can add as many stitches as required, but note that because of the last stitch one less must be added to the left of the panel.

Choice of yarn

When filet knitting was first in vogue it was intended to be worked in crisp, fine cotton and to look as like crochet or finely-darned filet net as possible. Today it has more potential and, in thicker yarns, could be incorporated with chain or ribbon threading or as a framework to carry other yarn textures and colours.

Pattern instructions

A simple insertion is shown in fig. 240b. To the actual pattern you must add two edge stitches at the right and one at the left, which along with the last stitch that forms an upright make the pattern equal at both ends.

For this pattern cast on 24.

1st and 3rd rows K2, make 3 spaces, K3 for a block, make 3 spaces, K1.

2nd and every alt row K every stitch except the 2nd loop of each y2on which is purled.

5th and 7th rows K2, make 2 spaces, K3 for 1st block, make 1 space, K3 for 2nd block, make 2 spaces, K1.

9th and 11th rows K2, make 1 space, K3 for 1st block, make 3 spaces, K3 for 2nd block, make 1 space, K1.

13th and 15th rows As 5th and 7th rows.

16th row As 2nd row.

Rep these 16 rows for the required length (see fig. 241a).

The matching lace edging shown in fig. 240c has one straight and another shaped edge.

Casting on and off for shaped edges

The extra stitches that are required on the fifth row are placed ready on the third row by casting on loops as shown for casting on during working (*see* **Casting on**). Cast off on the last row of the mesh in the usual way (see fig. 241b).

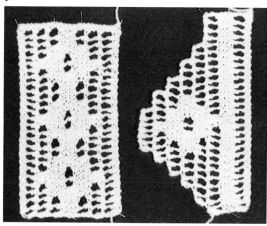

241 (*Left*) Filet lace insertion.
(*Right*) Filet lace edging

Finnish knitting

In Finland the traditional hand knitters did not hold a monopoly over the trade of woollen garments as another method was in existence. This was the coiling method whereby a shuttle was use to work the yarn. The coiling method produced a thick, two-sided fabric like double crochet, which could be made quickly and economically. In addition, owing to the larger amount of air that was trapped in the yarn by the coiling method, it was said that the man who wore knitted mittens chose unwisely, for the man that wore mittens made from the coiling method had warmer hands (see fig. 242).

fretwork type designs were particularly suitable to knit. Like most folk knitting, the idea for all the patterns was similar, but no two families used identical patterns. Geometrically inspired, the patterns move diagonally, each row or round naturally leading on as the pattern is built up; they are, therefore, easy to learn by sight rather than memory (see fig. 243).

The chart shows a traditional fretwork pattern in three different forms: a narrow border; a wider main border; and an allover pattern (see fig. 244a, b, c).

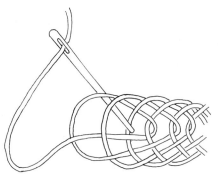

242 European form of making fabric from coiled loops

The coloured patterns that were in use in Finland were bold with one, or at most two, colours against a contrast background. With only two colours being used at any one time, the

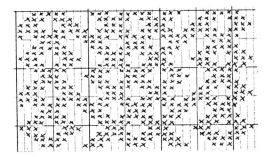

244a Chart for allover Finnish pattern

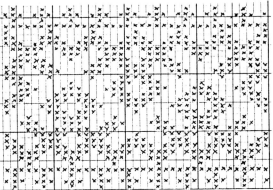

244b Chart for wide border

243 Finnish pattern

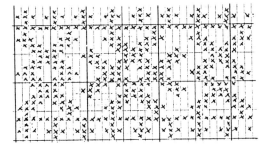

244c Chart for narrow border

Flat knitting

Flat knitting is worked in rows instead of rounds; the sections of garments are then seamed together.

Foreign terms

Publications from other countries often contain designs using a new technique, a new stitch pattern or an appealing finish. The vocabulary of knitting is small and with only a few key words the language problem should not present a barrier. These words are the most often used in instructions and they may be sufficient to help.

French-English

abbreviations du tricot	knitting abbreviations
aiguille(s)	needle(s)
aiguille auxiliaire	cable or spare needle
aiguille circulaire	circular needle
ainsie de suite	and so on
aller et retour	go and return, rows (not rounds)
assembler	join, make up
attente(att)	leave
aug dans une maille	knit into front and back of st
aug invisible	M1 tbl
augmentation (aug)	increase, add to
ayant	having
bandes de devant	front bands
bord en chainette	chain edge
bord perle	all edge sts knitted
bordures de devant	front borders
bouche	loop
bouton(s)	button(s)
boutonnière(s)	buttonhole(s)
bras	arm
casser le fil	break the yarn
ce point s'execute avec	work with multiple of
changement	change
chaque	each, every
col	collar
comme	as
commençant	begin
côté	side
côte	ribbing
coudre	sew
couleur	colour
couture	seam
croiser	to cross or twist
de * à *	from * to *
dernier (dern)	last
derrière (der)	behind, on the other side
dessous	under, below
dessous de	beneath
dessous de bras	under arm
dessus	over, above
devant (dev)	front
diminution (dim)	decrease
double jeté	yarn twice over needle
dos	back
droite	right
emmanchure (emman)	armhole
empiècement	yoke
encoloure	neck
endroit (end)	knit
à l'endroit	on right side (of work)
ensemble (ens)	together
envers (env)	purl
à l'envers	on back (wrong side)
epaule(s)	shoulder(s)
explication	instructions
exterieur	outside of (work, garment)
façon	make, shape
fermer	sew seams, close, shut
faire	make
faire un jeté	make a yon
faire vis à vis	reversing instructions
fermenture des mailles	cast off sts
fil(s)	yarn(s)
finnisant	completing, finishing
fois (fs)	time, times
former	shape
fourniture	materials
gauche	left
glisser (glis)	slip (st), pass
grande	large
grille	chart
hauteur	long, length
jeté a l'endroit	yon before K st
jeté a l'envers	yon before P st
jeté le fil	yon, throw the yarn
jeu de 4	set of 4 double pointed needles
jersey end	stocking stitch
jersey env	reverse stocking stitch
jusque	until
inversant les explications	reverse the instructions
lâcher une maille	drop a stitch
laisser (lais)	leave
lisière (lis)	edge st
longeur	width, breadth
maille(s) (M)	stitch(s)
maille à l'endroit torsée	K into back of st
maille à l'envers torsée	P into back of st
maille glisée à l'endroit	slip st knitwise
maille glisée à l'envers	slip st purlwise
maille impair	odd no of sts
maille pair	even no of sts
manche	sleeve
même	same

même travail	work as for
milieu	middle
montage	making up
monter	cast on
moyenne	medium (size)
nombre	number
on obtient	you have (no of sts)
ourlet	hem
overture	opening
partager	to divide
patron	extra large (size)
pendant	during, for
petit	small (size)
placer	to place
pôche(s)	pocket(s)
point (pt)	pattern (stitch)
point de côte 1 et 1	K1, P1 rib
point de riz	moss stitch
point fantaisie	unusual st pattern (instructions given)
point mousse	garter stitch
poursuivre	to go on with
premier, première	first
prendre	change, to take
puis	then, next
quelque	some, any
rabattre (rab)	cast off
rang (rg)	row
1 rg end	1 row knit
1 rg env	1 row purl
rg suivant	row following
rayé	striped
rayures	stripes
relever	pick up
remaillage sur en bord	K up sts from edge
repasser	to iron, press
répéter	repeat
reprendre	to return to
restant	remaining
sans	without
seconde	second
semblable	similar
separement	separately
simult	at the same time
soin	care
suivre	following
surjet double	Sl1, K2 tog, psso
surjet simple	K1, sl1, psso
temps	times
total	total
toujours (tjrs)	all, always
tourner	to turn
tous (ts)	all
travail (ts)	work (knit)
tricoter (tric)	to knit

German-English

ab	from
ab * wiederholen	repeat from *
abbildung	illustration
abheben	to slip
abketten der Maschen (abk)	cast off sts
abnehmen (abn)	decrease(ing)
abschragen	shape
Anfang	beginning
anschlagen (anschl)	cast on
Arbeit (arb)	work
Arbeitsfolge	knitting instructions
Arbeit wenden	turn work
armausschnitt	armhole
Armel	sleeve
auf	on
Auffassen	pick up
aufnehmen (aufn)	increase
Ausarbeitung	making up
aussen	outside
beenden	finishing
bei	at
beidseitig	both sides, each end
bleiben	remain
bis	until
Borte	border
dabei	at the same time
dann	then
darüberstricken	work across (knit)
dauern	last
davon	away
der	the
Doppel	double
Doppelumschlag	y2on
eine	one
einmal	once
einsetzen	insert
erste	first
Faden nach hinter Legen	yarn to back
Farbe	colour
Farbflächen	colour change
folgen, folgt (folg)	follow
für	for
Gang	round (circular knitting)
ganze Länge	total length
garn	yarn
gerade	straight
geschlossen Arbeit	round knitting (closed)
gestrickt	knitted
glatt Maschen	stocking stitch
glatte re	
glatt li	reverse stocking stitch
gleiche	like, equal
gleich zeitig	at the same time
Hals	neck
Halsausschnitt	neck opening, neckline
heruntergefallene Masche aufheben	pick up dropped stitch

hilfsnadel	stitch holder, cable or spare needle
hinter	behind
hoch	high
im Wechsel	alternately
immer	always
jede, jeder	each, every
jedoch	still
Kante	edge
Kettenrand	cable
Knopf	button
Knopfloch	buttonhole
Kragen	collar
Kraus gestrickt	garter stitch
lassen	leave
linke M (li M)	purl stitch
links	left
locker	loosely
Masche(n) (M)	stitch, stitches(es)
Masche links	purl stitch
Masche rechts	knit stitch
2 Maschen rechts zusammen	K2 tog.
2 Maschen überzogen zus, stricken	sl1, K1, psso
Maschenzahl teilbar durch	sts divisible by
Maase	measurements
Maschenprobe	tension (gauge)
mit	with
Mittel	middle
Muster	stitch pattern
Mustersatz	pattern repeat
nach	after
nach hinten einstechen	through back of stitch
Nadel (N)	needle
nähen	sew
Naht	seam
noch	still, yet
oben	at the top
obersten	top
Oberweite	actual chest measurement
offen	open
Öffnung	opening
ohne	without
Rand	side
Randmasche (Rdm)	edge stitch
rechte M (re M)	knit stitch
rechts	right
Reihe (R)	row
restliche (restl)	remaining
Rollkragen	polo collar
Rückenteil	back
Rückseite	wrong side of work
runde (Rd)	round
Saum	hem
schliessen	sew up, close
Schulter	shoulder
Schulterstück	yoke

Seitennaht	side seam
Spielstricknadel	double-pointed needles
Spitzmuster	lace pattern
Strickschema	diagram
stricken (str)	knit
Stricknadel	knitting needle
Strickring	circular needle
Strickschrift	knitting pattern
Tasche	pocket
Teil	part
über	over
Umschlag (U)	yarn over needle
Umschlag fallen lassen	drop yarn over needle
umlegen	fold over
und	and
unter	under
Unterarm	under arm
Veränderung	change
verbinden	join
verdrehte	crossed, twisted
verschränkt	back of stitch
verteilt	distribute
von	of
vor	in front of, before
Vorderseite	front of work
wechseln	turn, change
weiterarb (eiten)	continue
weiterhin	from now on
wenn	when
wie	as
wiederholen (wdh)	repeat
Zahl	number
zusammen (zus)	together
zwei	two
zweite	second
zweimal	twice

Italian-English

accavallare (acc)	slip, pass
accavallato (acc)	sl1, K1, psso
accavallato doppia	sl1, K2 tog, psso
alternamente	alternately
altezza totale (alt tot)	total length
altri	another
ancora	again
apertura	opening
attacare	attach, sew
assieme (ass)	together
aumente (aum)	increases
avviare (avv)	cast on
bordo	border
cambiare	change
centrale	central

chiudere	cast off
collo	collar
colore (col)	colour
come	as, like
con il filo davanti	with yarn at front
con il filo dietro	with yarn at back
confezione	making up
contemporaneamente	at the same time
continuare (cont)	continue
coste 1 x 1	K1, P1 rib
cucitura	seam
davanti	front
a destra	on the right
dietro	back
diminuire	to decrease
diminuzione (dim)	decrease
diritto (dir)	knit stitch
dir crociato	2 knit sts crossed
disegno	diagram
dispari	odd number of rows
distribuendo nel corso del ferro	spacing evenly across the row
doppia	double, twice
due	two
esecuzione	instructions
esequire	make, work
ferro, ferri(f)	row, rows also needle
ferro ausiliario(trecce)	cable needle
ferro circolare	circular needle
2 f e f pari	2nd and every alt row
filati, filo (fil)	yarn
finiture	finish, finishes
foretti	holes, ribbon slotting
gettato	yarn over needle
gilet	waistcoat
gioco di ferri	set of double-pointed needles
giro	round
golfino	jersey
gonna	skirt
in senso inverso	reverse shaping
incavo manica	armhole
iniziare(iniz)	begin
insieme(ins)	together
intrecciare	cast off
intrecciare a costa	cast off in rib
lana	wool
lato	edge, side
lavorare in tondo	work in rounds
lavorare su un numero di multiplo de	worked on a multiple of . . . . sts
lav le m come si presentano	K, K sts and P P sts
legaccio	garter stitch
maglia, maglie	stitch, stitches
maglia doppia	K into next st on row below
maglia rasata(m ras)	stocking stitch
maglia rasata rovescia	reverse stocking stitch
2 m ins a dir	K2 tog
2 m ins a rov	P2 tog

m dir ritorto	K through back of loop
m rov rotorto	P through back of loop
manica	sleeve
meta	half
morbidamente	loosely
nell stesso modo	in the same way
occhielli	buttonholes
occorente	materials
ogni	each, every
pari	even number (sts, rows)
passare	to pass, slip
passare 1 dir senza lav	sl1 st knitwise
passare 1 rov senza lav	sl1 st purlwise
per	for, through
piegare	fold, turn
piu	more
primo	first
prosequire (pros)	carry on, continue
punti divisi da	sts divided by
punto	stitch pattern
punto a coste	ribbing
punto a grano di riso	moss stitch
punto fantasia	unusual st patt with instructions
punti impegiati	stitch patterns used
punto legaccio	garter stitch
quindi	then
regolarmente	evenly, regularly
rimanente	remaining
rip il disegno	rep the patt
ripetere da * a *	repeat from * to *
riprendere	pick up
rovescio (rov)	purl stitch
scalfo manica	armhole
scieco	slope, shaping
sciarpa	scarf
scollo	neck
senze	without
sequito	following
a sinistra	on the left
spiegazione	explanation, instructions
successivo	following
sul diritto del lavore	on right side of work
sul rovescio del lavore	on purl (wrong) side of work
taglia	size
tenere in attesa	leave unworked
terminare (term)	end, finish
totale	total
traforato	lacy
treccia	cable
uguale	alike
ultimo	last
uncinetto	crochet hook
vivagno (viv)	edge st
volte	times
(una) volta	once

Frame knitting

No work is made on knitting frames today, except by children using a bobbin, knitting Nancy or old-fashioned cotton reel with pins or pegs around a central hole. At one time, however, frames played a large part in the manufacture of knitted goods (see fig. 245).

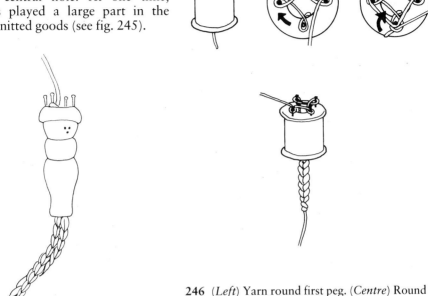

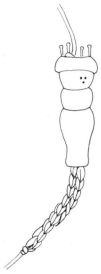

245   French knitting

246 (*Left*) Yarn round first peg. (*Centre*) Round other three pegs. (*Right*) Carry yarn across first peg and lift original loop over strand and off peg. (*Bottom*) Worked cord passes through centre opening

Basically, frames were round in varying sizes or straight wooden blocks with a slit centre. All had pegs or prongs around the opening, their closeness depending on the type of item to be made. The different shapes and sizes were used for different purposes from the production of girdles and cords on small round frames to stockings and caps on larger round frames and garments, sections of garments, and possibly even the masterpiece carpets on straight frames. Stocking stitch, garter stitch and ribbing could be worked, particularly on the straight frames, depending on the method of winding the yarn round the pegs. Coloured work, just as with the bobbin or cotton reel, could also be worked; it is probable that the large masterpiece carpets or colourful hangings made by journeymen for their guild, from approximately the middle of the seventeenth century until the eighteenth century, were made in this way.

Working peg knitting

Take the end of yarn through the centre opening and round the back of the first peg from right to left then across to the next peg from left to right (see fig. 246a).

Repeat this round each peg in turn (see fig. 246b).

On the second round take the yarn across the front of the peg immediately above the loop and lift the loop inwards over the newly-placed yarn and off the peg, using the tool provided or a fine, short knitting needle. Repeat on each peg (see fig. 246c).

Repeat the second round again and again until the resulting braid is the required length (see fig. 246d).

Plain braid
Work with only one colour throughout.

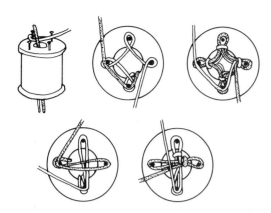

247 (*Top*) Alternately coloured cord.
(*Bottom*) Use opposite pegs for vertical stripes

Coloured braid

Alternate rounds of two colours produce a horizontally-banded braid. The stripes can be made more obvious by working more than one round in each colour. Additional colours can also be added. Thread all colours to be used through the centre at the start and carry those not in use up the centre of the braid as it is made (see fig. 247a).

For vertical stripes place colours on opposite pegs and always work with the colour on the peg (see fig. 247b).

Using braid

Braids can be coiled and slip stitched together to make small purses, mats, bags and other items. You can also use them as laces, for slotting through knitting decoratively and for creating small animals and figures.

French knitting

French knitting both took inspiration from and influenced other countries, with the French court being particularly instrumental in ensuring an interchange of ideas. Theodore Letto in 1525 wrote: 'Before 1527 the French possessed this talent [knitting], and regarded the Scots as their masters.' The French guilds were among the earliest to be set up – the Guild of Tournai was established in 1429 and that of Paris in 1527; the first Scottish guild of Dundee is thought to date before 1485. In addition, the French also took inspiration from the Spanish, whom the English credited with having invented knitting. In the Pyrenees coloured pattern work similar to the knitting of the Basque people was to be found.

Around Landes, a rural sheep rearing area, the

248 Basque girl knits as she guards the sheep

shepherds knitted while watching flocks (see fig. 248). Like other folk knitters, speed was essential in order for enough money to be made – the men of the region knitted on stilts so that they could see any danger approaching their flocks. On the sea coast of Brittany the fishermen knitted in Brioche stitch, using many interesting variations of the basic stitches.

Many lace patterns still in use today derive from the earliest knitting books for domestic knitters and still have French names. As these must have been translations of existing patterns, the original name may be of importance, despite the trend of the time to make an item fashionable by giving it a French name.

French lace patterns

Lace patterns particularly seem to have origins in France, possibly having been modelled on French lace.

Pyrenees pattern

First published in Britain around 1840, the pattern of this lace is dainty and suitable for the finest yarns (see fig. 249a).
Worked over a number of stitches divisible by 18, plus 1.
1st row (WS facing), P.
2nd row K2 tog, * yon, K1, K2 tog, yon, K2, K2 tog, yon, K1, yon, SSK, K2, yon, SSK, K1, yon, SK2togPO, rep from * ending last rep SSK in place of SK2togPO.
3rd row P2, * P2 tog tbl, yon, P2, P2 tog tbl, yon, P3, yon, P2 tog, P2, yon, P2 tog, P3, rep from * ending last rep P2 in place of P3.
4th row K1, * K2 tog, yon, K2, K2 tog, yon, K5, yon, SSK, K2, yon, SSK, K1, rep from * to end.
5th row P2 tog tbl, * yon, P2, P2 tog tbl, yon, P7, yon, P2 tog, P2, yon, P3 tog, rep from * ending last rep P2 tog in place of P3 tog.
6th row K3, * K2 tog, yon, K2, K2 tog, yon, K1, yon, SSK, K2, yon, SSK, K5, rep from * ending last rep K3 in place of K5.
7th and 8th rows As 3rd and 4th rows.
9th row P2 tog tbl, * yon, P2, P2 tog tbl, yon, P2, yon, P3 tog, yon, P2, yon, P2 tog, P2, yon, P3 tog, rep from * ending last rep P2 tog in place of P3 tog.
10th row K.

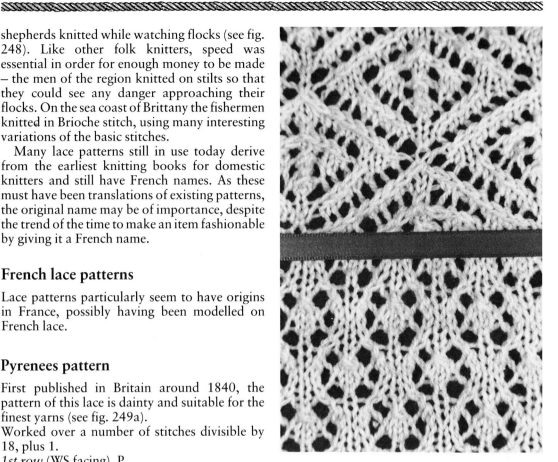

249 (*Top*) Pyrenees pattern
(*Bottom*) Fleurette pattern

11th row P1, * yon, P2 tog, P2, yon, P2 tog, P1, yon, P3 tog, yon, P1, P2 tog tbl, yon, P2, P2 tog tbl, yon, P1, rep from * to end.
12th row K2, * yon, SSK, K2, yon, SSK, K3, K2 tog, yon, K2, K2 tog, yon, K3, rep from * ending last rep K2 in place of K3.
13th row P3, * yon, P2 tog, P2, yon, P2 tog, P1, P2 tog tbl, yon, P2, P2 tog tbl, yon, P5, rep from * ending last rep P3 in place of P5.
14th row K4, * yon, SSK, K2, yon, SK2togPO, yon, K2, K2 tog, yon, K7, rep from * ending last rep K4 in place of K7.
15th row P1, * yon, P2 tog, P2, yon, P2 tog, P5, P2 tog tbl, yon, P2, P2 tog tbl, yon, P1, rep from * to end.
16th and 17th rows As 12th and 13th rows.
18th row K2 tog, * yon, K2, yon, SSK, K2, yon, SK2togPO, yon, K2, K2 tog, yon, K2, yon,

SK2togPO, rep from * ending last rep SSK in place of SK2togPO.

Rep from 1st–18th rows as required.

Originally the SSK would have been worked with an SKPO but this gives a cleaner line to the diamonds.

Fleurette

This lace, because of its size, fills a gap between tiny patterns and the larger major patterns and is only patterned on every right side row (see fig. 249b).

Worked over a number of stitches divisible by 6, plus 5.

1st row (WS facing) P.

2nd row K2, * K1, yon, SSK, K1, K2 tog, yon, rep from * to last 3 sts, K3.

3rd and every alt row P.

4th row K4, * yon, K3, rep from * to last st, K1.

6th row K2, K2 tog, * yon, SSK, K1, K2 tog, yon, sl2 knitwise, K1, p2sso, rep from * to last 4 sts, SSK, K2.

8th row K2, * K1, K2 tog, yon, K1, yon, SSK, rep from * to last 3 sts, K3.

10th row As 4th row.

12th row K2, * K1, K2 tog, yon, sl2 knitwise, K1, p2sso, yon, SSK, rep from * to last 3 sts, K3.

Rep 1st–12th rows as required.

In this lace the clarity of the lines has been improved by using the decrease made by SSK in place of a slipped and passed over stitch as was used when this was first printed.

Fringes

A fringe, either knotted or knitted, is often used to decorate an edge which is not seamed, as on a scarf.

Knotted fringing

Cut lengths of yarn a little more than double the finished required length. Take four or more ends at a time and fold in half over a crochet hook (see fig. 250a).

Draw the doubled ends through the edge and with the hook catch hold of the other ends and draw them through the first loop at the fold over of the ends (see fig. 250b). Draw the ends up and trim them as required (see fig. 250c).

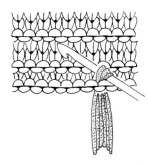

250a Insert hook through folded strands and edge

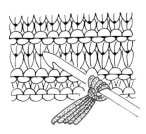

250b Draw fringe tails through loop

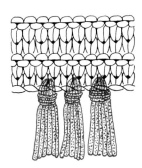

250c Finished fringe

Knitted fringe

To make a knitted fringe cast on and knit a strip to the required length, then cast it off so that some stitches can be unravelled to form long fringe-like strands. The edge which is not unravelled is stitched along the garment or scarf edge.

Cast on a number of stitches divisible by 3.

Depending on the depth required and the weight of yarn 6 or 9 sts will give a reasonable fringe. If the edge is to be knitted after working it may need to be longer.

1st row * K1, yon, K2 tog, rep from * to end.
Rep this row as required.
Last row Cast off 3 stitches only, break off the
yarn and draw through the last cast off st, then
slip from the needle and allow the remaining
stitches to unravel. The fringe can then be sewn
on to the garment.

If the fringe is to be knotted, cut the folded
strands evenly and draw together into equal
numbers of strands and knot to the next strand.

Coloured fringes

Two or more colours can be wound or knitted
together to give a coloured fringe.

Knotted fringes

Many yarns tend to cling to each other and spoil
a deep fringe by hanging together rather than in
straight lines. Prevent this by knotting the ends
towards the top, giving the yarn extra weight
and separating the strands into bundles (see
fig. 251). (*See also* **Looped Knitting** for a fringe
which can be knitted by regulating the depth of
the loops over a strip of card.)

251 Decorative fringes

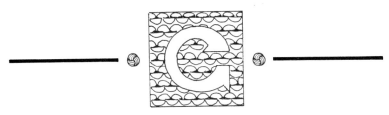

Garter stitch

See **Basic stitches**

Gauge

See **Tension**

German knitting

Knitting in Germany is a long-established craft and is forever documented in the picture of the knitting Madonna, *The Visit of the Angels* painted around 1390 by Master Bertram of Munich for the convent of Buxtehuder (now in the Kunsthall, Hamburg). Bertram has depicted the Madonna working a vest or full garment on four needles, with the neck edge neatened with stitches picked up around the otherwise finished garment.

Some of the earliest books about knitting patterns published in the early nineteenth century show patterns still in use today, often elaborate and lacy (*see* **German knitting patterns**).

Much German knitting is worked on four or five needles in the round, and some patterns rely on this technique for their execution; this, unfortunately, makes it difficult to translate them into patterns for use with two needles.

Patterned stockings have always been important to German knitters and in many areas are part of the national costume. Their decoration, like those of Austrian stockings, is often ingenious and highly skilled.

German stitch patterns

Many patterns still in use every day began in Germany.

Track of the turtle pattern

This pattern, which has many variations, was already in use in Germany by the beginning of the nineteenth century (see fig. 253). Worked over a number of stitches divisible by 15.

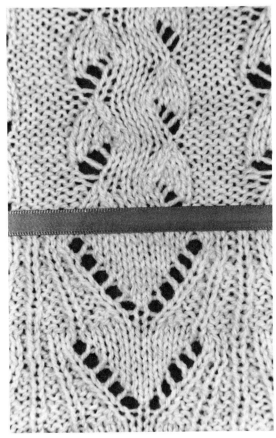

253 (*Top*) Track of the turtle pattern. (*Bottom*) Umbrella pattern

1st row (WS facing), K3, P9, K3.
2nd row P3, yon, K4, SSK, K3, P3.
3rd row K3, P2, P2 tog tbl, P4, yon, P1, K3.
4th row P3, K2, yon, K4, SSK, K1, P3.
5th row K3, P2 tog tbl, P4, yon, P3, K3.
6th row P3, K9, P3.
7th row K3, yon, P4, P2 tog, P3, K3.
8th row P3, K2, K2 tog, K4, yon, K1, P3.
9th row K3, P2, yon, P4, P2 tog, P1, K3.
10th row P3, K2 tog, K4, yon, K3, P3.
Rep 1st–10th rows as required.

Umbrella pattern

This delightful lace is an old pattern and has several well-known relatives including, bear track and grand shell (see fig. 253b).
Worked over a number of stitches divisible by 18 sts, plus 1.
1st row (WS facing) * P1, [P1, K3] 4 times, P1, rep from * to last st, P1.
2nd row * K1, yon, K1, P2 tog, P1, [K1, P3] twice, K1, P1, P2 tog, K1, yon, rep from * to last st, K1.
3rd row * P3, K2, [P1, K3] twice, P1, K2, P2, rep from * to last st, P1.
4th row * K2, yon, K1, P2 tog, yon (K1, P1, P2 tog) twice, K1, yon, P2 tog, K1, yon, K1, rep from * to last st, K1.
5th row * P3, [P1, K2] 4 times, P3, rep from * to last st, P1.
6th row * K3, yon, K1, P2 tog, [K1, P2] twice, K1, P2 tog, K1, yon, K2, rep from * to last st, K1.
7th row * P5, K1, [P1, K2] twice, P1, K1, P4, rep from * to last st, P1.
8th row * K4, yon, K1, P1, [K1, P2 tog] twice, K1, P1, K1, yon, K3, rep from * to last st, K1.
9th row * P5, [P1, K1] 4 times, P5, rep from * to last st, P1.
10th row * K5, yon, SSK, [K1, P1] twice, K1, K2 tog, yon, K4, rep from * to last st, K1.
11th row * P8, K1, P1, K1, P7, rep from * to last st, P1.
12th row * K8, P1, K1, P1, K7, rep from * to last st, K1.
Rep 1st–12th rows as required.

Gloves

Gloves may not have been knitted as long ago as socks, but they have been made for hundreds of years. Knitting, ideally suited to reproducing the intricate shape of the hand, was used for very special gloves for the clergy, often worked in silk with metallic thread ornamentation.

They are found in most folk knitting communities: with brightly-coloured edges in Lappland, in coloured wools in Shetland, in the soft sheep shades of Icelandic yarn and in patterned styles in Sweden and Norway. There are two ways of knitting gloves and mittens, round without seams or on two needles.

Gloves knitted round

Seamless gloves are usually knitted from the wrist upward; wrist ribbing is worked on the number of stitches cast on and may be inceased slightly before the start of the hand.

A gusset is usually worked in the most shapely gloves so that a triangular piece is knitted between graded increases equal to the increased width of the hand from the wrist beneath the thumb to the base of the thumb. These gusset stitches are left on a holder so that the thumb can be knitted after the remainder of the glove has been worked.

The gusset stitches usually form at least three-quarters of the stitches required for the thumb width; the remainder are picked up from stitches cast on immediately above the thumb division. These cast-on stitches, along with those left after you have taken the thumb gusset on to the holder, are the number required round up to the base of the fingers (see fig. 254a).

Work each finger separately, taking stitches from both palm and back. First finger and small finger both add two or three stitches on the inner side of the finger between front and back and on the other two fingers two or three stitches are picked up from this edge and an equal number are cast on for the opposite side. This gives a roundness that would not exist if only front and back stitches were used. These stitch finger dividers may be decreased over two or three rounds to form a narrower finger and a more comfortable fit (see fig. 254b).

The top of each finger is usually decreased on

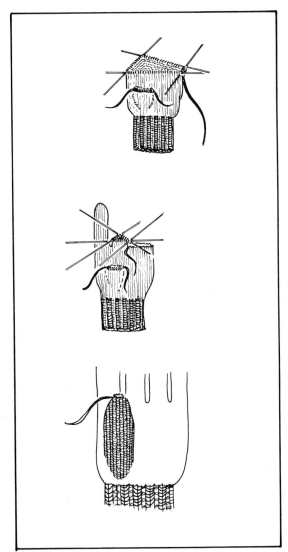

On two needles

With the decline in popularity of round knitting, patterns have been adapted so that gloves can be made on two needles. These do have to be seamed, however, and are therefore not quite as comfortable to wear.

Alternative two needle method

Gloves can also be knitted from side to side; you can work them from the palm upwards, casting on and off the numbers of stitches required for the different finger lengths (see fig. 255a).

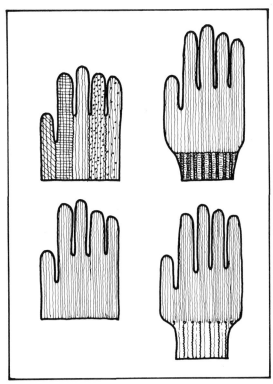

254 (*Top*) Thumb gusset and palm up to finger base
(*Centre*) Working the fingers
(*Bottom*) A shaped finger tip

255 (*Top right*) Knitted from side to side
(*Top left*) Using colours for separate fingers
(*Bottom*) Picked-up cuff

the last few rounds or gathered on to the finished yarn and drawn up to bring the finger to a tip. The thumb section is then worked in the same way: pick up the gusset stitches and a few stitches from those cast on behind the thumb (see fig. 254c).

Longer rows to include a wrist area are made by working shorter rows every two rows so that the wrist with less rows is tighter than the palm and back of the glove. This method is used for brightly-coloured gloves with a different colour or tone used for each finger (see fig. 255b).

Garter stitch is the best stitch for gloves

knitted in this way from the required tension point of view. You could use stocking stitch but you would need to treat the wrist differently to draw the stocking stitch in. You should do this by working a rib, picking up stitches from the lower edge of the glove and knitting away from the hand – the reverse way from the side-to-side palm and back (see fig. 255c).

Mittens

You can work mittens in the same way as gloves, omitting the fingers.

Short mittens

At the base of the fingers you can finish the top of the hand with a rib, allowing all the fingers to be free.

The fingers can be separated and worked as for a glove for a very few rounds then edged with rib. Alternatively, all the stitches can be continued to the top, then decreased at each side to form a narrower top section. With the top stitches grafted as for the toe of a sock, the mitten is exceedingly comfortable to wear.

Alternative thumb

Mittens or gloves can be made so that they fit the left or right hand by putting a gusset in. You can also make them to fit either hand by placing the gusset on the side fold line so that the side of the first finger is immediately over the centre of stitches behind the thumb opening.

No gusset gloves and mittens

Gloves and mittens can also be made without a gusset if extra width is allowed for above the wrist. The thumb division is worked in the same way.

Guernsey knitting

Wool has properties which make it ideal for outdoor wear. It can be mended, repaired, re-edged; it can be worked at home when there is time to rest or hands are idle from other chores

256 Fisherman wearing traditional guernsey or gansey

and is therefore economical; and, above all, it dries by body heat when it gets wet, in no way harming the wearer.

All these properties were of importance to the women who knitted the guernseys or ganseys in the fisher communities around the British coast and the western coast of Europe from the end of the eighteenth century onwards. Knitted in one piece on sets of long needles, and even on umbrella spokes in hard times, the garments were made in one piece. Worked round to underarm level, the back and front were then knitted separately, joined back into one at the shoulders and had sleeves picked up and knitted downwards from shoulder to wrist. A ribbed neckband, or buttoning neckband trimmed the neck edge (see fig. 256). Within this limited outline there were innumerable variations, even in the method of casting on.

Patterns, usually in knit and purl stitches only along with cables, were used in bands horizontally, in panels vertically or in yoked patterns, often of apparent complexity – at least to the layman's eye. Mock side seams often edged gusset shaping under the arms and in some areas no guernsey would have been complete without contrast patterned shoulder straps.

Many guernseys, as in Polperro in Cornwall, were knitted to augment the meagre income of the residents and were taken to a collecting base in the nearest large town, where more yarn was purchased, and carried home for the next batch of knitting.

In areas further from towns the patterns seem to be even more varied, where families had their own version, and where one woman vied with neighbours for the production of a design that would keep others guessing.

Wool varied from area to area but was usually dark or even black and was smoothly spun yarn of five-ply weight. Finer yarn was also used but whatever thickness used the needles were always exceptionally fine for the wool quality, producing a fabric that could 'turn' water and was less absorbent than softly spun and openly knitted yarn. It was commonplace to find that new guernseys were worn for weddings, then kept for best or Sunday wear until the next guernsey was knitted, older ones being worn for weekdays until they could be repaired no more. Even then they were not thrown away, for the thrifty houewife would rattle down the yarn and send her old guernseys to the mill to be turned into blankets.

Guernsey knitting patterns

The variety of patterns seems to have been never ending; even amongst the often-used diamonds and meshes, marriage lines and cable patterns, it is difficult to find two guernseys alike. Knitters would think of a variation as they worked and next time round would incorporate it in its new form.

Yorkshire pattern

Diamonds, symbolic of wealth and of the nets of the men, were to be found in many variations, as allover patterns, open, reversed stocking stitch or in moss stitch. Figure 257 shows a pattern from Yorkshire that uses a purled diamond contrasted against a moss stitch diamond.

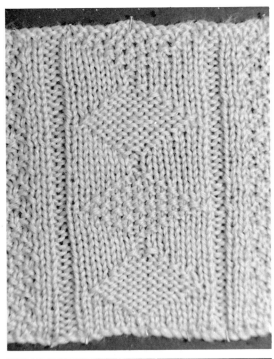

257 (*Top*) Yorkshire pattern.
(*Bottom*) Pattern from Norfolk.

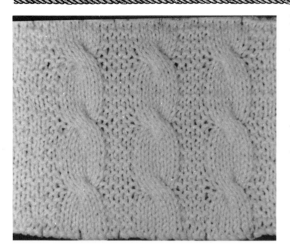

(*Above*) Scottish pattern from Musselburgh

Worked over a number of stitches divisible by 28.

The chart shows the repeat centred with double moss stitch panels at each side (see fig. 258).

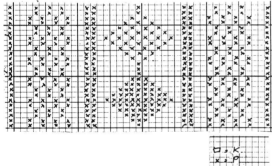

258 Yorkshire chart

Cromer pattern

An unusual and distinctive cable pattern comes from Cromer in Norfolk. It is a wide cable with a very individual look because it is backed by garter stitch bands, which, because they draw the fabric up, give the cable an interesting pucker. The cable panel is placed on a background of a seeded pattern of two purl stitches on a stocking stitch background, with position reversed throughout on alternate rows (see fig. 257b).
Worked over 34 stitches (see fig. 259).

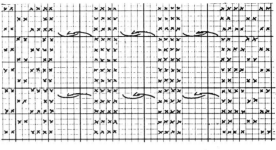

259 Cromer chart

The cable pattern is worked over 6 sts thus:
C6F – slip next 3 sts to CN, hold at front, K3, K3 from CN.

Fisher-row pattern

From Fisher-row, close to the old Lothian town of Musselburgh, comes a version of the fir tree pattern found in many Scottish patterns. As a panel it is edged by a broken ridge and is often teamed with cable ropes on alternative vertical panels (see fig. 257c).
Worked over a repeat of 18 sts (see fig. 260).

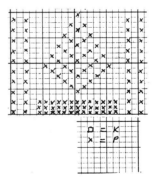

260 Musselburgh chart

Grafting

Grafting is a means of joining two edges of knitting together so that the stitches appear to be continous; it is also a way of avoiding the firm line created by seaming cast-off edges. It is often used to join shoulder seams, whether straight or sloping, and is ideal for sock and stocking toes and mitten tips.

Stitches can be grafted on or off the needles: which you choose to do is partly a matter of preference, but also determined by whether the type of yarn will allow stitches to drop readily once they have been slipped from the needle tips.

Grafting stocking stitch on needles

Place both sets of stitches one behind the other with wrong sides touching and the needle points at the right. There should be equal numbers of stitches on both needles. Break off the yarn on the front needle, leaving an end at least four times the length of the edge to be grafted. If insufficient yarn has been left at the side, join in another length along the side edge, darning the end in once the grafting is complete.

Thread the yarn into a wool needle and draw it purlwise through the first stitch on the front needle but do not slip the stitch off the needle. This process positions the yarn correctly and is required whenever two sections are being grafted. The start is different for sock or mitten toes where the stitches are part of folded work (*see* **Socks**).

* Insert the wool needle through the first stitch on the back needle purlwise, draw the yarn through and let the stitch slip off the knitting needle, then pass the wool needle through the next stitch on the back needle knitwise but do not let the stitch slip from the needle (see fig. 261a).

Insert the wool needle through the next stitch on the front needle knitwise and let it drop off the needle, then insert the wool needle purlwise through the next stitch on the front needle (see fig. 261c). Repeat from * until all stitches are worked off. Break off the yarn and darn the thread end into the side edge.

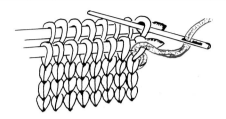

261a Draw the yarn purlwise through the first stitch on front needle

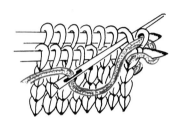

261b Draw the needle through the first stitch on back needle, letting the stitch slip off the needle tip

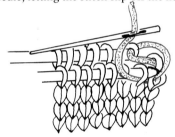

261c Pass it through the next stitch knitwise then knitwise through the first front stitch, letting it drop from the needle and then through the next front stitch, purlwise

Grafting reverse stocking stitch on needles

Turn the work so that both purl right sides are touching and the knit sides are outside. Graft as for stocking stitch and reverse the work on to its correct right side when the grafting is completed.

Grafting garter stitch on needles

To place the grafted row correctly a ridged line of stitches must show on both front and back needles when they are placed with wrong sides touching, as in fig. 262a.

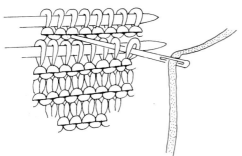

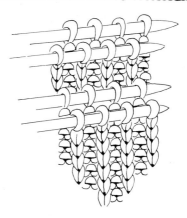

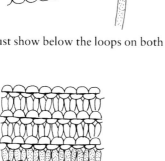

262a Ridges must show below the loops on both needles

263a Ribbing arranged on two needles

262b Tension must match knitting

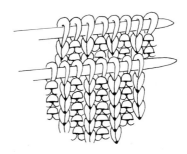

263b Like stitches on each needle placed on second needles

Insert the threaded wool needle through the first stitch on the front needle purlwise and leave on the needle.

* Insert the wool needle through the first stitch on the back needle knitwise and slip it off the needle, then pass the wool needle purlwise through the next st on the back needle, leaving it on the knitting needle.

Repeat from * on the front needle then work alternately on back and front, noting that the way of taking off the stitches does not alter as it does for stocking stitch but is the same on both needles (see 262b).

Grafting ribbing on needles

The simplest way is to slip all the knit stitches on the front needle on to a spare needle and all the knit stitches on the back also on to a spare needle (see fig. 263b). Graft all the knit stitches on front and back needles, then turn the work to the other side and work all the other stitches which will also be knit stitches on this side.

Grafting stocking stitch off needles

Place the two needles close together on a flat surface with wrong side downwards and the needle tips to the right. Only draw out the needles as the stitches are grafted, avoiding any risk of them slipping down a row. Keep the stitches absolutely flat and untwisted as they are worked; otherwise the grafting will not give a continuous line. Insert the threaded wool needle twice into every stitch with the exception of the first back stitch which is only passed through once.

Insert the wool needle through the loops of two stitches at the same time so that the touching edges are on the top of the needle as shown by the coloured thread in fig. 264a.

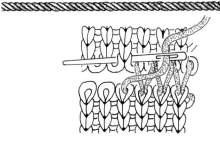

264a Grafting stocking stitch off needle

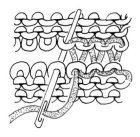

264b Grafting reversed stocking stitch off needles

Grafting reverse stocking stitch off needle

Place the edges face down on a flat surface and thread the yarn through the stitches so that the two sides of every two stitches that touch have the yarn over them on both front and back needles (see fig. 264b).

Grafting garter stitch off needles

Lay the work flat on each side of the knitting needles and gradually withdraw the knitting needles as the stitches are worked. Work so that the grafting thread is always over the top of the sides of two touching stitches on the back needle and under two threads on the front needle (see fig. 264c).

Grafting ribbing off needles

Place both edges as before, flat and with needles tips at the right edge. The method of threading the stitches is to combine the stocking stitch method over stocking stitch rib stitches with the reverse stocking stitch method over purled stitches.

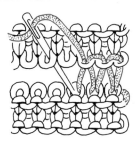

265 Grafting garter stitch off needles

Thread the yarn on knit stitches so that it passes under the touching sides of two stitches on both back and front needles and over touching sides of purl stitches on both back and front needle (see fig. 265).

The yarn in all the diagrams is coloured only to show the position that it must take for the stitches to look correct and continuous.

The yarn must also be threaded through the stitches in all methods of grafting so that the same distance between the rows is maintained between the two rows being grafted.

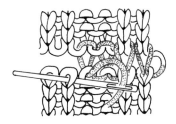

266 Grafting ribbing off needles

Guilds

Guilds were set up during the fifteenth and sixteenth centuries in many countries for the growing manufacture of knitted goods. These guilds, closely linked with the Church, trained apprentices to become journeymen and journeymen to become full members of the guild. To be promoted from journeymen to full members the men often made very complex 'masterpieces' as proof of their talent. Large items, tablecloths, bed coverings or wall hangings, intricately patterned and worked in many colours, were made, a few of which still exist. Before the 1939 war there were 28 such pieces in existence; today the whereabouts of only 18 are known.

267 17th century masterpiece

Held openings

Held openings are those which are to become buttonholes, pockets, heel flaps or any other form of opening which is to be edged by sewing or with picked up stitches for another section. You can work these quickly during the making of the sections by working over the required number of stitches with a length of contrasting coloured yarn of similar thickness, returning to the original yarn as soon as the stitches are worked. Tie the contrast yarn ends on the wrong side to make certain that the thread is not pulled out until required.

When the opening is required the contrast yarn can be withdrawn ready for the stitches to be used (see fig. 269).

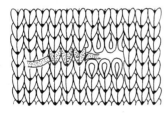

269 Draw contrast yarn out of opening

Hems

On stocking stitch the most usual hem is made by turning back the stocking stitch for the required depth and then hemming it into place along a line of stitches on the wrong side, preferably with matching yarn. Although adequate, this hem is bulky because the fold is made over the ridges of the purled rows (see fig. 270).

Prepared hem

Stocking stitch that has one row worked out of context, to form a ridge on the right side and a hollow on the wrong side, makes a neater fold back. The ridged row is worked at the depth required for the hem and can be worked as a knit row on the purled side or as a purled row on the knit side, whichever gives the closest point to the required measurement (see fig. 271a).

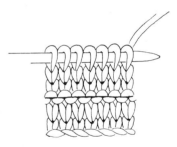

271a Knit fold line

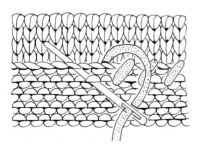

270 Hem folded; edge sewn in place

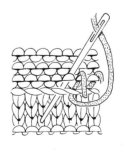

271b Hem on wrong side after folding

When the hem is folded back on to the wrong side along the fold line it can be slip stitched in place (see fig. 271b) to hang evenly as a finished hem.

As a variation of this hem, the rows before the fold line are sometimes all worked in reversed stocking stitch. The hem is finished in the same way and appears the same from the right side but places stocking stitch stitches against the reversed stocking stitch of the garment over all the hem area. It is suitable for particularly thick yarns (see 272).

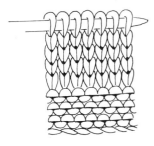

272 Reverse stocking stitch hem

Picot hem

This decorative edge forms a hem at the same time as giving a dainty finish to fine knitting.

Work to the depth required for the hem, ending with a wrong side row.

On the next row work eyelets thus:
Picot row K1, * yon, K2 tog, rep from * to end or to last stitch if there are an even number of stitches, then K1.

Continue in stocking stitch for the remainder of the garment (see fig. 273a). Fold the hem to the wrong side along the centre of the holes and slip stitch in place along one row of ridges on the wrong side (see fig. 273b).

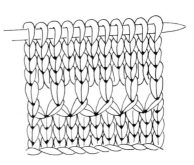

273a Picot hem

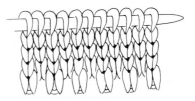

273b After turning to wrong side

Knitted up hems

To avoid sewing up a hem you can knit it up instead.

Cast on using a yarn of similar thickness to the garment yarn but in a contrasting colour. This yarn is removed when the hem is completed. Work the depth of the hem, then place a fold line by working a knit row on the purled side or a purled row on the knit side. Continue until the depth of the hem has again been knitted, so that when folded, the cast-on edge is in line with the

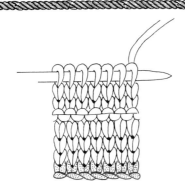

274a Contrast yarn hem

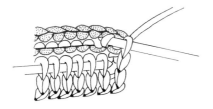

274b Knitting up loops showing on contrast yarn

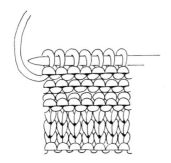

274c Finished hem on wrong side

last row worked, ending with a purl row (see fig. 274a).

Fold the hem up behind the needle holding the stitches and with wrong sides facing knit together one stitch from the needle with one loop of the stitch shown on the contrast yarn of the casting on row (see fig. 274b). Take care to knit up the loop directly below the needle stitch or the hem will be twisted.

When the row is complete the contrast yarn can be removed, leaving a completed edge (see fig. 274c).

Open edged hem

When a skirt or sweater is knitted downwards the hem will be at the opposite end of the work and may be less even than wanted if it is cast off.

Leave the stitches on the needle, then hem the stitch directly from needle to its matching stitch several rows below. The number of rows will depend on the depth of hem required (see fig. 275).

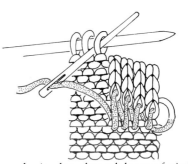

275 Hem edge in place through loops of stitches

Icelandic knitting

As in other northern countries, sheep in Iceland have developed outer coats that protect from the weather, and soft undercoats for warmth. The combination of these, spun without the firm twist of many wools, gives the softness so popular in the natural yarns, with colours ranging from cream through beige and rust colours to dark browns that are almost black. Today, coloured yarns with a similar soft spun texture are made for the fashion market, and the designs used are original, worked by Icelandic designers, rather than copies of Scandinavian influence, as was once the case. It is said that the soft untwisted form of the Icelandic wool was discovered accidently in 1923 when a farmer's wife, in a great hurry to knit a scarf for her husband, knitted with fleece which she had not had time to spin in the usual way. The result was so pleasing, so soft and warm, that it has been prepared in this way ever since. It is not sold in Iceland in wound balls but in thick flat coils.

Increasing

Increasing is the adding of stitches during knitting. Stitches may be added for three reasons:
- to give shape to the garment
- to add patterning, usually with a similar number of decreases
- to shape and pattern at the same time

There are also three different types of increases:
- single increases that add only one stitch
- double increases that add two stitches
- multiple increases that add more than two stitches

Single increases

Single increases can be divided into two groups: first, closed increases which do not interrupt the lines of worked stitches; secondly, open increases which leave a hole beneath the made stitch, and are usually placed to use the hole decoratively.

Barred increase

The barred increase is the most commonly used and is made by working twice into the same stitch, either knitwise or purlwise or a combination of knitwise and purlwise.

Knitwise Knit to the stitch from which the increase is to be made, knit into the front of the loop (see fig. 278a).

Without withdrawing the left needle from the stitch, knit into the back of the same loop (see fig. 278b).

277 Typical Icelandic sweater

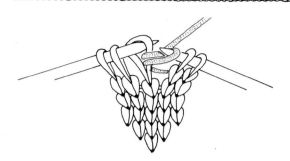

278a Knit into front of stitch

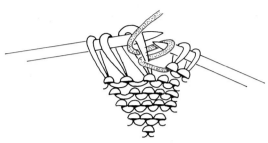

279a Purl into front

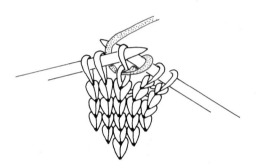

278b Knit into back of same stitch

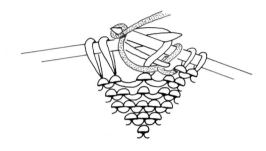

279b Purl into back of same stitch

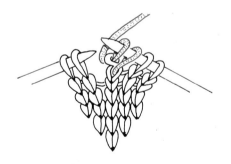

278c Completed increase

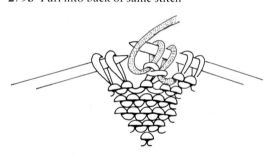

279c Completed increase

This produces two stitches from one and the made stitch lies to the left side of the original stitch with a bar of yarn across its base (see fig. 278c).

Purlwise Purl to the stitch out of which the increase is to be made and purl into the front of the loop (see fig. 279a).

Without withdrawing the left needle purl into the back of the same loop (see fig. 279b).

This produces two stitches from one and the made stitch lies to the left of the original stitch with a bar of yarn across its base (see fig. 279c).

Knitwise and purlwise Increasing on the rib involves keeping the rib as unaltered as possible while adding the new stitch.

On a knit rib where the increase is to be made on the following purled section knit into the front of the knit stitch (see fig. 280a).

Without withdrawing the left needle purl into the back of the same loop (see fig. 280b).

This gives an increased stitch to the left of the original stitch (see fig. 280c).

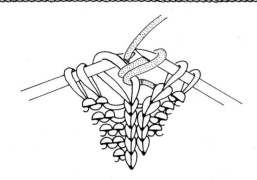

280a Knit into front of stitch

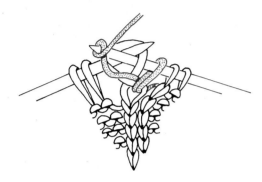

280b Purl into back of same stitch

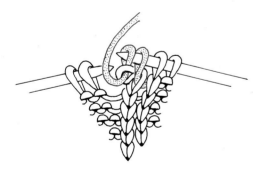

280c Finished increase

On a purl rib where the increase is to be made on the following knitted section purl into the front of the purl stitch.

Without withdrawing the left needle knit into the back of the same loop.

This again places the made stitch at the left of the original stitch.

Invisible increasing

As its name suggests this increase is almost invisible. It can be placed anywhere as long as there are at least two rows between it and another similar increase directly above.

An invisible increase can be placed so that it lies to the right or left of the stitch it is made out of; it can be used in any position on the knitted section provided there are at least two rows between it and the next increase if it is to be placed immediately above. On sleeve, side or leg increases it can be used whenever instructions state 'increase' and no further instruction is given.

Knitwise to right Knit to the stitch out of which the increase is to be made and with the right needle tip lift the loop below the next stitch on the left needle to the right (see fig. 281a).

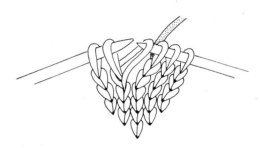

281a Lift loop below next stitch

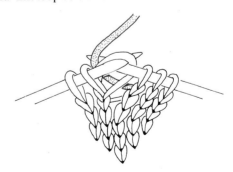

281b Knit lifted loop

Place the lifted loop on the left needle and knit it (see fig. 281b). Complete the increase by knitting the next stitch on the left needle, the stitch the increase was made out of.

Knitwise to left Knit to the stitch out of which the increase is to be made and knit the stitch itself before making the increase.

With the left needle tip lift the loop which is two rows below the last knitted stitch on the right needle towards the left (see fig. 282) knit it on to the right needle, giving a made stitch to the left of the stitch it was made out of.

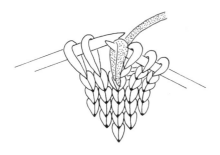

282 Knit up loop at left of stitch two rows below stitch on needle

Purlwise to right On purl fabric the invisible increase is made in a similar way to the knitted increase.

Purl to the stitch out of which the increase is to be made. With the right needle tip lift the loop of the stitch immediately below the next stitch on the left needle towards the right, then place it on the left needle and purl it, then purl the next stitch out of which the increase was made.

Purlwise to left Purl to and including the stitch that the increase is to be worked out of. With the left needle tip lift the loop of the stitch two rows below the last knitted stitch on the right needle towards the left and purl it. This gives an increased stitch to the left of the stitch it is made from.

Lifted increase
A lifted increase is made in two ways – an open version and a closed version. The closed version is made by working the made stitch through the back of the loop. It may be abbreviated to M1 or m1 and the given explanation may instruct that it is knitted or purled through the back of the loop. To differentiate between the open versions

(which in this book are given in abbreviated form as M1K and M1P), the abbreviation is given as M1K tbl or M1P tbl.

This increase, in any of its forms, is placed directly where it is required and is between two stitches, neither of which it is made out of.

Knitwise through back of loop Knit to the position for the increase and with the right needle tip lift the thread between the last knitted stitch and the next stitch on the left needle (see fig. 283a).

Slip the lifted loop on to the left needle (see fig. 283b).

Knit the lifted loop through the back of the loop (see fig. 283c).

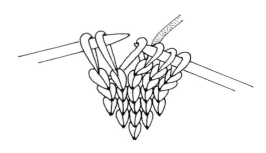

283a Lift strand between stitches

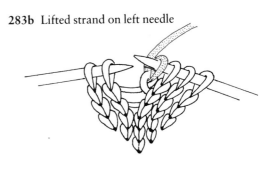

283b Lifted strand on left needle

283c Knit stitch through back of loop

Purlwise through back of loop Purl to the position for the increase. With the right needle tip lift the thread before the next stitch on to the right needle and slip it over the left needle and purl it through the back of the loop.

Pairing closed single increases

Increases, even closed increases, can be used to form patterns and require to be paired or to slope in opposite directions whether they are placed with only a few stitches between or at the ends of the same row.

Barred increases paired

As the barred increase lies to the left of the original stitch it must be carefully placed. When it is to lie one stitch in from either end you must make it by working twice into the first stitch and then into the second last stitch. If it was worked on the last stitch the increased stitch would be right at the end of the row (see fig. 284a).

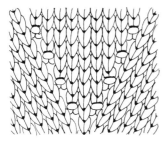

284a Paired barred increases

Invisible increases paired

This increase can be paired by working one right increase and one left increase. On the same row the right increase would be worked after the first stitch has been worked and the left increase on the next to the last stitch so that there is one edge stitch to knit beyond it (see fig. 284b).

284b Paired invisible increases

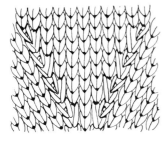

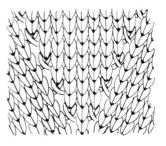

284c Paired lifted increases

Lifted increases paired

As this increase is made between stitches and can be placed exactly where it is required it can be worked inside or after the first stitch and before the last stitch (see fig. 284c).

Open increases

Open increases are used so that the hole left by the increase being worked on the following row is used decoratively. Either the lifted increase or the over increases that follow may be used in lace pattern making and are usually combined with a decrease which may be placed on the same row or delayed until a later row.

Lifted open increase

Like the closed lifted increase this is placed where it is required and is made between two stitches. It can be worked knitwise or purlwise.

Knitwise Knit to the point at which the increase is required. With the tip of the left needle lift the thread between the last stitch knitted and the next stitch and knit into it. This strand over the needle is worked as a stitch on the following row and leaves a hole beneath the lifted strand.

Purlwise Purl to the point at which the increase is required. With the tip of the left needle lift the thread before the next stitch and purl into it. The strand is worked as a stitch on the following row and leaves a hole beneath the lifted thread.

Over increases

An over increase is made by putting the yarn over the needle between two stitches. It may be placed between two knit stitches, one knit and one purl stitch, one purl and one knit stitch or two purl stitches.

Whichever stitch is worked, the yarn is taken to the front of the work and taken over the needle and into whatever position is required for the following stitch. Whatever type of stitches are on either side of the increase the abbreviation is the same and is yon.

In English publications different abbreviations are sometimes used to indicate which type of stitches precedes or follows. This is not necessary if the yarn is automatically taken to the correct position to work the following stitch and so causes fewer errors or misunderstandings.

Between two knit stitches The yarn is taken to the front, over the needle and is in the correct position to knit the next stitch (see fig. 285a).

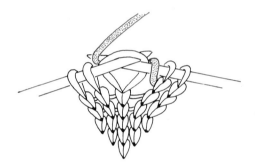

285a Yarn over needle between knit stitches

Between a knit and a purl stitch The yarn is taken forward, over the needle and back to the front under the right needle tip, ready to purl the following stitch (see fig. 285b).

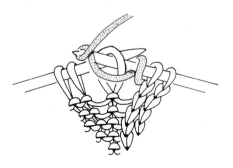

285b Yarn over needle between knit and purl stitches

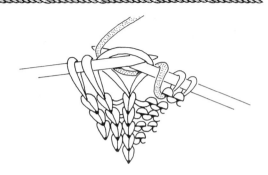

286a Yarn over needle between purl and knit stitches

Between a purl and a knit stitch The yarn is already forward so is only taken over the top of the needle and is then ready to knit the following stitch (see fig. 286a).

Between two purl stitches The yarn is already at the front so is taken over the needle and round back to the front, under the right needle tip, ready for the following purl stitch (see fig. 286b).

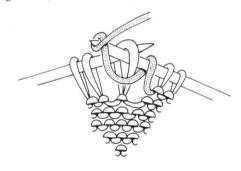

286b Yarn over needle between purl stitches

Exceptions

There are two exceptions to working the yarn over the needle from front to back as in the previous over increases. These are when it is worked on or between twisted stitches and when it is worked on purl rows only, whether they are used as the right side of the work or not. In both cases the hole is improved by the yarn being passed over the needle from back to front.

Between two twisted stitches knitwise Work to the position for the increase, knitting each stitch through the back of the loop. As the yarn is

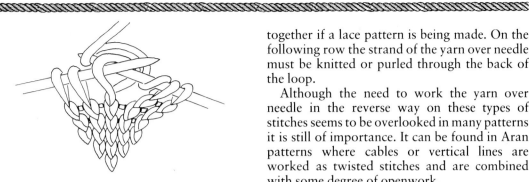

287a Between two twisted stitches knitwise

already at the back take it over the needle from back to front and under the right needle tip to the back again. It is now in the position for you to work the next stitch knitwise through the back of the loop (see fig. 287a).

Between two twisted stitches purlwise Work to the position for the increase, purling through the back of the stitches. The yarn is forward and should be taken back, then forward over the needle where it is in the correct position to purl the next stitch through the back of the loop (see fig. 287b).

In both cases on the following row the strand made by the yarn over needle is worked through the back of the loop.

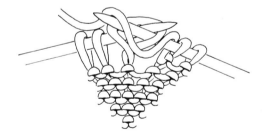

287b Between two purled twisted stitches

On reversed stocking stitch When an open yarn over increase is made on reversed stocking stitch and is worked on the purl rows only it is clearer if you work it in the reverse way, taking the yarn over the needle from back to front.

Work to the position for the increase. The yarn is forward and is taken back between the needles and over the needle either to purl the next stitch or to work the next two stitches

together if a lace pattern is being made. On the following row the strand of the yarn over needle must be knitted or purled through the back of the loop.

Although the need to work the yarn over needle in the reverse way on these types of stitches seems to be overlooked in many patterns it is still of importance. It can be found in Aran patterns where cables or vertical lines are worked as twisted stitches and are combined with some degree of openwork.

Double increases

Two stitches can be increased from one stitch by working either a closed increase or an open increase.

Closed double increase

Work to the stitch that is to carry the increased stitches. Knit into the front of the next stitch and into the back of it as for a single increase (see fig. 288a).

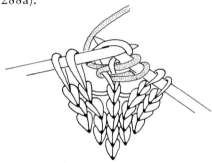

288a Knit into front and back of next stitch

Without taking the left needle out of the stitch knit into the front loop again (see fig. 288b).

288b Knit into front again

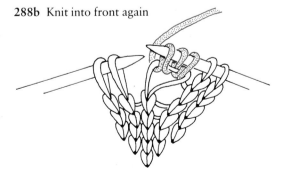

Purlwise the increase is worked similarly into the front back and front again.

Where tension makes this difficult to work it may be worked thus: knit into the front, then purl into the same loop again and knit into it once more.

The purled version purls into the loop, knits into it again then purls the third stitch into the same loop again.

Double open increase

The double open increase is made as for the open increase but is based on the yarn being put over the needle twice.

Knitwise Knit to the space where the two stitches are to be added. Put the yarn twice over the needle and complete the row. On the following row work to the two strands of the yarn round needle, purl into the first strand and knit into the second.

Purlwise Work to the position for the increase, put the yarn twice over the needle and complete the row. On the next row, knit the first yarn over needle loop and purl the second.

Multiple increases

Just as with double increases multiple increases can be made in closed or open methods.

Closed multiple increase

The number of times the stitch loop is able to be knitted or purled into is the only controlling factor in the number of stitches that can be made out of one stitch. As in the double increase, knit into the front then into the back and repeat until the required number of stitches has been worked.

The alternative method, which is easier where many stitches are required, is to knit and purl alternately into the same loop until the required number of stitches has been increased.

Multiple open increase

The multiple open increase can be made knitwise or purlwise by adding additional turns to the number of times the yarn is put over the needle.

On knit rows when the yarn has been put three times round the needle follow with a purl row

that knits the first over, purls the second over and knits the third over.

On purled rows which have the yarn put three times round the needle, follow with a knit row, purl the first over, knit the second and purl the third over.

For larger multiple increases work the overs in the same way, alternately knitting and purling the loops.

An alternative multiple increase

In lace patterns a large increase is occasionally made by casting on several stitches. This should be worked as shown in casting on while working (see fig. 104). The added loops, which become stitches in the following row, are twisted so that once on the needle they cannot unwind.

Indian knitting

Indian knitting is thought to precede Arabic knitting; a small section in the Victoria & Albert Museum in Kensington, London, shows a fabric in several colours. As it is disintegrating it is clearly possible to see that it has been worked with a continuous length of yarn, unlike the samples of Arabic knitting which are worked with short lengths of yarn and a single needle.

Interlaced stitches

Stitches that are to give the appearance of being interlaced must be lengthened. This makes the interlaced strands more obvious, and, in the case of groups of stitches that are interlaced, gives space to make the movement physically possible.

The method of lengthening may be to use a size larger needle or to wind the yarn more than once round the needle before knitting each stitch on the row to be interlaced (see fig. 289a b).

Once the stitches have been prepared, with extra loops dropped and their length increased, one strand can be lifted over another. In groups of interlaced stitches this will mean rearranging each group before it is knitted into place. In Indian cross stitch (*see* **Interlaced stitch**

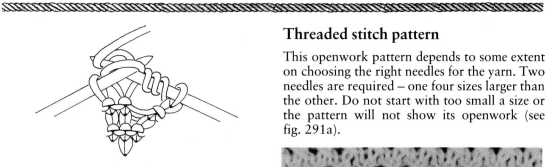

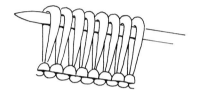

289a Wind yarn extra times round needle

289b Lengthen stitches by dropping extra loops

patterns), eight stitches are grouped together, four stitches crossing over four stitches.

To work this slip eight lengthened stitches to the right needle and with the left needle tip lift the fourth, third, second and first over the other four stitches then knit each stitch. Work each set of eight lengthened stitches in the same way to the row end (see fig. 290).

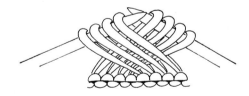

290 Interlacing four stitches through four stitches

Interlaced stitch patterns

The two methods of lengthening stitches so that you can cross or interweave them are used in the following two patterns.

Threaded stitch pattern

This openwork pattern depends to some extent on choosing the right needles for the yarn. Two needles are required – one four sizes larger than the other. Do not start with too small a size or the pattern will not show its openwork (see fig. 291a).

291 (Top) Threaded stitch pattern.
(Bottom) Indian cross stitch

Special abbreviation

Cr2 – cross 2 sts, insert tip of right needle through 1st st as if to P, K the 2nd st and leave it on the needle then K the 1st st through the back of the loop, slip both sts off the needle together. Worked over an even number of stitches. Cast on with large needle.

Preparation row (RS facing), With small needle, K.

1st row With large needle, P.

2nd row With small needle, * Cr2, rep from * to end.

3rd row With large needle, P.
4th row With small needle, K1, * Cr2, rep from * to last st, K1.
Rep from 1st–4th rows as required.

Indian cross stitch

Although usually worked over groups of eight stitches, this can be adapted to groups of six stitches if you prefer. It is a reversible fabric and can be worked in fine or chunky yarns (see fig. 291b).
Worked over a number of stitches divisible by eight.
1st row K.
2nd, 3rd, and 4th rows As 1st row.
5th row K1, * K1 winding yarn 4 times round needle tip, rep from * to last st, K1.
6th row * Sl 8 sts from left to right needle, dropping extra loops to lengthen each st, with left needle tip lift 1st, 2nd 3rd and 4th sts over the remaining 4 sts then move 5th, 6th, 7th and 8th sts to left needle and K each st back to the right needle in this order, rep from * to end. (*See* **Interlaced stitches** for method of crossing or interlacing the eight stitches.)
7th–10th row K.
11th row As 5th row.
12th row Sl 4 sts dropping extra loops, cross 2 sts over 2 sts and K these 4 sts, * sl 8 and cross 4 over 4 then K as for 6th row, rep from * to last 4 sts and work as for 1st 4 sts.
Rep 1st–12th rows as required.

Italian knitting

Like Europe, Italy has known knitting for many hundreds of years. Leaders in the field of fashion, the Italians also seem to be excellent pattern makers and many stitch patterns have entered the category of 'best sellers' throughout other knitting countries.

Amongst a nation which seems to be equally adept at crochet and knitting – an unusual combination – many of the stitch patterns fill the need for look-alike crochet stitches in knitting.

As early as the seventeenth century silk jackets were made in Italy, patterned with metallic yarns creating shining flower and scroll allover patterns, these designs were worked using the stranding method of colour work and showed a high skill on the knitters' part. Surprisingly they were made in sections, and one such garment can be seen at the Victoria & Albert Museum, South Kensington, London.

Italian stitch patterns

From the large tapestry-like patterns of the seventeenth century, the Italians have introduced many smaller stitch patterns, often giving a crochet-like appearance.

Shell mesh stitch

A dainty stitch that gives a clearly defined pattern (see fig. 292a).
Worked over a number of stitches divisible by 6, plus 1.

292 (*Top*) Shell mesh stitch.
(*Bottom*) Anemone stitch

1st row (WS facing), K.

2nd row K.

3rd row P1, * y2on, sl 2 with yarn forward, P3 tog, p2sso, y2on, P1, rep from * to end.

4th row K1, * K 1st of y2on loops and P 2nd loop, K1, P 1st loop of 2nd y2on, then K 2nd loop and K1, rep from * to end.

5th and 6th rows K.

7th row P3 tog, * y2on P1, y2on, sl2 with yarn forward, P3 tog, P2sso, rep from * ending last rep P1, P2sso in place of P3 tog, P2sso.

8th row K1, * P into 1st y2on loop and K 2nd loop, K1, K 1st loop of next y2on and P 2nd loop, K1, rep from * to end.

Rep 1st–8th rows as required.

Anemone stitch

This pattern, often used in single lines between garter or reverse stocking stitch lines, is also a pattern that can be self-coloured or worked in two or more colours giving a broken striped effect (see fig. 292b).

Worked over a number of stitches divisible by 4.

1st row (WS facing) with A, P putting yarn twice round needle for each st.

2nd row With A, sl4 sts to right needle dropping extra loops then return to left needle and into all 4 sts tog work K4 tog, P4 tog, K4 tog, P4 tog, rep from * to end.

3rd row With B, P2, P next and every st putting yarn twice round needle to last 2 sts, P2.

4th row With B, K2, * sl4 sts dropping extra loops to right needle then return to left needle and work K4 tog, P4 tog, K4 tog, P4 tog into all 4 sts tog, rep from * to last 2 sts, K2.

Rep 1st–4th rows as required.

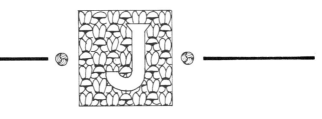

Jacquard knitting

Coloured, patterned knitting is called jacquard after Joseph-Marie Jacquard, 1752-1834, the inventor of the jacquard loom. This loom was the first to be able to weave figured cloths and revolutionized patterning. Based on a punch card system, allowing automatic weaving of any pattern, it was later adapted for knitted fabrics.

Joining yarn

In all flat knitting yarn should always be joined at the start of a row, never during the working of the row.

Leave an end of yarn from the finished ball at the side edge and start the new ball or different colour in the same way, leaving not less than 10cm (4 in.) of yarn hanging at the side. All ends can be darned into the side or into the nearest seam when the work is made up (see fig. 294).

Splicing yarn

On round knitting, yarn can be left at the round start and darned into the work when complete or, if care is taken, the yarn can be spliced.

Separate the strands of the yarns for not less than 12cm (5 in.) and cut away half of the strands of both old and new yarn. Lay the trimmed ends over each other and twist firmly together. They should equal the thickness of the yarn when twisted. Place this join over the start of the round or at a point that is neither central front or back. Ends can be trimmed away once the join is knitted into the fabric (see fig. 295).

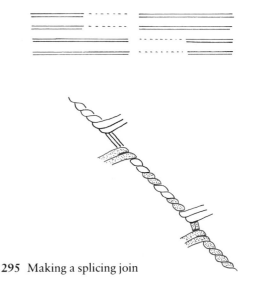

295 Making a splicing join

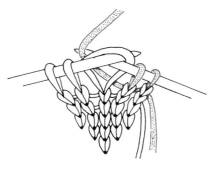

294 Joining in new yarn

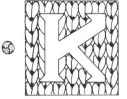

Kitchener's stitch

See Swiss darning in **Embroidering knitting**.

Knitting below stitches

Many patterns require stitches to be knitted into the stitch beneath the stitch on the needle. This is usually to create a longer stitch and a lighter fabric, the actual stitch on the needle being dropped and held by the new stitch. It makes a fabric similar to brioche fabric, although the actual working method is different.

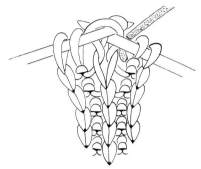

297a Knit into stitch below next stitch

Continental rib

Sometimes called fisherman's rib, and related to other stitches like brioche that belong to a family of stitches known in America as waffle stitches.

Both stitches that are knitted into the stitch below or purled into the stitch below must be worked with one preparation row before the pattern is begun. On ordinary continental rib it is sufficient to knit into the stitch below the next stitch on the left needle for alternate stitches on right side rows, the wrong side rows alternating and becoming knit stitches also.

Cast on an even number of stitches, and purl one row.

1st row * P1, K into the centre of the stitch below the next stitch on the left needle. This gives two loops on the needle and it is knitted by drawing the new loop under both stitch and the strand over it from the original stitch on the needle (see fig. 297a b).

This row is repeated throughout and forms a deep, soft 1 and 1 rib (see fig. 297c).

Although used less often the purled version is worked in a similar way. The rib will look identical if worked with every purl stitch on right and wrong side rows worked into the stitch below, the knit stitches being treated normally.

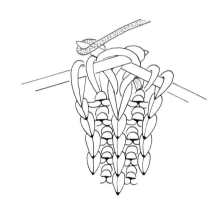

297b Put yarn round needle tip

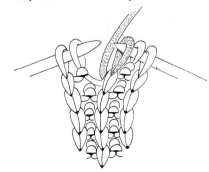

297c Draw through new stitch

To work purlwise

Insert the right needle through the centre of the stitch below the next stitch on the left needle from back to front (see fig. 298a).

Put the yarn round the right needle tip and purl the stitch (see fig. 298b).

When the stitch is dropped from the needle there are two strands – that of the stitch from the needle which drops one row and that of the stitch knitted into (fig. 298c).

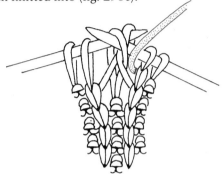

298a Purl into stitch below next stitch

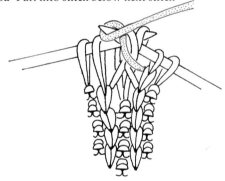

298b Put yarn round needle

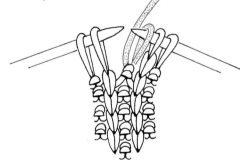

298c Draw through new stitch

Knitting below stitch patterns

Stitches that are worked by knitting into the stitch below the next stitch on the needle are easy to do and make interestingly different textures.

Allover cross stitch

A pattern that is lacy without being a lace pattern and is easy to work should be an asset to any knitter's store of information (see fig. 299a). Worked over a number of stitches divisible by four, plus three.

299 (*Top*) Allover cross stitch. (*Bottom*) Rambler stitch pattern

1st row (WS facing), P.
2nd row K2, K into st below next st on left needle and then sl the st above it, K2 tog, psso, * K into st below next st on left needle then into the st above it then again into the same st below to make 3 sts from 1 st, sl next st, K2 tog, psso, rep from * to last 2 sts, K into st below next st on left needle then K the st above it, K1.
3rd row P.

4th row K1, K2 tog, * K the st below the next st on left needle then the st above it then into the same st below again, sl1, K2 tog, psso, rep from * to last 4 sts, K into st below next st on left needle then st above it then into st below again, sl1, K1, psso, K1.
Rep 1st–4th rows as required.

Rambler stitch pattern

One of those delightful fabrics that lies flat, does not curl and can be used for garments and knitted items of every possible description (see fig. 299b).
Worked over a number of stitches divisible by 2, plus 1.
1st, 3rd and 5th rows (WS facing), K2, * P1, K1, rep from *, ending last rep K1.
2nd, 4th and 6th rows K1, * K into st below next st on left needle and allow the st above it to drop off the needle, P1, rep from *, ending last rep K1.
7th, 9th and 11th rows K1, * P1, K1, rep from * to end.
8th, 10th and 12th rows K1, P1, * K into st below next st on left needle as on 2nd row, P1, rep from *, ending last rep K1.
Rep 1st–12th rows as required.

Knitting Nancy

See **Frame knitting**.

Knitting terms

See **Abbreviations**.

Knit and purl stitch patterns

You can use knit and purl stitches for a great variety of brocade-like patterns of all shapes and sizes, without working any other knitting technique.

Triangle pattern

Found on many fishermen's guernseys, the triangle or flag pattern gives an interesting mixture of light and shade (see fig. 300a).
Worked over a number of stitches divisible by seven.

300 (Top) Triangle, flag or kilt pattern.
(Bottom) Garter stitch zigzag pattern

1st row (RS facing) K.
2nd row * K1, P6, rep from * to end.
3rd row * K5, P2, rep from * to end.
4th row * K3, P4, rep from * to end.
5th row As 4th row.
6th row * K5, P2, rep from * to end.
7th row * K1, P6, rep from * to end.
8th row P.
9th row * K6, P1, rep from * to end.
10th row * K2, P5, rep from * to end.
11th row * K4, P3, rep from * to end.
12th row As 11th row.
13th row * K2, P5, rep from * to end.
14th row * P6, K1, rep from * to end.
Rep 1st–14th rows as required.

Garter stitch zigzag pattern

Purled stitches could be used to replace the garter stitch which gives this pattern a more unusual texture (see fig. 300b).

Worked over a number of stitches divisible by 6.

1st row (WS facing) P.

2nd row * K3, P3, rep from * to end.

3rd row P.

4th row P1, * K3, P3, rep from * to last 5 sts, K3, P2.

5th row P.

6th row P2, * K3, P3, rep from * to last 4 sts, K3, P1.

7th row P.

8th row * P3, K3, rep from * to end.

9th and 11th rows P.

10th row As 6th row.

12th row As 4th row.

Rep 1st–12th rows as required.

Knit stitches

See **Basic stitches**

Knot stitch patterns

Knots can be formed in many different ways, including the true popcorn, (made all along the row and decreased on another row) and bobbles (each made singly before continuing to the next).

Peppercorn stitch

Quite distinctive, this pattern has an unusual way of forming a knot (see fig. 301a).

Worked over a number of stitches divisible by 4, plus 3.

1st row (WS facing), P.

2nd row K3, * K next st, [sl st just knitted back to left needle and K it tbl] 3 times, K3, rep from * to end.

3rd row P.

4th row K1, * K next st then return to left needle and K tbl 3 times more as in 2nd row, K3, rep from * to last st, K1.

Rep 1st–4th rows as required.

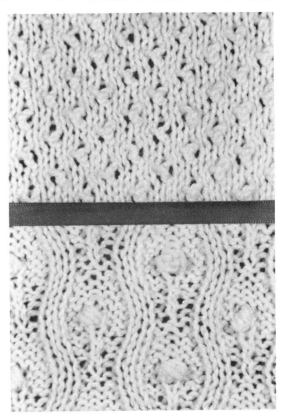

301 (*Top*) Peppercorn stitch.
(*Bottom*) Irish knot stitch

Puff stitch (see fig. 54b)

Although this may be thought to be a bobble pattern, technically it is a popcorn pattern.

Worked over a number of stitches divisible by 7, plus 2.

1st row (RS facing), P2, * [K1, P1] into each of the next 2 sts, P2, K1, P2, rep from * to end.

2nd row K2, * P1, K2, on the 4 puff sts [K1, yon] 3 times then K1, K2, rep from * to end.

3rd row P2, * [K1, drop yon of previous row] 3 times, then K1, P2, K1, P2, rep from * to end.

4th and 5th rows As 2nd and 3rd rows.

6th row K2, * [P1, K1] into next st., K2, P4 tog, K2, rep from * to end.

7th row P2, * K1, P2, [K1, P1] in each of next 2 sts, P2, rep from * to end.

8th row K2, * [K1, yon] 3 times, then K1, K2, P1, K2, rep from * to end.

9th row P2, * K1, P2, [K1, drop yon of previous row] 3 times then K1, P2, rep from * to end.
10th and 11th rows As 8th and 9th rows.
12th row K2, * P4 tog, K2, [P1, K1] into next st., K2, rep from * to end.
Rep 1st–12th rows as required.

Irish knot stitch

The order of decreasing makes this knot stitch pattern different from most (see fig. 301b).

Special abbreviations
incP – P into front and back of next st.
MK – make knot: into next st [K1, P1, K1, P1, K1] loosely then with tip of left needle pass the 2nd, 3rd, 4th and 5th sts on the right needle separately over the last made st, so finishing the knot.
Worked over a number of stitches divisible by 14, plus 5.
1st row (WS facing) K6, * P2, K1, P1, K1, P2, K7, rep from *, ending last rep K6 in place of K7.
2nd row P4, * P2 tog, K2, incP, Kb1, incP, K2, P2 tog, P3, rep from * ending last rep P4 in place of P3.
3rd row K5, * P2, K2, P1, K2, P2, K5, rep from * to end.
4th row P3, * P2 tog, K2, incP, P1, Kb1, P1, incP, K2, P2 tog, P1, rep from * to last 2 sts, P2.
5th row K4, * P2, K3, P1, K3, P2, K3, rep from * to last st, K1.
6th row P2, Kb1, * P1, K2, P3, MK, P3, K2, P1, Kb1, rep from * to last 2 sts, P2.
7th row K2, P1, * K1, P2, K7, P2, K1, P1, rep from * to last 2 sts, K2.

8th row P2, Kb1, * incP, K2, P2 tog, P3, P2 tog, K2, incP, Kb1, rep from * to last 2 sts, P2.
9th row K2, P1, * K2, P2, K5, P2, K2, P1, rep from * to last 2 sts, K2.
10th row P2, Kb1, * P1, incP, K2, P2 tog, P1, P2 tog, K2, incP, P1, Kb1, rep from * to last 2 sts, P2.
11th row K2, P1, * [K3, P2] twice, K3, P1, rep from * to last 2 sts, K2.
12th row P2, MK, * P3, K2, P1, Kb1, P1, K2, P3, MK, rep from * to last 2 sts, P2.
Rep 1st–12th rows as required.

Boxed bobble pattern
(illustrated in fig. 54a)

Each bobble in its own small square brings uniformity to this pattern.

Special abbreviation
MB – make bobble: into next st work [K1, Kb1, K1], turn, K3, turn, P3 then lift 2nd then 3rd sts over the 1st st and off the needle to complete bobble.
Worked over a number of stitches divisible by 6,
1st row (WS facing), K.
2nd and 6th rows P1, * K5, P1, rep from * to end.
3rd and 5th rows P.
4th row P1, * K2, MB, K2, P1, rep from * to end.
Rep 1st–6th rows as required.

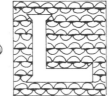

Lace holes

Lace patterns are made in several different ways. The most usual is that where open increases, single, double or multiple are matched with decreases totalling the same number of stitches but not necessarily worked alongside, or even on the same row.

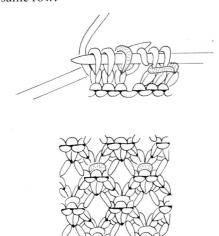

303 Open star stitch

Other methods of making lacy fabrics include:
- drawing stitches together, *see* **Trinity stitch,** fig. 11
- dropped stitches, *see* **Vertical drop stitch pattern,** fig. 195a
- knitting into row below, *see* **Allover cross stitch,** fig. 299a
- lengthened stitches, *see* **Anemone stitch,** fig. 292b
- lifting the running thread, *see* **Coral knot stitch,** fig. 358a
- passing one or more slipped stitches over other stitches (see fig. 303), for working

instructions *see* **Open star stitch, Lace Stitch Patterns.**
- using larger than usual needle to add to openness of stitches, *see* **Threaded stitch,** fig. 291a

Eyelet and faggot stitches

Both eyelets and faggot stitch patterns are made by using a single eyelet, an increase beside a decrease. It is the placing of the increases and decreases that determines whether an eyelet pattern or a faggot stitch pattern is made.

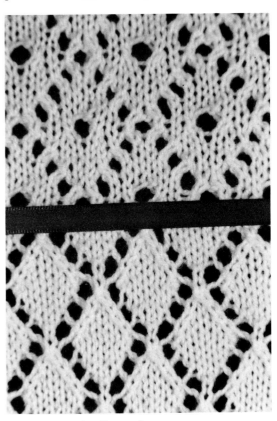

304 (*Top*) Eyelet diamond pattern.
(*Bottom*) Faggot diamond pattern

The differences

Eyelet patterns, placed immediately next to each other along a row, have the other divided from the next by the double strands of the decrease. This is their characteristic and must be retained. Faggot stitches, on the other hand, made by just the same open increase and decrease, if placed immediately after each other lose the narrow link that is the characteristic of the faggot stitch and become eyelets. Diagonally, both eyelets and faggot stitches can be used to form diagonal lines and the difference between the two is shown in fig. 304. (Instructions for fig. 304a *see* **Eyelet stitch patterns**, for fig. 304b *see* **Lace pattern stitches**.) In this form they can both be used on alternate rows – the eyelet having its small clustered strands by each openwork hole, the faggot stitch having a more slender, twisted link.

Worked vertically the opposite becomes true. The faggot stitch becomes an eyelet when worked horizontally, but the eyelet worked vertically on alternate rows becomes a faggot stitch and will only retain its character if worked no nearer than on every third row.

305 (*Left*) Chain edge. (*Centre*) Soft edge. (*Right*) Broken edge

Placing open increases and decreases

Increases and decreases, grouped vertically and worked on every row, give lace faggot patterns, the lace areas linked by as few strands as possible (see fig. 233).

Open increases worked beside or close to their matching decreases give simple lace patterns that, when worked on right side rows only with knit or purl wrong side rows, are easily worked (see fig. 307a).

Patterns that use only single threads to outline the openwork (and therefore can be as lacy as it is possible to make knitting) are worked with patterned rows on both sides of the fabric (see fig. 249a).

Multiple increases and decreases

Multiple increases can be matched with multiple decreases. However, this is not always the case, the decreases being worked more gradually on following rows.

Decreases

These may be used to reduce the increased stitches to the original number as invisibly as possible (see fig. 383a). Alternatively, they may be used to accentuate the slope created by the openwork placing (see fig. 307b). In this pattern

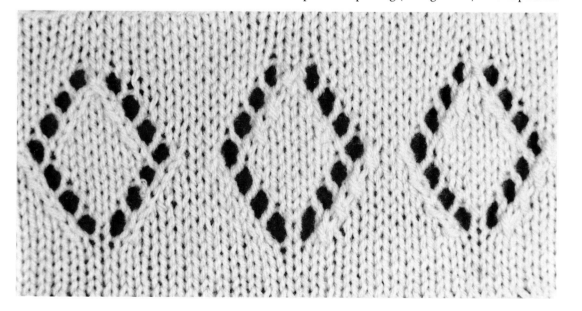

they slope with the line of openwork but they can be used to slope against the line of stitches when they are said to be 'feathered' (see fig. 306).

Outlines

In all lace faggot patterns the position of the lines that are used to form an outline beside openwork require planning. In working a diamond, the increase and decrease used for the lower half will not produce the same effect on the upper half where they must be reversed.

Three types of edges can be worked at the side of faggot stitch openwork:
● chain edge (fig. 305a)
● soft edge (fig. 305b)
● crossed broken edge (fig. 305c)

A table shows the methods used for each type of edge, showing the matching increase and decrease for the lower left and upper right side and for the lower right and upper left sides.

Lower left and upper right

chain edge	soft edge	crossed edge
Yon, SKPO.	Yon, K2 tog.	Yon, K2 tog tbl.

Lower right and upper left

K2 tog, yon.	SKPO, yon.	K2 tog tbl, yon.

Lace stitch patterns

Lace patterns include openwork fabric formed in many different ways and are endlessly inventive.

Feather and fan pattern

Infinitely variable, this pattern is easy for you to knit and remember. It can be used with the addition of colours and is suitable for many different thickness of yarn, although possibly it is at its best made in fine yarn (see fig. 306). The feathering is formed by the decreases drawing in

306   Feather and fan pattern

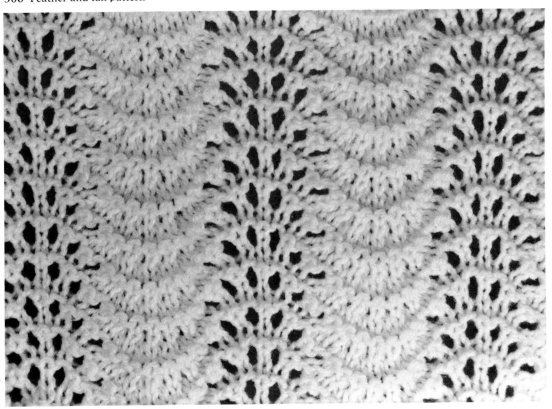

the stitches which are fanning out by the placing of the increases.

Worked over a number of stitches divisible by 18.

1st row (RS facing), K.

2nd row P.

3rd row * [K2 tog] 3 times, [yon, K1] 6 times, [K2 tog] 3 times, rep from * to end.

4th row K.

Rep 1st–4th rows as required.

Openwork diamond pattern
(for illustration see fig. 304b)

Lace that is not too lacy is always in demand and a basic faggot stitch diamond provides the answer.

Worked over a number of stitches divisible by 8, plus 1.

1st and every alt rows (WS facing), P.

2nd row K1, * K1, K2 tog, yon, K1, yon, SSK, K2, rep from * to end.

4th row K1, * K2 tog, yon, K3, yon, SSK, K1, rep from * to end.

6th row K2 tog, * yon, K5, yon, sl1 knitwise, K2 tog, psso, rep from * to last 7 sts, yon, K5, yon, SSK.

8th row K1, * yon, SSK, K3, K2 tog, yon, K1, rep from * to end.

10th row K1, * K1, yon, SSK, K1, K2 tog, yon, K2, rep from * to end.

12th row K1, * K2, yon, Sl1 knitwise, K2 tog, psso, yon, K3, rep from * to end.

Rep from 1st–12th rows as required.

Open star stitch (for illustration see fig. 303)

This lace relies on the grouping of stitches to form an openwork pattern. The group is gathered together by a strand lifted over other stitches.

Worked over a number of stitches divisible by 3, plus 3.

1st row (WS facing) K2, * yon, K3, with point of left needle lift the 1st of the K3, inserting needle from left to right, over the other 2 sts and off the needle tip, rep from * to last st, K1.

2nd row K.

3rd row K1, * K3 then lift lst st over other 2 as in 1st row, yon, rep from * to last 2 sts, K2.

4th row K.

Rep 1st–4th rows as required.

Laburnum stitch

This rather unusual pattern, on a purled background, uses a y2on to form the lace hole but requires it to be worked in reverse – that is taking the yarn to the back and over the top of the needle towards the front, round to the back again and over the needle back to the front where it is in the right position to purl the next stitch (see fig. 307a).

Worked over a number of stitches divisible by 5, plus 2.

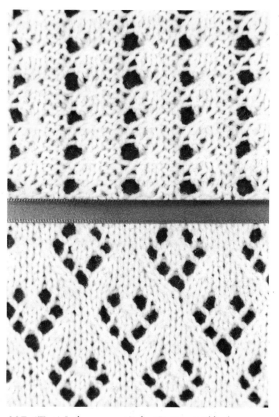

307 (*Top*) Laburnum stitch. (*Bottom*) Elfin lace

1st row (RS facing), P2, * sl1 knitwise, yarn back, K2 tog, psso, y2on, P2, rep from * to end.

2nd row K2, * P into back of 1st loop of y2on made on previous row then P into next loop, P1, K2, rep from * to end.

Elfin lace

This simple lace, with every wrong side row purled, is easy enough for beginners and is delightful when finished.

Worked over a number of stitches divisible by 8, plus 9 (see fig. 307b).

1st row and every alt row (WS facing), P.

2nd row K2, * yon, SSK, K6, rep from *, ending last rep K5 in place of K6.

4th row K3, * yon, SSK, K3, K2 tog, yon, K1, rep from * to last 6 sts, yon, SSK, K4.

6th row K4, * yon, SSK, K1, K2 tog, yon, K3, rep from * to last 5 sts, yon, SSK, K3.

8th row K2, K2 tog, * yon, K5, yon, sl2 knitwise, K1, p2sso, rep from * to last 5 sts, yon, K5.

10th row K6, * yon, SSK, K6, rep from * to last 3 sts, yon, SSK, K1.

12th row K4, K2 tog, * yon, K1, yon, SSK, K3, K2 tog, rep from * to last 3 sts, yon, K3.

14th row K3, * K2 tog, yon, K3, yon, SSK, K1, rep from * to last 6 sts, K2 tog, yon, K4.

16th row K5, * yon, sl2 knitwise, K1, p2sso, yon, K5, rep from * to last 4 sts, yon, K2 tog, K2.

Rep 1st–16th rows as required.

Trellis diamond pattern (see fig. 332a)

A simple diamond pattern enlarged to edge the solid areas with lace trellis.

Worked over a number of stitches divisible by 12, plus 1.

1st and every alt row (WS facing), P.

2nd row K1, * K1, [K2 tog, yon] twice, K1, [yon, SSK] twice, K2, rep from * to end.

4th row K1, * [K2 tog, yon] twice, K3, [yon, SSK] twice, K1, rep from * to end.

6th row K2 tog, * yon, K2 tog, yon, K5, yon, SSK, yon, SK2togPO, rep from * to last 11st sts, yon, K2 tog, yon, K5, [yon, SSK] twice.

8th row K1, * [yon, SSK] twice, K3, [K2 tog, yon] twice, K1, rep from * to end.

10th row K1, * K1, [yon, SSK] twice, K1, [K2 tog, yon] twice, K2, rep from * to end.

12th row K1, * K2, yon, SSK, yon, SK2togPO, yon, K2 tog, yon, K3, rep from * to end.

Rep 1st–12th rows as required.

Mrs Montague's pattern (see fig. 332b)

Worked as a present for Queen Elizabeth I on a pair of silk stockings, this pattern has always been in favour – and not just for stockings.

Worked over a number of stitches divisible by 16, plus 1.

1st and every alt row (WS facing), P.

2nd row K1, * K4, yon, SSK, K3, K2 tog, yon, K5, rep from * to end.

4th row K1, * yon, SSK, K3, yon, SSK, K1, K2 tog, yon, K3, K2 tog, yon, K1, rep from * to end.

6th row K1, * K1, yon, SSK, K3, yon, SK2togPO, yon, K3, K2 tog, yon, K2, rep from * to end.

8th row K1, * K2, yon, SSK, K7, K2 tog, yon, K3, rep from * to end.

10th row K1, * K1, K2 tog, yon, K9, yon, SSK, K2, rep from * to end.

12th row K1, * K2 tog, yon, K3, K2 tog, yon, K1, yon, SSK, K3, yon, SSK, K1, rep from * to end.

14th row K2 tog, * yon, K3, K2 tog, yon, K3, yon, SSK, K3, yon, SK2togPO, rep from * to last 15 sts, yon, K3, K2 tog, yon, K3, yon, SSK, K3, yon, SSK, rep from * to end.

16th row K1, * K3, K2 tog, yon, K5, yon, SSK, K4, rep from * to end.

Rep 1st–16th rows as required.

Leaf pattern (see fig. 333a)

The diamond shape becomes softer and more leaf-life when the decreases are worked away from the edges.

Worked over a number of stitches divisible by 8, plus 1.

1st and every alt row (WS facing), P.

2nd row K1, * yon, K2, SK2togPO, K2, yon, K1, rep from * to end.

4th row K1, * K1, yon, K1, SK2togPO, K1, yon, K2, rep from * to end.

6th row K1, * K2, yon, SK2togPO, yon, K3, rep from * to end.

8th row K2 tog, * K2, yon, K1, yon, K2, SK2togPO, rep from * to last 7 sts, K2, yon, K1, yon, K2, SSK.

10th row K2 tog, * K1, yon, K3, yon, K1, SK2togPO, rep from * to last 7 sts, K1, yon, K3, yon, K1, SSK.

12th row K2 tog, * yon, K5, yon, SK2togPO, rep from * to last 7 sts, yon, K5, yon, SSK.
Rep 1st–12th rows as required.

Trellis leaf pattern
(for illustration see fig. 333b)

An extension of the previous pattern with the leaf elongated and the trellis added.
Worked over a number of stitches divisible by 12, plus 1.
1st and every alt tow (WS facing), P.
2nd row K2 tog, * K2, yon, SSK, yon, K1, yon, K2 tog, yon, K2, SK2togPO, rep from * ending last rep SSK in place of SK2togPO.
4th and 6th rows As 2nd row.
8th row K2 tog, * K1, yon, K2 tog, yon, K3, yon, SSK, yon, K1, SK2togPO, rep from *, ending last rep SSK in place of SK2togPO.
10th row K2 tog, * yon, K2 tog, yon, K5, yon, SSK, yon, SK2togPO, rep from *, ending last rep SSK in place of SK2togPO.
12th row K1, * yon, K2 tog, yon, K2, SK2togPO, K2, yon, SSK, yon, K1, rep from * to end.
14th and 16th rows As 12th row.
18th row K2, * yon, SSK, yon, K1, SK2togPO, K1, yon, K2 tog, yon, K3, rep from *, ending last rep K2 in place of K3.
20th row K3, * yon, SSK, yon, SK2togPO, yon, K2 tog, yon, K5, rep from *, ending last rep K3 in place of K5.
Rep 1st–20th rows as required.

Rose trellis lace pattern (see fig. 334)

For very special knitting what could be better than this lace using trellis and eyelet patterns?
Worked over a number of stitches divisible by 20, plus 2.
1st row (RS facing) K1, * yon, K3 tog, yon, K2, yon, SSK, rep from *.
2nd and every alt row P.
3rd row K1, SSK, * yon, K4, yon, SK2togPO, yon, K3, yon, SK2togPO, yon, K4, yon, SK2togPO, rep from * to last 6 sts, K6 in place of K4 yon, SK2togPO.
5th row K2, * [yon, SSK] twice, K3, yon, SSK, K3 tog, yon, K3, [K2 tog, yon] twice, K1, rep from * to end.

7th row * K3, [yon, SSK] twice, K3, yon, SK2togPO, yon, K3, [K2 tog, yon] twice, K1, rep from * to last 2 sts, K2.
9th row K4, * [yon, SSK] twice, K7, [K2 tog, yon] twice, K5, rep from *, ending last rep K3.
11th row K5, * [yon, SSK] twice, K5, [K2 tog, yon] twice, K7, rep from *, ending last rep K4.
13th row K6, * [yon, SSK] twice, K3, [K2 tog, yon] twice, K9, rep from *, ending last rep K5.
15th row K2, * yon, SSK, K3, [yon, SSK] twice, K1, [K2 tog, yon] twice, K3, K2 tog, yon, K1, rep from * to end.
17th row * [K3, yon, SSK] twice, yon, SK2togPO, yon, K2 tog, yon, K3, K2 tog, yon, rep from *, ending with K2.
19th row K1, * yon, K3 tog, yon, K1, yon, K3, K3 tog, yon, K1, yon, SK2togPO, K3, yon, K1, yon, SSK, rep from *, ending K1.
21st row K1, SSK, * yon, K3, yon, K1, K3 tog, yon, K3, yon, SK2togPO, K1, yon, K3, yon, SK2togPO, rep from *, ending last rep K5 in place of K3, yon, SK2togPO.
23rd row K2, * [yon, SSK, yon, K3 tog, yon, K2] twice, yon, SSK, yon, K3 tog, yon, K1, rep from * to end.
25th row * K3, yon, SK2togPO, [yon, K4, yon, SK2togPO] twice, yon, rep from *, ending K2.
27th row K1, * yon, K3 tog, yon, K3, [K2 tog, yon] twice, K1, [yon, SSK] twice, K3, yon, SSK, rep from *, ending K1.
29th row K1, SSK, * yon, K3, [K2 tog, yon] twice, K3, [yon, SSK] twice, K3, yon, SK2togPO, rep from * to last 5 sts, ending last rep K5 in place of K3, yon, SK2togPO.
31st row K5, * [K2 tog, yon] twice, K5, [yon, SSK] twice, K7, rep from *, ending last rep K4.
33rd row K4, * [K2 tog, yon] twice, K7, [yon, SSK] twice, K5, rep from *, ending last rep K3.
35th row * K3, [K2 tog, yon] twice, K9, [yon, SSK] twice, rep from *, ending K2.
37th row K2, * [K2 tog, yon] twice, K3, K2 tog, yon, K1, yon, SSK, K3, [yon, SSK] twice, K1, rep from * to end.
39th row K1, K2 tog, * yon, [K2 tog, yon, K3] twice, yon, SSK, K3, yon, SSK, yon, SK2togPO, rep from * to last 2 sts, ending last rep SSK in place of SK2togPO.
41st row K2, * yon, SK2togPO, K3, yon, K1, yon, SSK, yon, K3 tog, yon, K1, yon, K3, K3 tog, yon, K1, rep from * to end.
43rd row * K3, yon, SK2togPO, K1, yon, K3,

yon, SK2togPO, yon, K3, yon, K1, K3 tog, yon
rep from * ending K2.
44th row P.
Rep 1st–44th rows as required.

Lapp knitting

Each area of folk knitting is interesting because
of the way in which the designs are given their
own characteristic style. Throughout all textile
production there are basic similarities and yet
each district or area gives to its knitting a look or
a technique of its own, each contributing to the
knowledge of knitters.

The colours of Lapp knitting are traditional
and – red, blue, yellow and the natural creamy
white of the wool. In addition the Lapps use a
simply worked but effective edge made by
carrying the yarns on the right side of the fabric.

To work Lapp edging

The edge is worked in two colours: A, the
background colour and B, a bright contrast. It is
worked over an even number of stitches.
1st row (RS facing), P1A, leave A at front and
P1B, drop B and * lift A over it, P1A, drop A and
lift B over it, P1B, drop B, rep from * to end of
row.
2nd row With A, P.

To adapt for round knitting the 2nd round
must be worked as a knit round. The yarn not in
use can be twisted with the yarn in use at the start
of the round and carried up the inside of the
work until required again (see fig. 308).

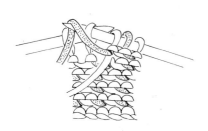

308 Lapp edging

Left hand knitting

Knitting for those naturally left handed may be a
trial but the problem can be overcome.

Most instructions can be reversed so that the left
hand does what is normally done with the right
hand, with rows worked from left to right
instead of from right to left.

This is, in fact, a mirror image of right-hand
knitting, and you can reverse diagrams by
placing a mirror opposite the diagram and
working from the reflection rather than from the
diagram itself.

Thumb casting on

To cast on by this method hold the needle with
slip knot in the left hand, looping the yarn round
the right thumb (see fig. 309a).

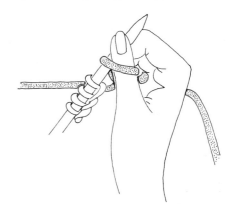

309a Put yarn round left needle tip

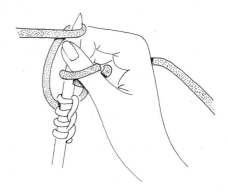

309b Pass yarn round left needle

Use your left hand to pass the yarn round the needle tip and drawn it through into a new loop using the needle and the right thumb, which helps the loop over the needle tip (see fig. 309b).

Two-needle casting on

Place a slip knot on the right needle and with the other needle in the left hand insert the needle through the slip knot. With the left forefinger pass the yarn round the right needle tip and use the right needle to draw through a new loop and place it on the right needle (see fig. 310a).

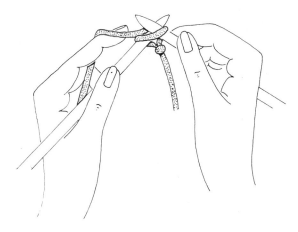

310a Put yarn round left needle tip

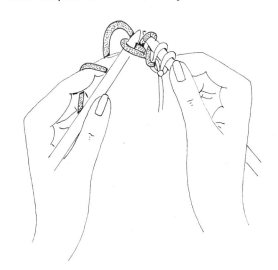

310b Draw through loop and place on right needle

Insert the left needle between the two stitches on the right needle and pass the yarn round the right needle tip and draw through the next new loop, placing it on the right needle (see fig. 310b).

Work as many new loops as are required in this way.

To knit stitches

Work from left to right along the row, using the left forefinger or left hand to pass the yarn round the left-hand needle tip and the left needle to draw the new loop through the stitch, placing it on the left needle (see fig. 311a b c).

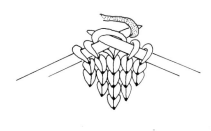

311a Put yarn knitwise round left needle tip

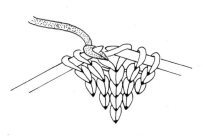

311b Use left needle to draw through new stitch

311c Finished stitch on left needle

To purl stitches

Reverse in the same way as for the knitted stitches. Hold the needle with the stitches on it in the right hand and work from left to right. Use the left forefinger or hand to pass the yarn round the left needle tip and the left needle to draw through the new loop, which is added to those on the left needle (see fig. 312a b).

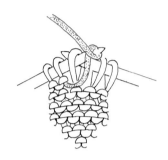

312a Yarn round left needle tip

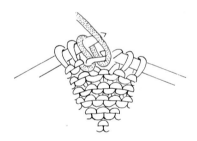

312b Use left needle to draw through loop

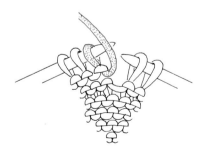

312c Finished loop on left needle

Lengthened stitches

See **Dropped stitches**

Linen

See **Yarns**

Loop knitting

Looped knitting gives a texture that adds contrast. It can be used to edge mitten or glove gauntlets, to work cuffs, collars and small areas of loops or it can be used as the main texture for jackets, rugs, pram and cot covers or cushions.

The length of loop can be controlled by winding round fingers or, for longer loops, by working the loop over a ruler or card template.

To work loops

There is more than one method of working loops, which can be made on garter stitch or stocking stitch and are usually worked on a wrong side row, so that they lie on the right side of the work.

On a wrong side row insert the right needle through the stitch that is to hold the loops, avoiding the edge stitch if possible, and hold the first, second and third fingers of the left hand immediately behind the needle tips. Wind the

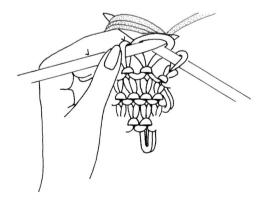

313a Wind yarn three times round left fingers and needle

yarn three times round the needle tip and fingers (see fig. 313a). Knit the stitch in the usual way drawing the strand of the new loop through the three loops so that one loop only is placed on the right needle (see fig. 313b).

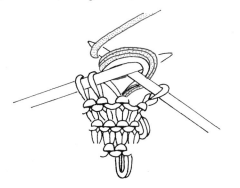

313b Draw through single loop

Slip this newly-made stitch back to the left needle, taking care not to let the long loops drop, and knit the stitch again, locking the long loops into place (see fig. 313c).

This version allows the loops to hang against the fabric on the right side.

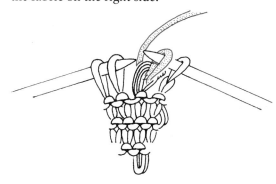

313c Loop on right needle ready to slip to left

Alternative methods

Work the loops in the same way but draw *all* loops through (not just one) and, before withdrawing left needle, slip the loops all back to left needle. Knit together the four loops on the left needle, made up of the three loops drawn through and the strand of the original stitch.

Length

The depth of the loop is controlled by the number of fingers that it is wound round. You can lengthen it by holding a piece of firm card behind the needle and winding the yarn round this rather than round your fingers.

Density

The amount of yarn in the loops makes a difference to the appearance. The yarn need only be wound once round card or fingers for a less loopy fabric.

Lurex

See **Yarns**.

Making up

The assembling of knitted sections or making up should never be rushed because it is a very important part of making a garment. Good knitting can be ruined by bad, hastily undertaken seaming, blocking and finishing.

Finishing sections

Before seaming, but after pressing and blocking if the yarn is suitable for these processes, work any details of each section. Add pocket flaps, sew on button bands or edges, sew in zips, or add Swiss darning or other embroidery. All are easier to do on a section than when the garment is complete.

Check the order of sewing up if following instructions. For actual seams, which to use and how to work them, *see* **Seams**.

For details of blocking, suitable yarns and how to press, *see* **Blocking and Pressing**.

To sew in zips by the easiest method, *see* **Zips**.

To add strengthening and information on buttonholes and buttons, *see both* **Buttonholes** and **Buttons**.

Man-made fibres

See **Yarns**.

Marker threads

Marker threads, loops of different coloured yarns, are of immense use in acting as guide points, for measuring, knitting or in making up.

To place loop

Slip a loop into place between two stitches. On knit rows keep the tail of the marker towards the front and on purl rows towards the back. In this way the marker can be moved with each row, keeping the same position on the row but not becoming knitted in to the actual fabric.

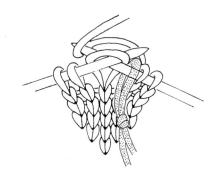

315 Marker loop on needle before stitch being worked

Using markers

Marker loops can be used in many ways: to mark which rows have carried increases, so that the total number of increases can be seen at a glance; to mark positions on the row, quarter centre or threequarter intervals or positions for the start of a pattern or the placing of a motif; for measuring and for points of seaming such as for the base of an armhole on unshaped sides of a sweater that are also without shaped armholes.

On round knitting they can be used to mark the beginning of the round and in knitting any garment a different coloured marker from the start of the round can be used to mark the other side or half way point of the round.

Measuring

For successful knitting measuring must be exact.

On garment sections

Whenever possible measure by working the same number of rows on backs and fronts, on sleeves or any two sections that are meant to match. Use a row counter and take the added few minutes required to be certain. This is a more sure way than relying on a tape or ruler.

When sections are measured use a ruler that is firm and place the section on a flat surface rather than using a tape on the arm of a chair or another surface that is not really flat or large enough.

Measure in the centre of a section, not along a slanted, sloped or shaped edge.

On people

Measuring the person who is to wear the garment is always the best way of ensuring that sleeves and body are the required length. Printed instructions always give general measurements, not taking into consideration longer or shorter sleeves, long sleeves and short bodies or any of the many variations that are so essential to make a good fit.

Measure with a tape, taking centre back and centre sleeve measurements. As a check, under-arm to wrist can be taken but avoid measuring over a bulky garment that adds to sleeve length by being taken on a sloping line. Tapes do stretch with wear so be safe and discard a tape that is really worn and has become distorted.

Make a note of measurements and check against the instructions, noting alterations. Success is based on leaving nothing to chance and always making preparations before beginning to knit.

Medallion knitting

Although medallion knitting is no longer in fashion as it was in the eighteenth and nineteenth centuries, it has a large contribution to make to the understanding of shape. Today it is mostly used in the construction of shawls.

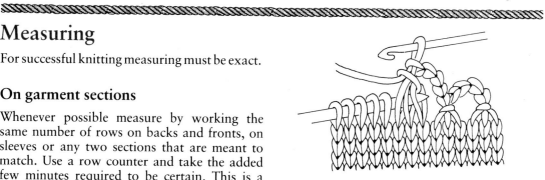

317 Working a chain medallion

At its height medallion knitting was responsible for many hand-knitted heirlooms – the small, often lacy patterns joined into bedspreads. But medallions were used on their own for many other items, such as endless variations for bonnet back sections, lace mats, doileys, table mats and traycloths.

Medallion knitting is worked from the centre outwards, usually on several double-pointed, short needles. The number of needles is determined by both shape and size of the item, which might be round, square, or other geometrical shape with as many sides as required. More than four needles were used for shapes with more than four sides so that one needle could be allocated to each side. For a design that was extended to being larger than usual more needles were also required.

The benefit of working from the centre out, even for a square, is to be found, not only in the growth of the pattern which repeats in each quarter, but in the fact that the edge can be patterned and fluted or shaped and cast off with a looped or picot edge, so completing the lace effect. Besides the rectangular shape, circles were worked on two knitting pins, cast on along the radius and worked in short rows in sections. They were pivotted on the central point, allowing a lace edging to be worked at the same time as the rest of the item and removing the need for a seam along last and first rows. Cast on with an open edge cast on, the contrast could be withdrawn and the last row of stitches grafted to the first.

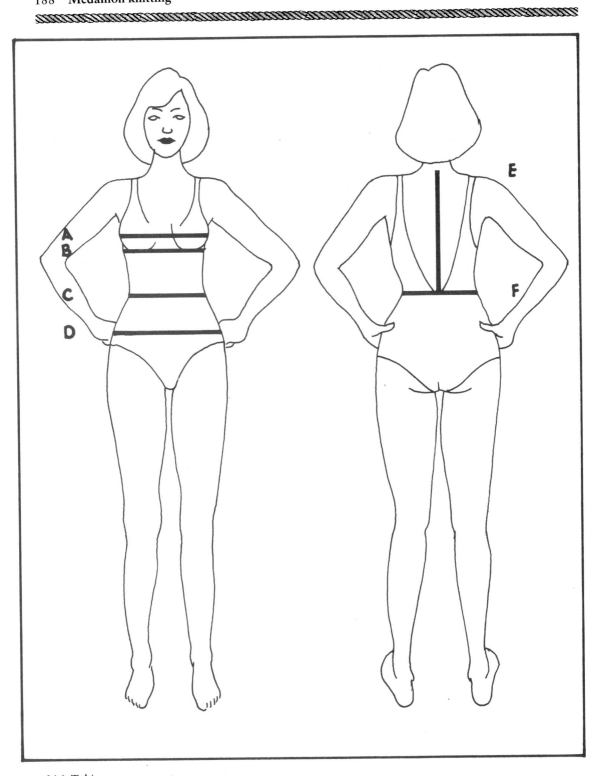

316 Taking measurements

Making a start

The first few rows of any medallion can be the most awkward. At this point very few stitches are on each needle and they tend to slip readily. There are two ways of solving this.

Cast on all the stitches for the first round on one needle; work one row, then knit off the required number of stitches on to three or four needles. Even if the pattern states more than four needles the total number can always be added when there are enough stitches to make this easier.

The second method is to make a small circle with a crochet hook and, once the circle is formed, work over it, making the required number of stitches into the circle for the 1st round. If these stitches are kept on the shank of the crochet hook they can be transferred directly on to knitting needles once the complete number has been made into the circle.

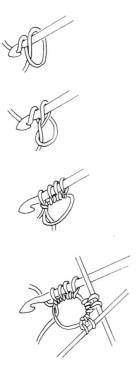

318 Working the centre stitches with a crochet hook

Shaping medallions

The shape of any medallion depends on the increases and where they are placed. Although there are basic rules for this, their success can depend on the tension and yarn used. A design that may work in one yarn or on one size of needles may be distorted on another size or in a different yarn. This may mean that instead of lying flat it will curl by being too tight or too slack at the outer edge. It can be remedied by adding to or subtracting stitches from the point at which it starts.

Circles

Basically, a round can be worked with eight increases on every other round. the same size can be made by placing sixteen increases every fourth round, or in soft lacy wool patterns thirty-two increases on every eighth round. The arrangement of these can be used in the design construction and may only achieve its true shape after blocking. The increases may also be worked so that they add stitches in a way that is not obvious.

Flat disc

This is worked by placing eight increases on every alternate round or row out of line with the previous increase (see fig. 319a).

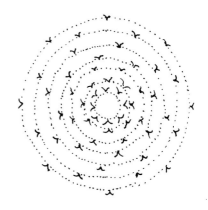

319a Increases required to make a flat disc

Radiant

In the radiant circle the inceases, after the sixth round or row are placed on every fourth round or row and increased to sixteen (see fig. 319b).

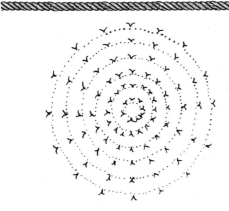

319b Increases required to form a radiant circle

Target

Like an archery target the increases start as eight, after six rounds become sixteen and double to thirty-two after another six rounds. The thirty-two increases are then retained and worked every eighth round, gradually widening with more stitches between each increase (see fig. 319c).

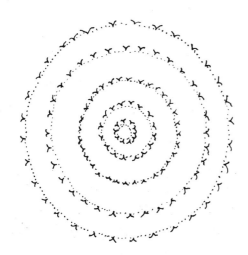

319c Increases required to form a target circle

Square

The square is a fascinating shape, its construction being possible in so many different ways. This is no less true of a square worked from the centre outwards (*see also* **Basic shapes** and **Diagonal knitting**).

Geometric

A shape that is ideally suited to medallion knitting allowing the pattern to repeat in the four quarters.

Paired increases can be used, or an openwork vein placed between the increases, or double increases can be worked narrowing the area used (see fig. 320a).

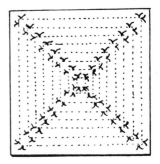

320a Geometric square

Windmill

The square can be layered or given a windmill sail effect by working it as for the geometric square, then adding to the number of stitches between in the increases at the corners (see fig. 320b).

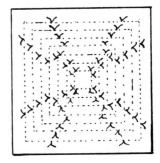

320b Windmill square

320c Maltese cross square

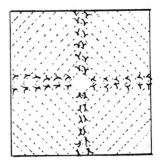

Maltese cross

The only alteration to the planning of this square is to place the quarters radiating from the centre instead of using the diagonal lines from the centre. But the difference to the appearance, however, may be immense (see fig. 320c).

Pentagonal shape

The five lines of increases for this five-sided figure require ten increases in all and, because of the additional number on the eight of circle or square, need to be worked on first the alternate round then the third round alternating in this way to the outer edge (see fig. 321a).

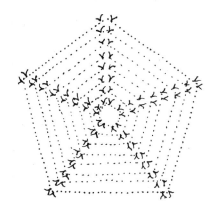

321a Pentagonal shaping

Hexagonal shape

For a six-sided figure twelve increase points are required and can be worked on every third round or row (see fig. 321b). Other multi-sided

321b Hexagonal shaping

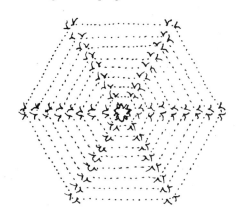

figures can gradually be built up in the same way. For patchwork-type knitting, figures with an uneven number of sides are less useful but they can be used in the construction of small lace mats or coasters.

Swirl centres

All shapes can have a swirled arrangement of increases based on the same number of sections as they have sides, with the exception of the square and circle, which should have eight swirl sections to retain the shape.

The increase is placed at the start of the round or row and as each increase is worked the extra stitch is worked before the next increase (see fig. 322a).

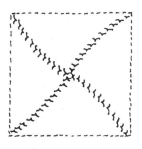 

322a Square swirl   **322b** Round swirl

Multiple shapes

Shapes within shapes are quite common in medallion knitting and give great design potential.

A circular swirl is used to form a beautiful shawl base, each section of the swirl starting with a yon increase. This yon increase also provides a method of working a flat circle, worked in rows instead of rounds. It uses a means of joining invisibly by seaming the open increase to the last stitch of the joining section. The outer area is either worked in lace, which is designed to carry on the round shape, or can be worked as a lace edge in the latter method, work off the total number of stitches by knitting together the lace edge rows with a stitch from the total on every other row.

A square can also be used as a centre to make

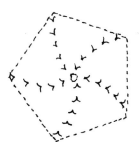

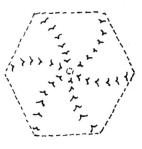

322c Pentagonal swirl   **322d** Hexagonal swirl

an eight-petalled shape on the outer section. Experimenting with an idea will always provide new ideas and new combinations of shapes.

Metallic yarn

See **Yarn.**

323 A mitred corner

Mitring corners

Mitred corners are an effective way of using shape to complete a design, whether as a self-coloured band or as a contrasting patterned edging. Cuffs, collars, necklines, openings and hemlines can be highlighted in this way.

Working methods

A corner is mitred or shaped by increasing or decreasing so that the band is turned at an angle to the original edge. The degree of turning depends on the number of increases or decreases worked and whether they are placed on every row, every alternate row or more widely on every third or fourth row.

Increases are used if you are working the band from the inner measurements to a larger outer measurement. Decreases are made if you are working the reverse way with the largest edge measurement first, becoming smaller in edge measurement on an inner edge.

Paired decreases or increases can be placed together on the mitring line or can be separated and worked on either side of one or more stitches. Alternatively you can use one double increase or decrease on every row or every alternate row. The choice of which increase or decrease you use will determine the finished appearance (see figs 166–171 and 270).

Mittens

See **Gloves.**

Mohair

See **Yarns.**

1 Fisherman's gloves. These red and black gloves are a fine example of
  Sanquhar knitting; they were made in 1882 by John MacKay, a fisherman.
  (City of Aberdeen Art Gallery and Museum)

2 White knitted bedspread, *c.* 1750-1800.

3 Medallion with picot flower.

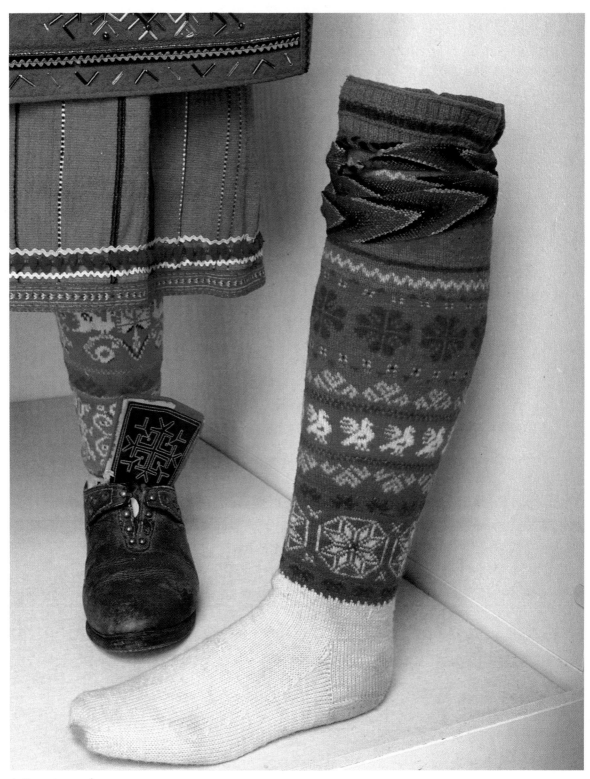

4 Estonian sock.

5(a) Two-coloured fisherman's rib.

5(b) Double-checked fabric.

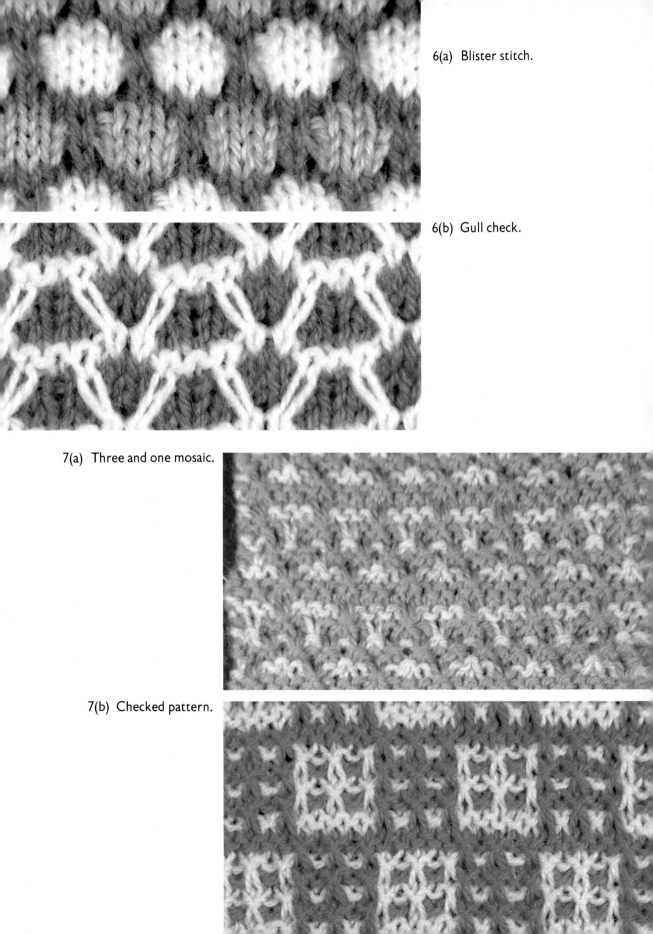

6(a) Blister stitch.

6(b) Gull check.

7(a) Three and one mosaic.

7(b) Checked pattern.

8 Peruvian knitting.

9(a) Dice check pattern.

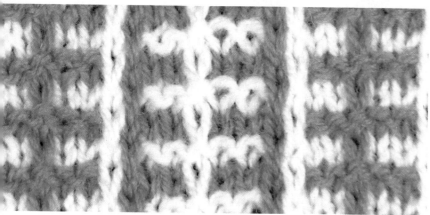

9(b) Cross colour strip.

10(a) Shell dip stitch.

10(b) Contrast shell stitch.

11 Early Fair Isle knitting *c.* 1850. The cap and purse are knitted in soft shades of silk, coloured with lichen and plant dyes. *(National Museum of Antiquities of Scotland, Edinburgh)*

Mosaic knitting

Mosaic knitting is not a special technique but rather the special use of a technique. It is a form of slipped-stitch pattern building used to work patterns in two colours, but with only one colour used on any one row. This means that no knowledge of stranding or weaving is necessary to work the many patterns satisfactorily.

Stitches are made to look as though they carried one colour into another area of the same colour. In fact this is due to the slipping of some stitches and the yarn in use being carried behind the slipped work, always on the wrong side of the fabric so that the construction is invisible from the right side.

The pattern is worked on a smooth stocking stitch base or the more textured garter stitch and is often easily varied from one to the other if preferred.

A simple pattern shows the working method, and further patterns are to be found in **Mosaic stitch patterns**.

Working Macedonian mosaic stitch

This is a small pattern, worked on a number of stitches divisible by four, plus three and is worked in garter stitch on a stocking stitch background.

To make the entire pattern in stocking stitch read P for K on 4th, 6th and 8th pattern rows.
1st row (RS facing), with A, K.
2nd row With A, P.
3rd row With B, K3, * sl1 with yarn back, K3, rep from * to end.
4th row With B, K3, * sl1 with yarn forward, K3, rep from * to end.
5th row With A, K2, * sl1 with yarn back, K1, rep from * to last st, K1.
6th row With A, P2, * sl1 with yarn forward, P1, rep from * to last st, P1.
7th row With B, K1, * sl1 with yarn back, K3, rep from * to last 2 sts, sl1, K1.
8th row With B, K1, * sl1 with yarn forward, K3, rep from * to last 2 sts, sl1, K1.

This forms the first pattern and it is repeated in reverse order to place the solid line of three stitches over the space between two lines on the previous repeat. All stitches are slipped purlwise

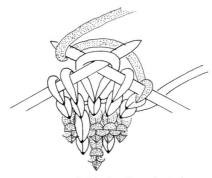

324 Carrying yarn behind a slipped stitch

because they are part of a pattern and are to be worked on the following row.
9th and 10th row With A work as given for 1st and 2nd rows.
11th and 12th rows With B, work as given for 7th and 8th rows (see fig. 324).
13th and 14th rows With A, work as given for 5th and 6th rows.
15th and 16th rows With B, work as given for 3rd and 4th rows.
Repeat these 16 rows for the required length. (See fig. 325)

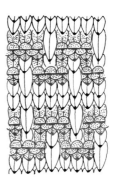

325 Macedonian mosiac pattern

Mosaic stitch patterns

The simplest patterns make mosaic knitting look unbelievably complex at first but, as so often happens in knitting, the pattern is easily understood and begins to follow one row after the other very easily once the first row is set.

Three and one mosaic pattern

An obvious basic pattern is three stitches in contrast reversed to one stitch with three in background colour. It can be varied in so many ways and provides a starting point for many often-used patterns. In this pattern, worked in two colours, it is given a less well-known appearance (see colour plate 7(a)).

Worked over a number of stitches divisible by 4, plus 3.

Cast on with A.

1st and 2nd row (RS facing), With A, K.

3rd row With B, K3, * sl 1 with yarn back, K3, rep from * to end.

4th row With B, K3, * sl1 with yarn forward, K3, rep from * to end.

5th row With A, K1, * sl1 with yarn back, K3, rep from * to last 2 sts, sl1, K1.

6th row With A, K1, * sl1 with yarn forward, K3, rep from * to last 2 sts, sl1, K1.

7th row With B, K2, * sl1 with yarn back, K1, rep from * to last st, K1.

8th row With B, K2, * sl1 with yarn forward, K1, rep from * to last st, K1.

9th and 10th rows With A, as 3rd and 4th rows.

11th and 12th rows With B, as 5th and 6th rows.

13th and 14th rows With A, K.

15th and 16th rows Rep 11th and 12th rows.

17th and 18th rows Rep 9th and 10th rows.

19th and 20th rows Rep 7th and 8th rows.

21st and 22nd rows Rep 5th and 6th rows.

23rd and 24th rows Rep 3rd and 4th rows.

Rep 1st–24th rows as required.

Checked pattern

Small geometric patterns are always easy to use and this one shows the possibilities for larger patterns worked by the same technique (see colour plate 7(b)).

Worked over a number of stitches divisible by 10, plus 2.

1st and 2nd rows With A, K.

3rd, 7th and 11th rows (RS facing), With B, K1, * K5, [sl1 with yarn back, K1] twice, sl1 with yarn back, rep from * to last st, K1.

4th, 8th and 12th rows With B, K1, * [sl1 with yarn forward, K1] twice, sl1 with yarn forward, K5, rep from * to last st, K1.

5th and 9th rows With A, K1, * [sl1 with yarn back, K1] twice, sl1 with yarn back, K5, rep from * to last st, K1.

6th and 10th rows With A, K1, * K5, [sl 1 with yarn forward, K1] twice, sl1 with yarn forward, rep from * to last st, K1.

13th and 14th rows With A, K.

15th, 19th and 23rd rows With B, K1, * [sl1 with yarn back, K1] twice, sl1 with yarn back, K5, rep from * to last st K1.

16th, 20th and 24th rows With B, K1, * K5, [sl1 with yarn forward, K1] twice, sl1 with yarn forward, rep from * to last st, K1.

17th and 21st rows With A, K1, * K5, [sl1 with yarn back, K1] twice, sl1 with yarn back, rep from * to last st, K1.

18th and 22nd rows With A, K1, * sl1 with yarn forward, [K1, sl1 with yarn forward] twice, K5, rep from * to last st, K1.

Rep 1st–24th rows as required.

Necklines

Necklines can reach up around the ears or plunge almost to the waistline; they can be a slashed straight line, edged with moss stitch or garter stitch as part of the garment; they can be neatly round with a small doubled edge of ribbing picked up and knitted on or they can be faced with a mitred square, striped for maximum effect. They can be as unimportant to the garment as possible, giving place to a stitch pattern or coloured motif, or they can be used as the design point, enlarged to be eye catching. They can also be a very good place to try out many techniques such as mitring, embroidery, short rows or darts for a large shawl collar, or evenly picked up stitches giving a tailored band.

Needles

See **Equipment**.

Norwegian knitting

Unlike other regional knitting, the knitting of Norway can be precisely dated because it was specifically introduced by King Christian IV during the seventeenth century when he was responsible for setting up orphanages and organized education for the poor. Like Finland and Sweden, however, the rural areas used needle-coiled stitches to make a thick fabric, and it was not until the eighteenth and nineteenth centuries that knitting became widely popular.

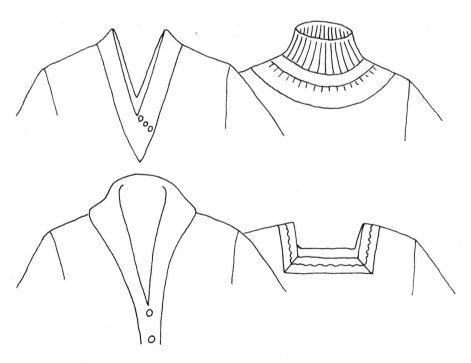

328 Traditional Norwegian pattern

Much Norwegian patterning was based on the eight-pointed star, introduced to Shetland after the second World War, but was worked only in light natural wool against dark grey. The main patterns were placed on a ground of seeded pattern, small single or double stitch patterns used as an allover base or ground pattern. Traditionally, the Norwegian *Luskofte* or lace jacket was decorated by the addition of embroidered braid sewn on to neck opening and cuff edges which, when trimmed with metal filigree buttons, added to the richness of the garment.

Norwegian garments were traditionally knitted with the right side facing, round, up to the neckline and were then stitched and cut to form armholes. Sleeves were also knitted round and sewn into the cut armhole with the top edge of the sleeve being neatly stitched into place over the cut and stitched armhole edge, making a self binding.

Norwegian stitch patterns

Since the nineteenth century the Norwegians have used many variations of the famous star pattern from the region of Selbu. It has been worked in small forms on the robust stockings worn with breeches and has been enlarged for the tourist trade of today in ski wear, now patterned in many bright colours.

Allover pattern

Worked over 34 stitches and 34 rows. To work as a repeating pattern work from A to B and repeat from B to C as required. Use red on white or yellow on royal blue for dramatic effect (see fig. 329).

Single motif

An unusual motif based on the eight-pointed Selbu star, this can be worked singly in Swiss darning or can be used scattered over a sweater, depending on how much work is chosen.

The motif is complete over 35 stitches and 39 rows (see fig. 329).

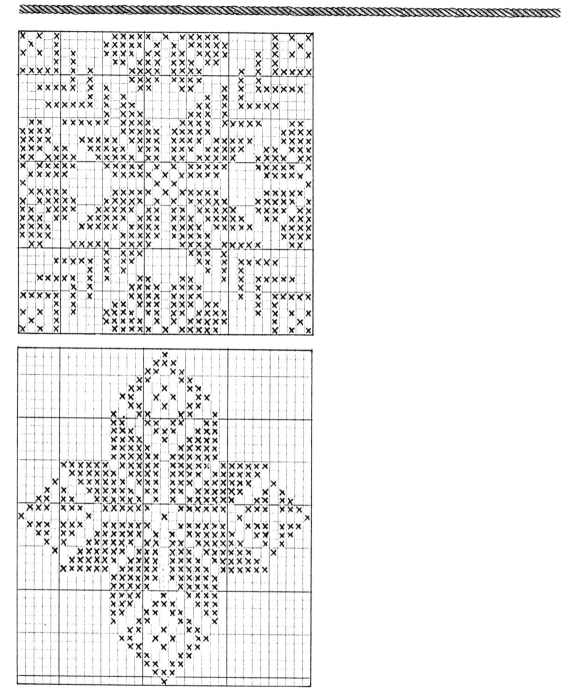

329 Norwegian pattern charts

Nylon

See **Yarns**

Openings

Whenever possible complete openings before seaming garment sections together (*see* **Making up** and *also* **Cut and sew knitting**).

Edgings that are to be neatened by having stitches picked up along their edges can be prepared by placing marker loops or pins at evenly-spaced intervals along the edge. It is then easier to lift a few stitches between each marker than to judge the correct number along an undivided row (*see* **Picking up stitches**).

Overs

See **Open increases**

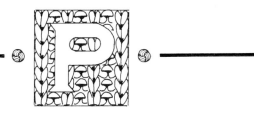

Pattern building

Stitch dictionaries are ideal places for finding ideas for patterns, but building from the ideas, learning what repeated rows will do to a basic idea, and changing a decrease here and an increase there can also produce new patterns.

Basic diamond

The basic faggot stitch diamond pattern shown in fig. 304b can be the start of an exciting adventure – a simple openwork pattern and

what it may become. For the working instructions for all the following patterns used in this section *see* **Lace stitch patterns**.

First steps

A first step might well be to increase the amount of lace and in this pattern the central diamond is retained but stitches added to each repeat become an extra means of emphasizing the shape (see fig. 332a).

Enlarging the repeat without adding to the lace gives a well-known pattern once knitted by Mrs Montague in stockings for Queen Elizabeth I.

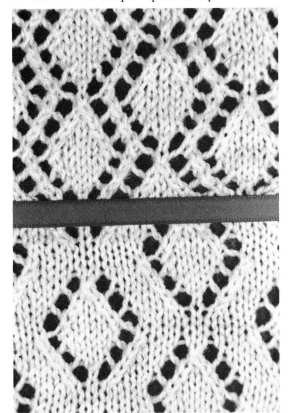

332 (*Top*) Trellis diamond pattern.
(*Bottom*) Mrs Montague's pattern.

333 (*Top*) Leaf pattern. (*Bottom*) Trellis leaf pattern

It has been popular with knitters ever since (see fig. 332b).

Further steps

There is usually more than one way in which to experiment with any pattern and the original diamond takes a different shape if the decreases around its edge are moved to its centre (see fig. 333a).

Add the same trellis to this design and also repeat the second and twelfth rows several times and the lace is extended (see fig. 333b).

A final stage

Keep the trellis line to emphasize the shape, keep the stocking stitch fabric between the shapes like Mrs Montague's pattern but alter the centre to eyelets. Such simple changes, one leading on to the next, bring about Rose Trellis lace (see fig. 334).

Reversing the experiment

There is no need always to enlarge and extend. Cut back and remove the openwork, reduce the size of the pattern repeat and obtain Rosebud pattern (see fig. 224a) (for instructions *see* **Eyelet stitch patterns**).

Cut again and the loss of the centre stitch brings about Elfin lace (fig. 307b).

Not every pattern can extend in every direction but only trial and error shows what can be made and sometimes even the change from stocking stitch to garter stitch can produce interest.

Pearl knitting

Pearl was the word used for purl knitting at one time. It is thought to have been so named because purl stitches stand out like beads or pearls on stocking stitch fabric.

334 Rose trellis lace

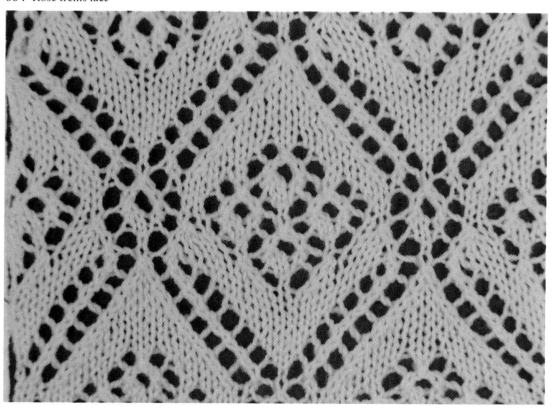

Peg knitting

See **Frame knitting**

Peruvian knitting

Peruvian knitting today is exported to many other countries, being both decorative and colourful. Many of the small textile motifs used in the coloured knitting are similar to woven textiles, not always in easy, knittable shapes.

At one time Peruvian knitting was thought to be exceedingly old, pre-dating the Spanish influence. This work, which looked like knitted stitches, was later be a type of needlework, worked over a fine base net rather than the Eastern and European methods of using short lengths of yarn in a single needle (*see* **Arabic knitting**).

Plain knitting

Used to differentiate between plain and purl or knit and purl.

Picking up stitches

Stitches may need to be picked up for two reasons:
- because they have been dropped accidentally
- because stitches are required to be picked up from a finished section to be knitted in a different direction or to complete an unfinished edge.

Accidentally dropped stitches

On stocking stitch or reversed stocking stitch pick up stitches with the knitted side of the work facing. The movement of drawing the loop through the stitch is less awkward on this side. (See fig. 335a)

Insert the right needle tip into the dropped loop and also through the 1st strand of yarn above it.

Use the left needle tip to lift the stitch over the

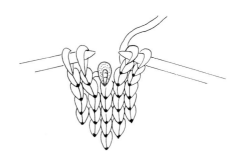

335a Dropped stitch and strand immediately above

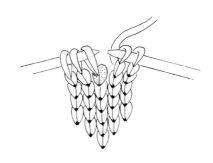

335b Use needle tip to draw strand through loop

strand, making the strand into the next loop (see fig. 335b).

When stitches have dropped many rows, repeat this for every strand to be worked back into place, taking care to lift the strands in their exact order.

When all the strands have been lifted, slip the last loop back on to the left needle ready for working on the next row. On garter stitch the purl method must be used alternately with the knit method to keep the edged surface correct. This can be worked by turning the work so that the stitch is always treated as a knit stitch, first on one side then on the other. Alternately, for the purl loop, use the right needle tip to lift the dropped stitch. Pass the same needle through the lifted stitch and use the tip to catch the strand and draw it through the stitch loop.

Pick up the remaining stitches alternately knitwise and purlwise, slipping the last lifted stitch back on to the left needle ready for working (see fig. 336b).

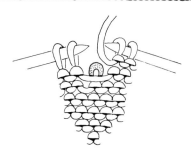

336a Dropped stitch with strand behind

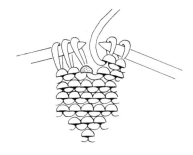

336b Hook strand through to right side

Using a crochet hook

Even for those who do not crochet it can be easier to pick up stitches with a crochet hook.

On the knit side of the fabric insert the crochet hook through the dropped stitch and catch the strand immediately above it with the hook (see fig. 336c).

Draw the strand through the stitch on the hook, forming a new loop and allowing the picked up stitch to slip over it and take its place beneath it as the previous row. Repeat this for each strand to be lifted.

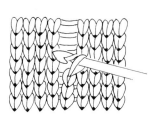

336c Use hook to draw strand through loop

Picking up stitches for edging

Whether stitches are being picked up from a small pocket top or from a long centre front edge it is always easier to pick them up evenly if the edge is divided into evenly spaced sections before knitting up begins.

Unless the edge is to be worked immediately, mark it with marker threads, loops of coloured yarn that can be loosely knotted and will not fall out or be in danger of being pulled out before the edge is completed (see Fig. 337).

It is then easy to divide the total number of stitches to be picked up by the number of divisions made and place stitches between the markers, rather than have to drop all the stitches and try again because the required number did not fit into the length of the edge on the first attempt.

337 Edge divided with marker loops

Placing picked up stitches

Stitches can be picked up between stitches or through the actual stitch, on side edges through loops or knots. The number of stitches required will determine whether both spaces and stitches are required to act as the base for a picked up stitch. Tension, yarn and needle size in relation to the size used for the garment will all contribute to how many stitches are required. A small tension swatch worked on needles and with yarn to be used for the edge in the chosen stitch will give an exact measurement of how many stitches are required to fit a particular edge.

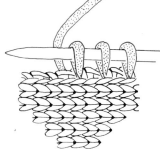

338a Picking up stitches through side knots

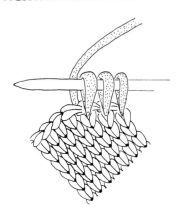

338b Picking up stitches from cast-off stitches

On necks and similar curves more stitches will need to be worked around the curve than on the straight edge. Stitches picked up from other stitches and from the row end knot are neater than stitches picked up through spaces between stitches and the side loops, where there is more chance of leaving a large gap or unsightly hole.

For evenness

Where there is any difficulty in picking up stitches use needles one or two sizes smaller, changing to the required size for the edge after the stitches are all lifted.

Knitwise or purlwise

Stitches are usually knitted up, but where the finished texture is to be purled, stitches can be purled up.

Knitwise
Insert the needle from the front to the back with the smooth side of stocking stitch facing. Pass the yarn round the needle tip and draw it through as a loop or new stitch. Work along the edge until the required number of stitches are on the needle.

Purlwise
Insert the right needle from back to front through the stitch with right side of work facing, put the yarn round the needle point and draw through a new stitch.

Continental method

Stitches can be picked up without your knitting or purling them up. Many knitters lift the loops required on a long hooked needle, finer than the needle to be used for knitting, only joining in the yarn on the first row to be worked.

Alternatively, the yarn can be drawn through and the new stitch formed by using a fine Tunisian needle, replacing this with knitting needles when the stitches are all lifted.

Clean lines

On reverse stocking stitch or any other fabric that is not stocking stitch a neat, clear line can be given to the picked-up edge if the stitches are lifted knitwise and knitted, only becoming reversed stocking stitch or another pattern after the first row.

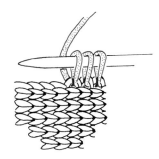

339a Picking up stitches between side knots

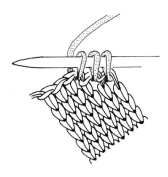

339b Picking up stitches between cast-off stitches

Picot knitting

Knitters are never willing to see a fashionable fabric that they are unable to make because it uses a different craft. When Irish crochet was at its peak, knitters found ways of using the stitches they understood to create similar fabrics to crochet. The result is Picot knitting, which consists of flower motifs or small picot point circles attached to a lace ground. Picot casting off uses the same technique (*see* **Decorative casting off**).

Lace ground

The lace background is formed by strips of small half circles joined to each other to form a looped fabric. Each single loop or ring is edged with a number of picot points made by casting on and off several stitches, and is known as a crown picot.

To work a strip

The strip consists of as many crown picots as are required to give the width of the fabric being made.
Cast on a number of stitches divisible by 5.
1st row K.
2nd row Each crown picot is worked along this row making the individual picots as the loops are formed. * Cast on 2 sts and then cast off 2 sts, making 1 picot. Slip st on right needle back to left needle and rep from * 3 times more then K and cast off next 4 sts, joining the 1st loop to the cast-on edge (see fig. 340a).

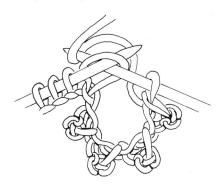

340a Join picots into circle or crown with several cast-off stitches before next crown

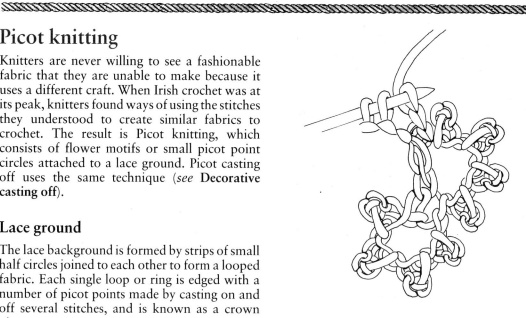

340b Repeat crowns for required length to form a strip

Work other picot point loops in the same way, joining each to the cast on edge by knitting and casting off 4 sts (see fig. 340b).

The next strip is worked along the 1st strip thus:
Slip the st rem on the right needle to the left and make 4 small picot points as for the 1st crown picot. To join to the 1st strip pick up and K 1 st between the 2nd and 3rd picot of the 1st crown, then cast off 1 st and pass the rem st to the left needle. The following rings are worked in the same way joining each between the centre 2 picots of the next crown towards the end of the row. Other rows are worked in the same way, always joining into the centre of the crowns on the previous strip. The size of the ground, its degree of openness and the number of picots in each crown can all be altered to give different appearances.

Picot points can be worked over more than two stitches but, unless for use in a motif, worked over too many stitches they become untidy and not small points as intended. The number of picot points can be altered if you place three, four or five round each ring. When an odd number of picots is worked the rings must join into the centre picot rather than into the actual ring (see fig. 341b).

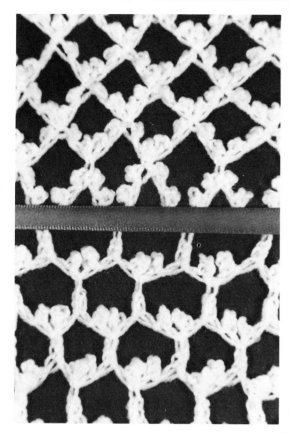

341 (*Top*) Strip after strip forms picot lace background. (*Bottom*) Background with only three picots per crown

Motifs

The motif is built round a small picot point ring, made in a similar way to the half ring or crown picot.

Cast on 3 sts then cast off 3 sts to form the 1st picot, work 5 more points in the same way. Join into a circle by drawing a loop of yarn through the base of the 1st picot, break off the yarn and pull through this loop, forming a complete picot ring which can be used as it is or used as a flower centre (see fig. 342a).

Adding petals

Petals are formed round the small picot ring, each petal touching the ring only at each side of a picot.

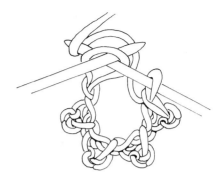

342a Flower circle is made by one complete ring or crown joined by casting off last stitch

Use the last st worked in joining the circle of picots as the base st for the 1st petal and place it on the left needle.
1st row Cast on 1 st, (2 sts on needle), K1, K into front and back of 2nd st.
2nd row K3.
3rd row K2, K into front and back of last st.
4th row K4.
5th row K3, K into front and back of last st.
6th–9th rows K.
10th row Cast off 1 st, K3.
11th row K4.
12th row Cast off 1 st, K2.

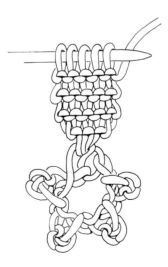

342b Petals can be added by knitting on from the single stitch

13th row K3.
14th row Cast off 1 st, K1.
15th row K2.

Cast off 1 st, leaving 1 st on needle. To complete petal pick up and K 1 st between next 2 picots, then cast off 1 st, leaving 1 st on needle. Slip this stitch to left needle and work the remaining petals in the same way. Repeat until the circle is complete and finish off by drawing yarn through last joining stitch (see fig. 342b).

Complex flowers

Other shapes of petals can be worked by altering each petal shape, by working further rounds of petals, joining each into the space between the 1st round; centres can be enlarged by the addition of small picot circles. Buds can be formed from single petals as can leaves, larger leaves being made by increasing and decreasing at both sides of the basic petal shape. Tiny flowers can be added to a spray of larger flowers by clustering several small picot circles into one group.

Uses

Originally, picot knitting in fine cotton on finer needles was used for small items, babies' bonnets, mittens and for making artificial flower buttonholes. The technique, however, can be used to make lacy evening wear, stoles, lace sleeves and yokes, lace edgings and even decorative pictures.

Pleats

Pleats can be knitted into fabric in two ways:
- by using the curl of knit stitches against purl stitches.
- by working a slip stitch on alternate rows and drawing the yarn across the slipped stitch on the wrong side.

Kilt pleats

Purled triangles on a knitted background worked in vertical rows cause the edge of the repeat where knit meets purl to roll over on to

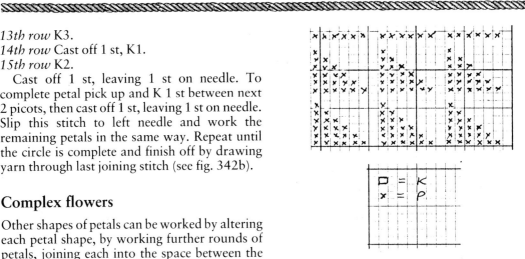

343 Chart for kilt pattern or flag

the purled stitches giving a pleat-like impression. It is often used on children's garments to give a pleat that is less bulky than a true pleat formed from three thicknesses of fabric.

The width of the repeat can be adapted as required but a chart for this type of pattern will look like fig. 343 (for pattern *see* **Knit and Purl stitch patterns, fig. 300a**).

Slipped stitch pleats

Any edge can be made to fold by your working a slip stitch vertically in line on alternate rows. You can work it on the right side or wrong side but you must draw across it on the wrong side of the work. Within reason the more firmly the yarn is drawn across the slipped stitch the more readily the edge will fold and retain its fold in washing and in wear (see fig. 344).

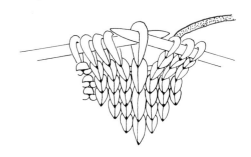

344 Pleat stitch slipped on right side

Ribbed slip stitch pleating

The line of the slip stitch edge can be emphasized by the use of ribbing; this allows the folded fabric to lie back against a purled surface. The slipped stitch is better not worked on the last or first stitch of a knitted panel but on the second or third stitch, depending on the width of the rib.

The rib shown is worked over a number of stitches divisible by 7 plus 3.

1st row (RS facing) K3, * sl1 with yarn back, K1, P2, K3, rep from * to end.

2nd row P3, * K2, P5, rep from * to end.

Rep 1st and 2nd rows as required (see fig. 345).

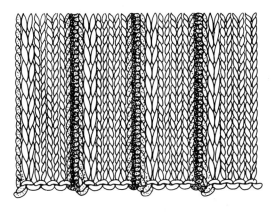

345 Ribbed pleat

Casting off

The forming of the pleats can be aided, when casting off, if stitches which are to be folded over are cast off together so that the fold is made permanently.

Ply

The terms 2, 3 or 4 ply describe the number of single threads of twisted yarn that are used to form the complete strand, not the thickness of the yarn. Four ply can be used to describe a sock yarn that knits to a tension of about seven stitches to 2.5cm (1 in.) on 3 1/4mm needles or a chunky yarn that is made of four single threads wound together and knits to a tension of three stitches to 2.5cm worked on 6mm needles.

Pockets

Pockets can be made in all shapes and sizes but can be divided into two distinct types; pockets that are added, partly or completely during knitting; and those that are made separately and sewn into place on the right side.

Patch pockets

You can add pockets of any shape after the garment is complete, using the actual garment as the pocket backing. Unless the pocket is edged by contrast stitches or pattern you should sew them on with care, matching row for row with the background.

Where an edge has been knitted on or when the pocket is to be stitched into place and the edge left to show as a ridge, stitch carefully following one row on the base fabric.

Knitted-in pockets

Pockets can be fashionable and, as an integral part of any design into which they are knitted, must be in keeping with the design.

Straight pockets

A straight pocket is worked by knitting the pocket lining before beginning the section it is to become part of. Left on a stitch holder it is ready to be joined into place as soon as the rest of the section is worked to that point.

Work to the position for the pocket then slip the same number of stitches as are worked for the lining on to a holder. With the right side facing, work the pocket lining into place, and complete the row.

The flap that is to become the lining can be slip stitched into place when the section is complete; take care that the edges are exactly vertical and horizontal along one row and up one vertical stitch at each side. The stitches that have been left on a holder are dealt with after the section is complete and can be ribbed or patterned as required (see fig. 346a).

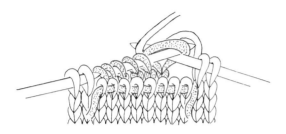

346a Working a straight pocket

A straight pocket may also be added to a held opening by working a contrast yarn over the stitches to be used for the pocket opening. Complete the section before removing the contrast yarn and use the stitches that this opens up to form edging and pocket lining.

You can make a bulkier pocket, suitable for heavier weight jackets and coats, by picking up the lower stitches and working the depth required for the lining. A similar flap worked from the top stitches makes a pocket in double thickness, with edges that can be stitched together after the garment is complete (*see also* **Held openings**) (see fig. 346b).

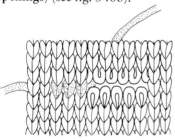

346b Placing a held pocket opening

Diagonal pocket

A diagonal pocket can be worked in a similar way to a knitted-in straight pocket, the lining being worked first. If the pocket is to be placed in from the edge, then the lining may be part of the side and is worked up to the highest edge of the diagonal and left on a stitch holder.

Work the pocket front, placing the diagonal when the depth of the pocket is reached. When the diagonal is completed, both sets of stitches can be worked across together (see fig. 346c).

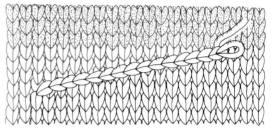

346c Making diagonal pockets

Side seam pockets

A side pocket may also be placed with its edges on the side seams of a garment. The lining for this pocket may be single and knitted in as part of the back or added to both back and front for a double thickness pocket. Alternatively, this type of pocket can be made of matching material and sewn into place during making up.

Edges

The edges of pockets can be decorated in many ways other than the usual ribbed edge. A doubled band can carry pattern on the outside, knitted in or added in embroidery, or the pocket can be bound with a striped or self-coloured diagonal braid or crochet trim.

Flaps can also be added and should be knitted in with the stitches above the pocket or, for a wider flap, knitted in several rows above the pocket and overlapping the pocket and overlapping the pocket width by a few stitches on each side.

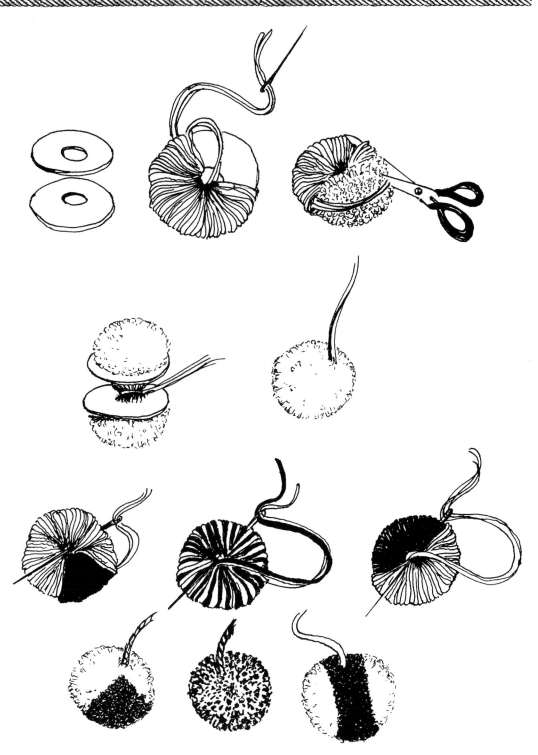

347 Pompons

Pompons

Pompons are a finish that can be used to trim baby garments, tie ends, caps and socks. On their own they can be made into toys and decorations for table or Christmas tree.

To make a self-coloured pompon

Cut two firm card rings the diameter of the pompon required. Cut a central hole through both circles about one-third of the diameter.

Place both cards together and wind the yarn round the card gradually filling the centre. Work until the yarn must be threaded into a needle to pass through the centre and continue working round until the central hole is completely filled.

Ease the cards apart and cut all the strands between the circles. Do not remove the cards until a double strand of yarn has been tied very firmly round the centre of all the strands. Remove the card and trim the ends of yarn all over the surface to form a neat ball.

Placing colours

For a multicoloured ball with flecks evenly mixed all over the surface use two or three ends of yarn from different balls and wind them round together.

For a striped effect

Wind several complete rounds of one colour then change and completely fill the circle evenly all round with a second colour. Stripes can be added in this way until the centre is filled.

Splodged balls

For colour in one area only wind strands round the circle, keeping the contrast yarn to one area only.

Popcorn patterns

See **Bobbles and popcorns** and *also* **Bobble and popcorn stitch patterns.**

Pressing

See **Blocking and pressing**

Purl stitches

Purl stitches are the stitches which along with knitted stitches are used for all knitting patterns (*see also* **Basic stitches**).

Quilting stitch patterns

See Quilted lattice in **Surface stitch patterns** *and* Cluster quilting pattern in **Tied stitches.**

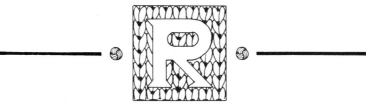

Raglan seams

Raglan seams can become a design feature by being emphasized rather than worked invisibly.

Decreases and increases

Worked from the armhole upwards, you can use the decreases to outline the seam line, either by taking the same slope as the seam or reversing it (*see* **Paired decreases**). A double decrease used on every fourth row instead of a single decrease used on alternate rows makes a more noticeable cluster of stitches. Alternatively, work a double decrease on every alternate row along with a single increase, which, if an open increase will outline the seam with a line of openwork holes (see 350a b).

Increases can be used in this way when the

350 (*Left*) Openwork shaping.
(*Centre*) Clustered multiple increases or decreases.
(*Right*) Patterned band between seams

garment is worked from the shoulders downwards forming openwork ladders that can be used for further decorative trimming of ribbon, braid or threaded contrasting yarns.

Pattern bands

Bands can also be used to decorate a raglan seamed garment and can be placed between seams or cast on at the start of the seam and worked in with one or other side of the work (see fig. 350c).

Reading instructions

Knitting instructions are usually formulated to mean exactly what they say and to be easily understood by the knitter. Some guide lines may be helpful to beginners.

Materials

Alterations made to any design will automatically alter the quantites of materials stated and should be considered from the start. Buy extra yarn while the same dye number is obtainable. Dye lots do differ and, even if only slightly, will mark the finished garment.

Every design is made specifically for the yarn that is stated. Using other yarn may not give similar results. If yarn is substituted it is essential to test that it does knit to the given tension in the instructions. If it does not or only nearly obtains the given tension, the garment is unlikely to be satisfactory.

Needle sizes are only given as a guide. Change to another size if necessary to obtain the correct tension.

Measurements

Check measurements before beginning to knit to see that they are the sizes required. If lengths are to be altered note them down on the instructions.

Tension

Tension is all important and is not given as a mere guide like the needle sizes (*see also* **Tension**).

Sizes

Most instructions are printed in more than one size. A note may indicate how the different sizes are shown. They may start with the smallest outside round or square brackets and place the others in increasing size inside brackets thus:
36(38: 40: 42) or 36[38: 40: 42]
They may even be printed thus:
36(38)(40)(42).

Underline the size that is being worked before beginning so that no error is made while working.

Check also before beginning that the number of sections that have to be made and read through the instructions to see that all abbreviations are understood.

Special abbreviations

Any special abbreviation or an abbreviation that is used in a different way from usual is given before the knitting instructions begin.

Asterisks

Asterisks, both single and in increasing numbers, are used to mark special sections. They are usually placed before a section that is to be repeated, the words filling in the number of times the pattern is to be repeated. They can also be used for an entire section that is to be repeated at another point. Used more than once in this way they are altered in number so that the section cannot be used in the wrong place. In this way it may read: work from * * twice more and further on work from * * * to end.

Repeats

Although most patterns use the asterisk inside row by row instructions for groups of stitches that are to be repeated it may be necessary to place repeats within repeats; this is usually done by using a different type of bracket from those used for size variations. When sizes are placed in round brackets ( ), the repeat may be placed in square brakcets [ ].

Read all instructions carefully and note where punctuation is placed. K1 P1 K1 in next st, does not mean the same as K1, P1, K1 in next st.

Reinforcing knitting

Strengthening knitting is necessary round buttonholes, on seams where the fabric is open and likely to drag on the knitted stitches, on the knitting behind buttons and on lower edges of garments intended for hard wear.

Seams

Stitching tape behind seams will stop lengthening or drag. Backstitch the tape firmly along the knitted seams, securing the tape to seams at each end if possible.

Lower edges

Fisherman's guernseys were often reinforced by having both cast on and following four or five rounds or rows worked with doubled yarn. This makes for an edge that will withstand being endlessly dragged on and off and stops the breaking of single threads (*see also* **Buttonholes and Buttons** for strengthening methods).

Repairing knitting

Knitting has long been a popular way of making garments because the knitted fabric is economical and easy to mend. Edges can be removed altogether and replaced and holes can be filled with knitting like stitches or, if large, with actual knitted patches.

Replacing stitches

Unpick the broken strands until the hole is a reasonably even shape.

Thread matching yarn into a wool needle and secure at the lower right corner, leaving an end to darn in later. Work twice into the stitches at both top and lower edge like elongated Swiss darning. Take the yarn to the right side through the 1st stitch then up and under the two sides of the stitch immediately above, down and to the wrong side through the stitch immediately below (see fig. 351 a). Work in this way until a web of double strands covers the hole.

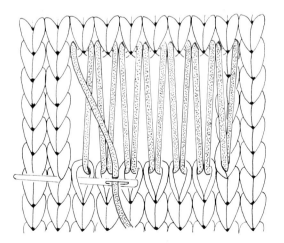

351a Weaving vertical strands across hole

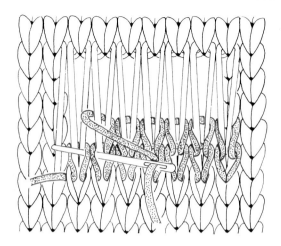

351b Work stitches round double strands

For large holes work over a darning 'mushroom' or other firm, very slightly round or flat surface. Beginning at the lower left corner work along the strands creating stitches as in Swiss darning, working row upon row until the hole is filled (see 352b).

Patches

A knitted patch can be picked up along the base of a large hole and knitted until it is the same number of rows as the area to be patched, matching the tension as nearly as possible. Leave the stitches. Finish by joining the row ends to the stitches by invisible seams.

Reworking edges

To remove a worn edge draw out a thread several rows above the worn area. Cut the yarn close to the side and the stitches will open on either side of the pulled thread. Ease the end of the thread out of the stitches so that all the stitches are free (see fig. 352).

Slip the stitches on to a fine needle and when all the stitches are on the needle and turned the correct way change to the correct needle size and work the rows that have been removed before casting off.

This method can also be used to shorten or lengthen skirts, sweaters or sleeves.

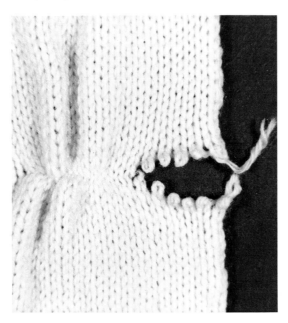

352 Drawing out yarn to cut and leave open stitches

Ribbing

See **Basic stitches**

353 (*Top left*) sport's rib. (*Top right*) moss patterned rib. (*Bottom*) ripple rib

Ribbing stitch patterns

Ribbing, so essential to form elastic fabrics, can be much more than just that. Ribbing can be decorative and can also be used to form allover fabrics.

Sports rib

One single row is all that this delightful fabric requires for its production. Alike on both sides it could almost be said to form itself (see fig. 353).
Worked over a number of stitches divisible by 4, plus 3.
1st row * K2, P2, rep from * to last 3 sts, K2, P1.
Rep this row as required.

Moss patterned rib

Ribbing but with a pattern as well gives this a rich, textured appearance (see fig. 353).
Worked over a number of stitches divisible by 7, plus 3.
1st row (RS facing) P3, * K1, P1, K2, P3, rep from * to end.
2nd row K3, * P2, K1, P1, K3, rep from * to end.
3rd row P3, * K2, P1, K1, P3, rep from * to end.
4th row K3, * P1, K1, P2, K3, rep from * to end.
Rep 1st–4th rows as required.

Ripple rib

A simple version of fisherman's rib, this uses less yarn and consists of one knit row and one patterned row (see fig. 353).
Worked over an even number of stitches.
1st row (RS facing), Sl1, K to end.

2nd row Sl1, K into the st below the next st on the left needle and let the st above it slip off the needle as the new st is moved onto the right needle, P1, rep from * to last st, K1.
Rep 1st and 2nd rows as required.

Ribbon slotting

For use or for decoration, ribbon slotting provides a knitted-in edge to carry ribbon of any width.

Narrow edging

The usual trim for baby garments is made by working eyelets along a row and is sometimes separated from the remaining patterned stitches by being framed on each side with a garter stitch row.
Worked over an odd number of stitches.
1st, 2nd and 3rd rows K.
4th row P.
5th row K1, * yon, K2 tog, rep from * to end.
6th row P1, P each yon and each st to end.
7th and 8th rows K.
Continue with garment as required (see fig. 354a).

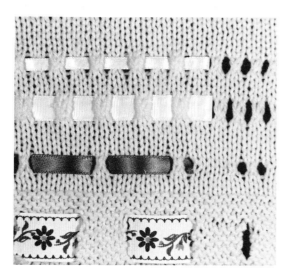

354 (*Top*) ordinary ribbon slotting. (*2nd row*) lengthened slotting. (*3rd row*) spaced slotting. (*Bottom*) vertical ribbon slots for wide ribbon

Wider edge

A similar edge can be worked by replacing this 5th row for the smaller holed version.
Alternative 5th row K1, * y2on, K2 tog, rep from * to end. On the next row P only 1 loop of each y2on made on the previous round and drop the 2nd making the stitch longer, and P the stitch between y2on also (see fig. 354b).

Arranged holes

Holes need not be placed as close together or they can be arranged in groups. Two eyelets placed together with a wider gap before the next pair give the opportunity of slotting the ribbon so that it shows over the larger gap or so that it barely shows at-all.
Pattern row K1, * yon, K2 tog, K6, rep from * to end.
In this slotting the yon is worked as a purl stitch on the following row.

Wide slotting

Slotting wide enough for any ribbon can be worked by dividing the work into sections and working each section until it is the required depth. Once all the sections are knitted they can again be joined into one row (see fig. 354 *3rd row*).
This type of edge benefits from having the last and first stitch on every slot knitted on both sides of the fabric, irrespective of the background stitch, to avoid the slit edges from curling (see fig. 354 *Bottom*).

Vertical slotting

Small eyelets worked vertically must be at least 3 rows apart but can be used for ribbon-slotting in this way.

Wide vertical holes

Wide holes that are placed vertically can be worked to any width just as a buttonhole is worked. Use the single row buttonhole for neatness.
Other ribbon-slotting can be made using the embroidered eyelet or the bold eyelet, (*see* **Eyelets**).

Ridged stitches

Ridged or corded stitches can be formed in several ways, using a variety of techniques.

Cording or piping stitch

This is worked in much the same way as a knitted-up hem, but is much less deep. The number of rows forming the cord can be varied and the 'hem' or cord made can be used in place of piping, its roundness accentuated by being threaded with double or triple yarn or, if suitable, with piping cord (see fig. 355a).
Worked over any number of stitches.
1st, 3rd, 5th and 7th rows (RS facing) K.
2nd, 4th and 6th rows K1, P to last st, K1.
8th row K1, * with yarn in front insert the right needle tip down into the top of the purl st 4 rows below the next st on the left needle, lift the st and

place it on the left needle and P it tog with the next st to it, rep from * to end of row, working the last st and the last picked up loop tog knitwise.
Rep 1st–8th rows as required.

Ridged stitch

Ridged stitch or double garter stitch as this pattern is sometimes called does give a delightful ridged pattern and is not unlike brioche stitch in its working. Because the yarn is wound twice round for every stitch on every row the strands must be knitted in the correct order (see fig. 355b).
Worked over any number of stitches.
Preparation row K winding yarn twice round needle on every stitch.
Pattern row K 1st loop, * K 2nd loop of 1st st tog with 1st loop of next st, rep from * to end.
Rep pattern row as required.
This gives a reversible fabric and is best worked on larger needles than usual for the thickness of yarn used.

Corded ribbing

Corded ribbing is worked by making a stitch by lifting the running thread between stitches and compensates for the made stitch by immediately working a decrease, resulting in a corded rib that is easily worked and produces a rich pattern (fig. 356 *Top*).
Worked over a number of stitches divisible by 4, plus 2.
1st row K1, * SSK, lift running thread before next st and K it tbl, P2, rep from * to last st, K1.
Rep this row as required.

Shadow ridges

This horizontal pattern grew from the wrong side of a slip stitch tweed pattern and is most effective worked in graded colours or in rainbow shades, one for each ridge (fig. 356 *Bottom*).
Worked over a number of stitches divisible by 2, plus 1.
1st row (RS facing), P.
2nd row K1, * P1, K1, rep from * to end.
3rd row P1, * yon, sl1 with yarn back, yarn forward, P1, rep from * to end.

355 (*Top*) Cording stitch. (*Bottom*) Ridged stitch

356 (*Top*) Corded ribbing.
(*Bottom*) Shadow ridge pattern.

4th row K1, * sl1 with yarn forward dropping yarn over needle made in previous row, K1, rep from * to end.
5th row P1, * sl1 with yarn back, P1, rep from * to end.
6th row K1, * sl1 with yarn forward, K1, rep from * to end.
Rep 1st–6th rows as required, working every 6 rows in different shades if preferred.

Right side

The side of any pattern that is used as the facing side when the garment is finished, as opposed to the wrong side or inside.

Round knitting

See **Circular knitting**

Rounds

Each stitch on a round worked once when using a set of three, four or more double-pointed needles or a circular needle which completes one round.

Rows

On flat knitting one row is every stitch worked on one needle. Rows are worked to and fro, as opposed to rounds, which are worked continually from right to left.

Ruched knitting

Ruched knitting does not use any special technique but is formed by increasing along a row, working rows on the greater number of stitches, then decreasing along a row to return the stitches to the original number.

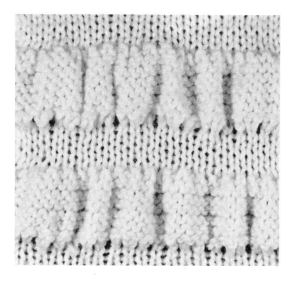

357 Ruched knitting

Worked without too many rows between the increased and decreased rows the extra fullness gives a gathered or ruched appearance (see fig. 357).

To work ruching

1st row and every alternate row P.
2nd, 4th, 6th, 10th and 12th rows K.
8th row Knit into front and back of each st.
Change to one size smaller needles.
14th row * K2 tog, rep from * to end.
Change back to the original needle size and repeat from 1st–14th rows as required.
The patterned rows on the increased stitches can be patterned with a small dot stitch or eyelet hole which accentuates the difference in fabric.

Running thread stitch patterns

You can lift the running thread between stitches to make a stitch and also to leave a small openwork hole.

Coral knot stitch

A stitch that, although not a true lace, is lacy and yet has additional texture in the patterned knit row worked on the wrong side (see fig. 358a).
Worked over an even number of stitches.
1st row (RS facing) K1, * K2 tog, rep from * to end.
2nd row K1, * K1, insert needle under running thread, the thread between the last st worked and the following stitch. K the lifted thread, rep from * to last st, K1.
3rd row P.
4th row K.
Rep 1st–4th rows as required.

Diagonal scallop stitch

To make this textured pattern the running thread is lifted but is not knitted and is then passed over the stitches and off the needle tip, creating a pattern from a stitch that has never been worked (see fig. 358b).
Worked over a number of stitches divisible by 4, plus 2.
1st and 3rd rows (WS facing), P.
2nd row K1, * insert right needle tip under the

358 (*Top*) Coral knot stitch.
(*Bottom*) Diagonal scallop stitch

thread between the last st and the next from behind, K next 2 sts, then with left needle point lift the lifted thread over the 2 K sts and off the right needle point, rep from * to last st, K1.
4th row K3, * lift running thread from behind on to right needle as for 2nd row, K2 and lift lifted stitch over and off right needle tip, K2, rep from * to last 3 sts, lift running thread, K2, pass lifted st over, K1.
Rep 1st–4th rows as required.

Scottish knitting

Scottish knitting is amongst the earliest knitting known in Britain and before the fifteenth century was already an established trade with its own guild in Dundee followed by one opening in Kilmarnock. The hand knitting of stockings became a vary large scale trade; in Aberdeen at the beginning of the nineteenth century the revenue from the stocking industry totalled £100,000. Today, the Scottish knitting heritage can be seen at the exhibitions at the Royal Highland show, near Edinburgh, where fisherman's guernseys, fine hose and the most delicate lace shawls still vie with one another for first place. Each area brings its own contribution, with patterned sock tops surpassing any other, and with gloves so perfect in detail that some have become museum pieces.

In the south, Sanquhar will long be remembered for its small fine check knitting patterns, once used in the making of gloves; unfortunately, even by the eighteenth century the knitting output ceased to be as prolific and today there is little left of the once-thriving industry.

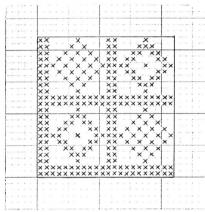

361 Chart for Sanquhar pattern

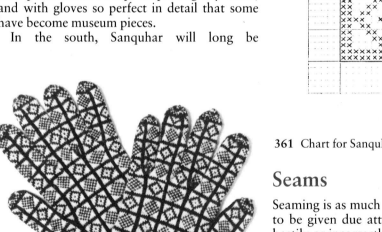

360 Sanquhar gloves

Seams

Seaming is as much a skill as knitting and needs to be given due attention; do not work seams hastily or incorrectly. None of the best methods is difficult, and good knitting deserves the final touch of good making up.

Backstitch seam

The backstitch seam can be used on any edge that is uneven, whether owing to pattern or shaping. It is not invisible and should be kept only for seams that cannot be worked with a less obvious method such as the invisible seam.

A backstitch seam must be worked to give an even line on the finished garment. This requires your watching both sides of the seam to place the needle between the stitches – never through the strands, which makes for unevenness. When working along unshaped edges always follow the line of one vertical line of stitches and on one row of stitches when working across stitches.

To work a backstitch seam
Place both right sides of fabric touching and thread wool needle with matching yarn. Secure end at right side and take needle through to front of fabric one stitch width along edge (fig. 362a).

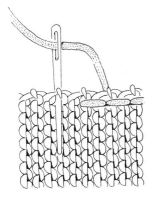

362a Pass needle from back to front a stitch ahead

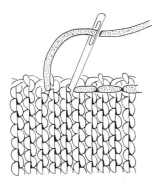

362b Pass needle to back at end of last stitch

Take the needle back to the other side at the beginning of the stitch, that is back along itself (fig. 362b). Repeat this until the seam is finished. Never make a stitch without checking that no yarn has been split with a stitch and that the stitches are in line.

Invisible seam

An invisible seam is invaluable. Particularly on unshaped seams or seams that are shaped inside an edge stitch, draw the stitches on both sides together leaving no sign of the seam on the right side.

At its best on stocking stitch this seam can be adapted for reverse stocking stitch and for garter stitch.

To work an invisible seam
Place both edges facing with the right side uppermost and work the seam on the right side. It can be worked either upwards or downwards, although the diagram shows it being worked upwards.

Secure the yarn at the lower edge, or leave an end to darn into the seam after it is made.

Pass the needle under one strand between stitches on one side and draw the yarn through (see fig. 363).

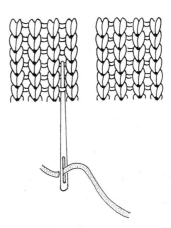

363 Insert needle between first and second stitches under strand

Take the needle across to the other side and lift the strand immediately opposite, again drawing the yarn through (see fig. 364).

Return to the first side and pass the needle under the next strand and then under the next strand on the second side.

As the yarn is drawn up firmly between the two sides the stitches will draw the two edges smoothly together. They should not draw the

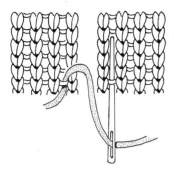

364 Repeat on opposite side

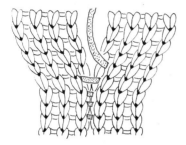

365 Drawing edge firmly together

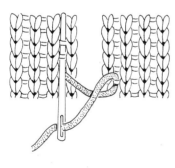

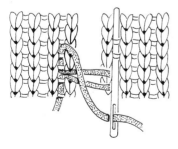

366 Pass needle under two strands

seam smaller than the surrounding stitches but they must be firm enough so that the seamed edges cannot be drawn apart to show the stitches (see fig. 365).

A seam for ribbing

Ribbed edges must be drawn together so that the edge stitches touch and there is no bulky wrong side stitches that can show at lower edge or cuff.

To work a ribbed seam

Place both sections to be seamed together with right sides touching and work the seam on the wrong side.

Secure the yarn at the lower edge.

Insert the threaded wool needle from back to front through both edge stitches, then from front to back through the next stitches, taking the needle through both thicknesses (fig. 367).

Continue to work along the seam in this way, alternating between passing through to the front and to the back, moving one stitch on with each movement until the seam is complete.

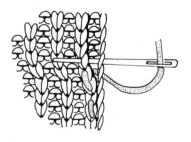

367 Ribbed seam

Layette seam

This seam is particularly good for small baby garments and is intended to be worked where the edge has had the first stitch slipped knitwise on every row and the last stitch knitted (*see* **Edges**).

Place both edges with wrong side facing and secure the yarn at the lower edge or leave an end to be darned into the seam when it is finished.

Lift the small edge bead or knot on one side

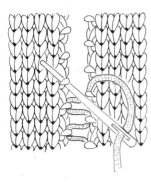

368 Joining slipped stitch edges

and lift the next bead stitch, always entering the stitch from the seam edge on each side. Draw the edges together so that they cannot be pulled apart as the seam is worked (fig. 368).

Seamless knitting

See **Circular knitting.**

Shapes

See **Basic shapes,** also **Medallion knitting.**

Shaping

See **Decreasing knitting,** also **Increasing knitting.**

Shawls

Square, round and triangular shawls have comprised most knitting techniques throughout the years and have also been worked in countless stitch patterns. The Shetland shawl is probably the best known and is a masterpiece of skilled knitting construction; it makes best possible use of both pattern and technique. Old magazines and early knitting books supply other ways of forming a shawl and many were extended ideas culled from medallion knitting.

Square shawls

The Shetland shawl is worked from the lace edge inwards and can present something of a puzzle because it has no obvious cast-on edge. This is, of course, not strictly true, for the lace must begin somewhere. To do this, cast on by the open-edge method, at the narrowest point; the first stitch of the first row can later be grafted to the last row, leaving no trace of a firm, cast-on edge.

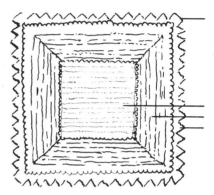

369 Working a square shawl without seams

The next patterned section of the Shetland shawl edges the centre and is picked up along the edge of the lace, often in four separate sections. Worked with an open edge along the sides of the sections, forming a mitre, the edges can be joined, again without an obvious or restricting seam.
For open edges *see* **Edges.**
The centre is an extention of one side and is grafted to the opposite side, while the other two sides are joined to the centre by a unique means of forming what appear to be eyelet holes. This method repeats the same holes made after the start of the centre and just before it is finished off. Again the result shows no seams.
An alternative shawl without seams can be made on medallion lines, working from the centre out and working deliberately without seams. Mitre the corners of the inner lace edge and work off the lace edge by casting on a few stitches at its starting point. Knitting together the last stitch of the lace with a stitch from the inner edge on every alternate row.
To go to the other extreme, a square shawl can also be made by working all three sections, outer

lace, inner edging and centre separately and stitching each together when knitting is complete.

Not all square shawls have so many sections and many no less beautiful shawls can be made by your making a centre and edging only.

Diagonal centres

For square shawls a diagonal centre, patterned or not, has always been popular, possibly because when made with a lace edge, worked by beginning every row with a yon increase, loops are already in place when it comes to sewing on or picking up stitches for an edging. After the total width is formed the yon is retained to match the first half but is followed by a decrease to reduce the shawl back to its corner stitch.

Circular shawls

Circular shawls can be worked on two needles with a seam or without a seam; on a set of needles and a circular needle for the outer wider areas; or on a set of long needles only.

Two needle circles

Worked in rows, a shawl can be made by your casting on the radius of a circle and working in sections or wedges. Gradually, work over more and more stitches until the rows are worked over all the stitches that were cast on. Repeated, the wedges complete a circle and are joined to the first row along the cast-on edge.

Alternatively, a shawl on two needles can be made from the centre out, the work being

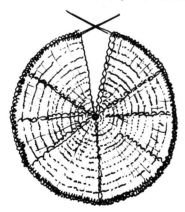

370 Working a circular shawl on two needles

increased to form a circle. The use of a lace increase up the edge, formed by a yarn over needle increase, gives a way of seaming almost invisibly, so that the pattern is not spoilt by the interruption of a noticeable seam. Both of these variations can be edged with lace. Work the lace at the same time as the rows; alternatively, by casting on a few stitches for the start of the lace on the last outer row, working the stitches off by decreasing one stitch from the lace edge with one stitch from the total number of stitches on the outer edge, on alternate rows.

Seamless circles

A circle without seams causes no knitting problems and allows the entire circle for the design, without your having to incorporate the seam. This is the medallion method of forming a shape (*see* **Medallion knitting**).

Triangular shawls

Triangles are easily planned, knitted from the point to the long edge or cast on along the long edge so that the rows gradually become shorter. Edging methods and lace edgings knitted up along the edge can be used in just the same ways as on round or square shawls.

Dressing a shawl

Traditionally, the finishing of a shawl, called the dressing, gives it perfect shape as no amount of pressing can do. Dampened for several hours in a wet towel the shawl was placed on a clean, flat, padded surface and drawn out very carefully until each stitch lay in the perfect position and every lace point was drawn out to its full extent, exactly level with the next. Pinned in this position and allowed to dry at its own speed out of sunlight and direct heat the shawl retained the shape and was soft with every strand of yarn rounded and unflattened by an iron.

Washing

Shawls washed gently in warm water in which soap has already been dissolved, rinsed very thoroughly in warm water, and redressed keep their beauty and usefulness for may years. (*See also* **Shetland knitting**.)

Sheaths and sticks

Sheaths and sticks, fishes and goose quills, feathers and straw, have all been used by knitters at one time or another as a means of anchoring the right-hand needle, leaving the fingers of both hands free to work swiftly at the needle tips where the working area of yarn and stitches takes place.

Sticks of one shape or another were perhaps the most usual form of needle holder used from as early as the late fifteenth or sixteenth century onwards. But the shapes are many and varied as are the forms of decoration. Many, possibly not of local manufacture, are inlaid and skilfully carved, while others have been made by a lad for his lass in a more personal but less skilful style. Twisted or turned, carved and shaped they leave a very distinctive picture of knitters of the past.

Shape was important for speed, and many of the designs are specially adapted to fit into a waistband or cleft to fit over a belt.

Quills were often used, sewn into material covers, or straw was stitched inside a holder to act as a pad. Leather pads are still extensively used in Scandinavia and are to be found in use in Scotland and also in Shetland. The leather is punched to take the needle end, and the pad, stiffened with horsehair, is known as a 'wispa'.

Knitting terminology has also been integrated into colloquial language. When a knitter said he didn't have 'a clue' he was very hard up, for the wooden clue-holder was an accessory onto which the ball, or clue, was hooked so that it could unwind without interference or without rolling on the floor.

Another aid to finding a straying ball, particularly after dark when there was only fire or candle light, was to wind the ball round a goose's dried windpipe. Dried peas were placed in the windpipe and as they rattled against the skin, the knitter could gauge how far the ball had rolled.

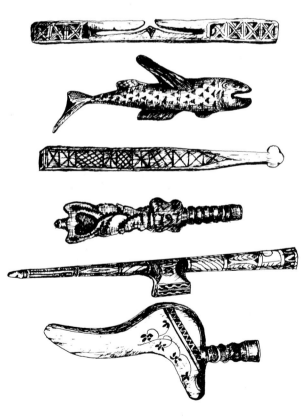

371 Knitting sheaths and sticks

Shetland knitting

For over four hundred years the Shetland Islands, lying midway between Britain and Iceland and closer to Norway than Scotland, have been the home of a thriving hand knitting industrty. Unlike the Outer Hebrides, where weaving takes precedence, knitting has been the mainstay of many homes. In the early years socks and stockings accounted for the main trade, but by the nineteenth century gloves and berets, sweaters and pullovers in the many shaded patterns were predominant. Fair Isle patterns also took their place in fashion, along with fine lace, developed initially for stocking knitting.

Several factors have made Shetland knitting outstanding, each dependent on the other.

Wool

The Shetland sheep provide the wool that, when loosely spun, gives a lightweight yarn. The yarn is available today in many colours, although once only natural sheep colours, of which there are many, were used.

372 Shetlander wearing X and O pattern

The fleece, particularly from the fine neck area of certain sheep, provides wool that can, in very special hands, be spun to incredible fineness. With such fine yarn at their disposal, the islanders desired to knit lace of the most exquisite design, much more ethereal than the lace knitted from the usual island wool.

Ability

The islanders, besides being spurred by economic necessity, possess a long heritage of knitting and an understanding that has grown with their trade. Unspoilt by designers and non-knitters with business acumen, Shetland knitting is, as it has always been, in the hands of the people who make it. Every year consideration goes into every piece of knitting; minute refinements are made for speed – an essential requisite where income is concerned; for garment softness; and to reduce making up.

Finish

With shawls, lace, stockings and soft garments, the finish is accentuated to turn the knitting into a well-presented item for purchase. Whatever the item, it is finished by being thoroughly dampened then stretched to even out fibres and stitches alike. Shawls are threaded on to drying frames, point by point, socks and gloves and stockings are placed over wooden-shaped boards and jerseys and pullovers over a specially-made horse, which can be adjusted for size and width. Then, out of direct sunlight, the breeze from the sea gently dries out the dampness, leaving a perfectly shaped, smooth, untwisted fabric, ready for sale in any part of the world (see fig. 372).

Lace knitting

At the end of the nineteenth century and the early years of the following century the finest of lace knitting reached its peak. Lace knitting graced many a wedding in the form of a bride's veil, became a family heirloom, or was even seen at court as a lace train.

The reputation for the ring shawl, a two metre square (6 ft) shawl that could be drawn through a wedding ring, lives on. Few spinners, today, can achieve the necessary fineness: two cobweb-like strands must be twisted together to make a yarn, seemingly no thicker than a hair. (For constructions of shawls without the bulk of cast on edges see **Shawls**.)

Lace patterns

The lace patterns used for the ring shawls belong to the knitters themselves, and have not been turned into instructions. They are, however, based on simple lace techniques, on faggot patterns and eyelets, single, double and multiple increases and decreases. Often worked in garter stitch, only the more complex use patterning on both sides of the work. The majority are essentially knittable like 'feather and fan' with all its varied arrangements and related patterns.

The names of some of the patterns have also caused controversy and confusion. Some names clearly indicate the shape of the stitch – such as cat's paw or feather and fan stitches; others have been more misleading. When a Shetlander proudly showed a pattern to her students which she called 'old shale' they thought that she was describing a pattern that depicted the curve of the wave left on the beach. In fact, they had misunderstood her dialect, since the pattern was meant to depict a shell. In this way, other patterns have been misnamed and recorded for posterity, despite inaccuracies or misinterpretations.

Short rows
See **Darts**.

Silk
See **Yarns**.

Silk knitting

Silk knitting was first carried out on the continent and reached Britain with the arrival of knitted silk stockings. Compared with hose made from wool, stockings were far superior and held in high demand by those who could afford them. Silk knitting is thought to have been at its height in the seventeenth century; perhaps the most famous example, of its use as a garment is the vest worn by Charles I at his execution in 1649. The vest is the only silk example in a British museum, although thought to be British, some experts suggest that it is Italian, following on the earlier and much less perfect silk knitting from Italy. In Norway there are several examples of similar vests, knitted in brocade-patterned turquoise silk, some with gilt or silver embroidery at the neck. In the Kundstindustrimuseet in Oslo these garments of the same high standard as the London vest or shirt, have been attributed to England but originated from Denmark, where there was an organized knitting trade. Today silk is still used, mostly with other yarns, or in couture boutique-designed wear.

Skirts

See **Basic shapes.**

Sleeves

See **Basic shapes.**

Slip knot

A slip knot is the means by which the first loop for casting on is made.

To work a slip knot

Hold the yarn in your left hand, no nearer the end of the yarn than 20cm (8 in.) and twist the

373a Make a loop and draw strand through centre

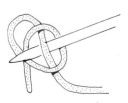

373b Place loop on needle and draw it up firmly

yarn to form a loop, with the end to the ball crossing the back of the loop (fig. 373a). With a knitting needle, slip the tip under the strand across the loop and draw the strand through as a loop over the needle tip. Draw it up to fit the needle (see fig. 373b).

Slipped stitches

Stitches that are slipped are passed from the left needle to the right without being worked, the yarn being passed either behind or in front of the slipped unworked stitch. Slipped stitches are used in several different ways:

- as part of a decrease
- in pattern making
- with the yarn across the front of the stitch to be seen on the right side of the work
- with the yarn on the wrong side so that it cannot be seen on the right side

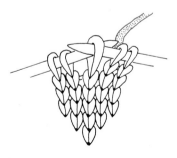

374a Slip stitch purlwise when it is to be worked on the following row

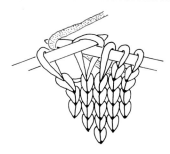

374b Slip stitch knitwise when it is to be part of a decrease

Decreases

When a slipped stitch is used for a decrease it is always slipped knitwise for knit stitches and purlwise for purl stitches.

For methods or working slipped decreases, single and double, *see* **Decreasing**.

Pattern forming

Stitches that are not being decreased or removed from the fabric but are to be worked again on the following row are always slipped purlwise on knit rows and knitwise on purl rows.

To work a slipped stitch

Work to the stitch to be slipped, hold the yarn on the wrong side of the fabric and slip the next stitch purlwise from left needle to right needle without working it, then complete the row.

If the yarn across the stitch is intended to be seen on the right side the yarn is held at the front (or on the right side) while the stitch is slipped.

Self-coloured patterns

When the pattern is to be worked in one colour only the slipped stitches may be used for several reasons:

Vertically arranged

Stitches that are slipped with the yarn on the wrong side form stitches that are longer than the stitches on either side and therefore stand out from the background. This makes a design feature and forms patterns like fig 375 (*Top*) which shows ridged rib (for working instructions *see* **Slipped stitch patterns**).

375 (*Top*) Ridged rib with yarn behind slipped stitch. (*Bottom*) Scallop stitch with yarn carried across right side

Horizontally arranged

Passing the yarn across the front of the fabric where it can be seen alters the appearance and gives a strand which is used in pattern forming as in scallop stitch fig. 375 (*Bottom*), for working instructions *see* **Surface stitches**. A pattern designed with right side strands can also be seen in fig. 376.

Add colour

Colour added to slipped-stitch patterns opens up vast possibilities for stitch patterns, whether the yarn is carried across the right side or hidden on the wrong side.

376 (*Top*) Woven herringbone pattern.
(*Bottom*) Mock ribbing

Lengthened slipped stitches

A slipped stitch need not be carried up over only two rows. Lengthened by having the yarn wound more than once round the tip and dropped in later rows allows stitches to be placed in very different places.

Slipped stitch patterns

Slipped stitches are used to form patterns in many ways, with elongated vertical stitches, with yarn carried in one colour over another colour, with strands of yarn across the front of the stitch like a woven fabric, or with coloured strands carried to new positions.

Ridged rib (see fig. 375 *Top*)

This simple slipped stitch pattern is only the starting point for many other patterns based on self-coloured stitches that are slipped, keeping the yarn on the wrong side.
Worked over a number of stitches divisible by 5, plus 4.
1st and 3rd rows (RS facing) K4, * sl1 with yarn at back, K4, rep from * to end.
2nd row P4, * sl1 with yarn forward, P4, rep from * to end.
4th row P.
Rep 1st–4th rows as required.

Woven herringbone pattern

All pattern making is a matter of adding light and shade to a basic fabric, by strands, nobbles, lines or twists. In this pattern two tones are very noticeable (fig. 376a).
Worked over a number of stitches divisible by 4, plus 2.
1st row (RS facing), K2, * sl2 with yarn forward, K2, rep from * to end.
2nd row P1, * sl2 with yarn back, P2, rep from * to last st, P1.
3rd row Sl2 with yarn forward, * K2, sl2 with yarn forward, rep from * to end.
4th row P3, * sl2 with yarn back, P2, rep from * to last 3 sts, sl2 with yarn back, P1.
5th–8th rows Rep 1st–4th rows once.
9th row As 3rd row.
10th row As 2nd row.
11th row As 1st row.
12th row As 4th row.
13th–16th row Rep 9th–12th rows.
Rep 1st–16th rows as required.

Mock ribbing

Without any of the elasticity of real ribbing, this makes a warm fabric for outdoor clothes (fig. 376b).
Worked over number of stitches divisible by 4 plus 2.
1st row (WS facing) K2, * P2, K2, rep from * to end.
2nd row P2, * sl2 with yarn forward, P2, rep from * to end.
Rep 1st and 2nd rows as required.

Dice check pattern (see colour plate 9(a))

This check, which is very popular for working in endless colour schemes, shows how slipped stitches can be used to hide all the threads carried across stitches on the wrong side of the work. Worked over a number of stitches divisible by 4, plus 2.

Cast on using A.

1st row (WS facing) With A, P.

2nd row With B, K1, sl1 with yarn back, * K2, sl2, with yarn back, rep from * to last 4 sts, K2 sl1, K1.

3rd row With B, P1, sl1 with yarn forward, * P2, sl2 with yarn forward, rep from * to last 4 sts, P2 sl1 with yarn forward, P1.

4th row with A, K.

5th row With C, P2, * sl2 with yarn forward, P2, rep from * to end.

6th row With C, K2, * sl2 with yarn back, K2, rep from * to end

Rep 1st–6th rows as required.

Cross colour stripe

A texture that will appeal to many and that is rather fun to knit. Worked in strongly contrasting colours, it makes a bold pattern but can be muted in tones of one colour or cream with a pastel shade.

Worked over a number of stitches divisible by 14, plus 9.

Cast on with A.

Preparation row With A, K.

1st row (RS facing), with B, K1, * sl1 with yarn back, K5, [sl1 with yarn back, K3] twice, rep from * to last 8 sts, sl1 with yarn back, K5, sl1 with yarn back, K1.

2nd row With B, K1, * sl1 with yarn forward, K5, [sl1 with yarn forward, P3] twice, rep from * to last 8 sts, sl1 with yarn forward, K5, sl1 with yarn forward, K1.

3rd row With A, K1, * [K3, sl1 with yarn back] twice, K5, sl1 with yarn back, rep from * to last 8 sts, K3, sl1 with yarn back, K4.

4th row With A, K1, * [P3, sl1 with yarn forward] twice, K5, sl1 with yarn forward, rep from * to last 8 sts, P3, sl1 with yarn forward, P3, K1.

Rep 1st–4th rows as required.

Barred stripe

This is a small pattern but uses the strand on the right side in an interesting way (fig. 377 *Top*). Worked over a number of stitches divisible by 4, plus 2.

Cast on with A.

Preparation row With A, P.

1st row (RS facing), With B, K1, * sl2 with yarn forward, K2, rep from * to last st, K1.

2nd row With B, K1, * P2, sl2 with yarn forward, rep from * to last st, K1.

3rd row With A, K3, * sl2 with yarn forward, K2, rep from * to last 3 sts, sl2 with yarn forward, K1.

4th row With A, K1, * sl2 with yarn forward, P2, rep from * to last st, K1.

Rep 1st–4th rows as required.

377 (*Top*) Barred stripes.
(*Bottom*) Thick and thin checked pattern

Thick- and thin-checked pattern

In this, the reverse form of slipped stitches from the previous pattern are shown. All the strands are kept to the wrong side and the colours show A on B and B on A (see fig. 377 *Bottom*).
Worked over a number of stitches divisible by 4, plus 3.
1st row (WS facing) With A, P.
2nd and 4th rows With B, K3, * sl1 with yarn back, K3, rep from * to end.
3rd row With B, P3, * sl1 with yarn forward, P3, rep from * to end.
5th row With B, P.
6th, 7th and 8th rows With A, rep 2nd, 3rd and 4th rows.
Rep 1st–8th rows as required.

Smocked knitting

See **Tied stitches**

Socks and stockings

Stocking knitters have been at work for at least five centuries. Through the years stockings have been made of every type, from coarse worsted stockings to loosely-knitted enormous stockings known by children as 'elephant' stockings, which were 'fulled' or shrunk to the correct size, giving a hard wearing, near-waterproof fabric. Stockings have been knitted in silk for the influential and wealthy and in the finest wool and lace stitches to the dictates of fashion. Stocking knitters also made their own long white funeral stockings, which were placed beneath their shrouds when they laid down their needles for the last time; then they were ready for the journey to where, in the words of a small Dales boy, 'it's a' Sundays and n'a knitting'.

In Greece and Estonia, in Turkey, and as far away as Tibet, coloured-patterned stockings blaze with the brilliance of the yarns, while in central Europe the shapely stockings of Bavaria, Germany and Austria carry intricately woven patterns reminiscent of early Celtic interwoven designs.

Knitting socks and stockings

Naturally, with stockings from every point of the compass there are as many ways of knitting them, from the toe up or the top down, with heels added after the sock is complete, picking up stitches from a held opening (see **Held openings**), or worked without seam, shaped in every section like a second skin.

Proportions

The proportion of a stocking that is to be seen, as in knee length stockings, is important. A patterned flap that is deep dwarfs the leg, while a narrow turnover looks as if it were a mistake better omitted.

Approximately 7-10cm (3-4 in.) is deep enough for the patterned area, which is best edged narrowly with rib or a decorative edge such as a picot hem.

Socks without turnovers are twice the length of the foot to the base of the top ribbing, which might be 7-10cm long. Boys' knee length stockings are twice the length of the foot to the top edge with any fold back top unfolded. An adult knee length stocking with patterned fold over top is three times the foot length plus the patterned top. As a rough guide the leg shaping begins the depth from the top equal to the length of the foot.

Shape

Shape can be dealt with in many ways, the leg is usually shaped on both sides of a centre back seam stitch. The type of leg determines the number of increases, for the sock of an adult man with a well-muscled calf requires more shaping from knee to a slim ankle than that for a young boy whose leg may still be almost straight.

No shaping

Diagonal rib has also been used to make socks and stockings without any shaping above the toe. Worked round the rib, it expands sufficiently to cover leg curves and heel, although is much less comfortable than a well-made heel, instep and leg.

Patterned flaps

The patterns used for stocking tops could easily fill a book on their own and are often ingenious examples of the knitters' skill and ingenuity (see fig. 378 or the deer's head and antlers in fig. 379, a pattern worked in the north of Scotland).

Diced and ribbed patterns are always popular, and rib is often used, not only for the turnover top, but in a simpler related form for the leg of the stocking as well.

Cable patterns and twisted stitch are also used, and many Austrian and Bavarian patterns use patterns like figs 16 and 19.

378 Sock top pattern: Scottish entrelacs pattern

Knitted-in garters

Beneath a turnover top, at least 2-3cm (1 in.) of ribbing, often worked on finer needles, grips the top of the leg.

379 Sock top pattern: deer's head pattern

Seam stitches

After the flap and top ribbing are worked, change to larger needles and work a seam stitch, placed in the centre back, to the heel; work any shaping on either side of it using paired decreases, (*see* Paired decreases in **Decreasing knitting**).

Heels

The heel is worked by dividing the stitches, half on two needles to be used for the front upper section of the foot and the other half plus the seam stitch on one needle. The seam stitch must be in the centre of the heel, which is knitted on two needles for its required depth. Because of the amount of friction on the heel of any sock, the flap should be strengthened. This can be done by adding a strand of the same yarn like a woven stitch (*see* **Woven stitches**). In this way it is never knitted in but bends in front of or behind alternate stitches. A more usual pattern is made by slipping stitches with the yarn on the wrong side. The first stitch of every row should also be slipped to form a chain edge, ready for picking up stitches for the instep.
The slipped stitch pattern is worked as follows:
1st row Sl1 knitwise, * K1, sl1 purlwise with yarn on wrong side, rep from * to last 2 sts, K2.
2nd row Sl1 purlwise, P to end.
The heel flap should be as long as it is wide when finished.

Turning the heel

To change the direction of the knitting from the leg to the foot it is necessary to turn the heel; this can be done in many different ways. The most usual method is to work from a narrow base until the heel width is taken up, roughly the shape of an actual heel.

Round heel

Over a heel of 29 stitches this can be worked as follows:
1st row K17, sl1 knitwise, K1, psso, turn.
2nd row P6, P2 tog, turn.
3rd row K7, sl1 knitwise, K1, psso, turn.
4th row P8, P2, tog, turn. Continue in this way,

always taking together the last stitch of the heel with one more stitch from the side, unworked stitches before every turn. Work until all the heel stitches have become part of the turned, shaped section. Now work the stitches picked up along the sides and, with the stitches left for the foot top, work the foot.

Dutch heel

The Dutch heel, also a very useful version, is square and has the same number of stitches on every row. It can be made any width but the example below is worked over 29 stitches.
1st row Work to the centre stitch and then knit 5 stitches beyond, sl1 knitwise, K1, psso, turn.
2nd row Sl1 knitwise, P11, P2 tog, turn.
3rd row Sl1 knitwise, K11, sl1 knitwise, K1, psso, turn.
4th row Sl 1 knitwise, P11, P2 tog, turn.
Rep 3rd and 4th rows until all the heel stitches are worked.

Side gussets

The gussets are formed by picking up stitches from the sides of the heel flap, taking the inner loop of each stitch. Draw the stitches tightly together, particularly at needle joins so that holes are not formed. The stitches are picked up along one side of the heel, the stitches left on the two needles are worked across and the round is completed by your picking up a similar number of stitches along the other side of the heel flap.

The stitches are usually re-arranged so that half the heel stitches and those picked up are on two needles and the remaining stitches are on the third.

The gusset decreases can now be worked at the end of the first needle and the beginning of the third needle and are best worked at least one stitch from the end of the needle.

The decreases are worked until both the needles holding picked-up stitches together equal the number of stitches on the other needle.

Foot

Once this number of stitches has been reached the foot can be worked in rounds until it is the required length, minus the length necessary for working the toe decreasing. Particularly in a patterned stocking, the foot may not be worked in rounds. In this case pick up the gusset stitches at each side of the heel and the decreases in just the same way, but working upper and lower foot separately to the toe. This allows the pattern to be kept constant to the toe area, but gives a smooth stocking stitch foot, comfortable to walk in. It does, however, mean seaming the sides of the foot once the stitches are decreased for the toe.

Toe

Again stitches may need to be rearranged so that the instep needle holds twice the number of stitches on the other two needles.

The decreases for the toe may depend on the shape of the toe but are most usually worked on alternate rounds. They are placed one stitch in from the end of the first needle; one stitch in from both ends of the instep needle; and one stitch in from the beginning of the third needle, when the start of the round is still in the centre of the sole. When the correct length, graft the toe to join it without having a bulky, irritating toe seam.

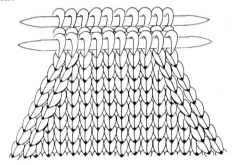

380a Flat toe shaping

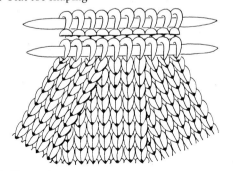

380b Six section toe

Alternative toe shaping

Shorter toe areas can be worked by arranging the decreases more often along the round.

Worked in line with each other the decreases can look like fig. 380b, the number of stitches between the decreases becoming one less on every decrease round; in the diagram they are shown on alternate rounds but for an even shorter toe can be worked on every round. In fig. 381 they are placed eight times round the toe and are not worked in line giving a more haphazard appearance.

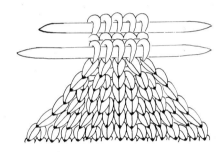

381 Four section toe

Grafting

Toes are grafted in the same way as stocking stitch grafting except that the initial movement differs. This is due to the toes being worked over two sides of knitting that are already in progress, instead of two sections, both of which have edge stitches.

To work the preparation stitches

Place all the stitches on two needles, equally divided.

Have the points at the right edge with the yarn from the back needle and thread the tail of yarn into a wool needle.

* Insert the wool needle through the first stitch on the front needle as if to purl the stitch and leave the stitch on the knitting needle.

Insert the wool needle through the first stitch on the back needle as if to knit, leaving the stitch on the needle. The rest of the casting off is worked as given for stocking stitch casting off

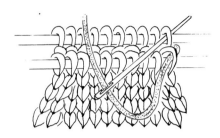

382 Toe grafting

(see **Grafting**) and is repeated from the * until all the stitches have been joined.

Draw the end through the last stitch and darn into the wrong side of the work, trimming off any yarn left.

Spanish knitting

Spanish knitting is reputed to be the source for much British knitting, but there seem to have been many influences from north and east, other than through the route from Arabia, along the southern coast of the Mediterranean and Spain.

The Spaniards, in turn, seem to have been influenced by the Moors, and some of the small Spanish coloured patterns bear resemblance to Moorish art, textiles and mosaic or tile patterns.

In the tomb of Fernando de la Cerda at Burgos near Castille, pillows were found with skilful knitted covers made of silk and patterned in green and purple, white and gold. As Fernando de la Cerda died in about AD 1275 the knitting must date before that time.

Liturgical gloves, often with gold trimming, were also imported from Spain, and there are references to Pope Innocent IV being clad in knitted gloves at his burial in 1254. Amongst other items, gloves were also found in the tomb of the Bishop of Ross in Fortrose Cathedral on the Black Isle, north of Inverness, and were made during the fourteenth century.

Later, Spanish lace became both fine and much treasured and many of the lace patterns that were traditionally used in Spain live on today (see **Spanish stitch patterns**).

Spanish stitch patterns

Spanish stitch patterns are amongst the oldest and most beautiful, although not always the most used today. Their beauty may lie in the fact that pattern is often worked on both rows, right and wrong side rows, and is therefore thought of as being more difficult.

Antique diamond pattern

Based on garter stitch this ancient pattern must be worked in a fine yarn (fig. 383a).

Worked over a number of stitches divisible by 10, plus 1.

1st row (RS facing) K1, * yon, SSK, K5, K2 tog, yon, K1, rep from * to end.

2nd row P1, * P1, yon, P2 tog, K3, P2 tog tbl, yon, P2, rep from * to end.

383 (*Top*) Antique diamond pattern.
(*Bottom*) Madeira mesh pattern

3rd row K1, * K2, yon, SSK, K1, K2 tog, yon, K3, rep from * to end.
4th row K1, * K2, P1, yon, P3 tog, yon, P1, K3, rep from * to end.
5th row K1, * K2, K2 tog, yon, K1, yon, SSK, K3, rep from * to end.
6th row K1, * K1, P2 tog tbl, yon, P3, yon, P2 tog,K2, rep from * to end.
7th row K1, * K2 tog, yon, K5, yon, SSK, K1, rep from * to end.
8th row P2 tog, * yon, P1, K5, P1, yon, P3 tog, rep from * to last 9 sts, yon, P1, K5, P1, yon, P2 tog.
Rep 1st–8th rows as required.

Madeira mesh

This lace pattern is a traditional Spanish lace and is a contrast to the many laces which have lace holes but no textural interest (fig. 383b).
Worked over a number of stitches divisible by 6, plus 7.
1st–6th rows K2, * yon, P3 tog, yon, K3, rep from * to last 5 sts, yon, P3 tog, yon, K2.
7th–12th rows K2, * K3, yon, P3 tog, yon, rep from * to last 5 sts, K5.
Rep 1st–12th rows as required.

Stripes

Stripes are one of the easiest ways of adding colour to a plain garment. They can be random or controlled, wide or narrow, over all, or in small sections or even worked in patchwork fashion.

Stripes on stocking stitch

On the smooth side of stocking stitch a row of contrast makes a neat line and can be made wider at will for the required effect (fig. 384a).

384a Stocking stitch stripes

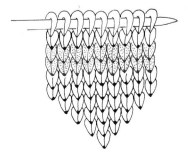

Stripes on reverse stocking stitch

Worked on reverse stocking stitch, the added row of colour is broken by loops of the original colour.

If two rows are worked together, each outer edge will be a broken line showing the original colour inside it and the ridge where the two lines of contrast meet will give a solid effect (fig. 384b). A design feature can be made of this broken row of loops, or you can avoid the effect by working one knit row on reversed stocking stitch before continuing with the contrast colour in reverse stocking stitch as before (fig. 384c). Similarly, work a purl row if the contrast is joining in on the right side in stocking stitch.

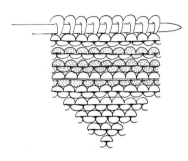

384b Reverse stocking stitch stripes

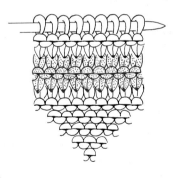

384c Uneven stripes avoided by use of knitted row

It is not, however, necessarily wrong to join so that the contrast loops show; it simply forms another type of stripe and can give greater contrast when used along with smooth-edge stripes.

Ribbed stripes

Stripes worked on ribbing will have the same effect. On knit rows or lines they will give a smooth joining line and over vertical purl stitches will show an uneven line, linked with the original colour (fig. 385a). This can be used deliberately or can be removed by working the first row of the new colour as a knit row over knit and purl stitches, before returning to the rib. The final row of the colour, or the first row on which the original is again used, must be treated in the same way (fig. 385b).

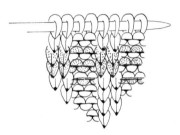

385a   Uneven stripes in rib

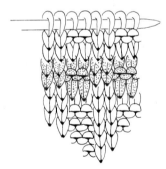

385b   Avoided by use of knit row

Working stripes on round knitting

Stripes worked on round knitting can be as wide as you like or consist of only one round, but the original yarn must be ready to be lifted at the beginning of the next round for which it is required. This is because the end of the round and the beginning of the next round are close together.

Yarn twisted at the start of the round with other colours used throughout the knitting will be carried up the inside as the knitting is worked and will be at hand when required.

Working stripes on flat knitting

Stripes on rows of knitting cannot be worked quite so easily because a new colour worked once over an odd number of rows will be at the wrong end of the work if the other colours or colour are worked over an even number of rows. Colours can still be carried up the side of the work by being twisted with other colours until they are required; but, unless the yarn is to be broken off and rejoined, two-colour stripes must be worked in even numbers.

Avoiding constant yarn breaks

When you are working in narrow stripes and the colour is constantly broken because it is at the wrong end of the needles, slip the stitches onto a circular needle and begin at the end where the coloured yarn you need is. When the yarn is at the same end as the other yarn when a row is finished, the needles are turned in the usual way and the next row is worked.

Wide stripes

Very wide stripes can be worked without the yarn being carried up the side. Join in a new colour several stitches before the end of the yarn before it and twist them on every stitch to anchor the new yarn. On the next row use the new yarn, twisting the previous yarn and the new yarn over each other for the first few stitches. Then the previous yarn can be cut off and there will be no endless darning in of ends when the actual knitting is complete.

Patchwork stripes

Where stripes are to stop and start during the working of a row, treat as for coloured knitting and twist every colour over the next at colour joins or changes.

Surface stitches

Strands of yarn or complete stitches are used in many patterns to decorate the surface of knitting. You may work these using several different techniques, lifting stitches over other stitches, drawing stitches through from the wrong side, or lifting strands that have been left on the right side just for this purpose. These techniques may sound complex but all are easy to work and should be no drawback to you when you attempt to knit the patterns.

Quilted lattice

This is a self-coloured lattice that leaves a strand on the right side ready to be lifted and worked into place on the next right side row (fig. 386 *Top*). The diagrams show the way in which this is worked.

Worked over a number of stitches divisible by 6, plus 3.

1st row (WS facing), P.
2nd row K2, * sl5 with yarn forward, K1, rep from * to last st, K1.
3rd row P
4th row K4, * insert needle under strand across front of work and K next st under strand, K5, rep from *, ending last rep K4 in place of K5.
5th row P1, sl3 with yarn back, * P1, sl5 with yarn back, rep from * to last 5 sts, P1, sl3 with yarn back, P1.
6th row K.
7th row P.
8th row K1, * insert needle under strand across front of work and K next st under strand, K5, rep from * ending last repeat K1 in place of K5.
9th row P2, * sl5 with yarn back, P1, rep from * to last st, P1.
10th row K.
Rep 3rd–10th rows as required, finishing the pattern after a 4th or 8th row.

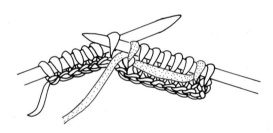

387a Working second row

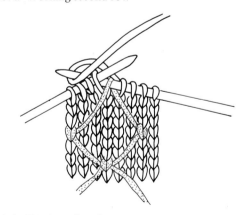

387b Working fourth row

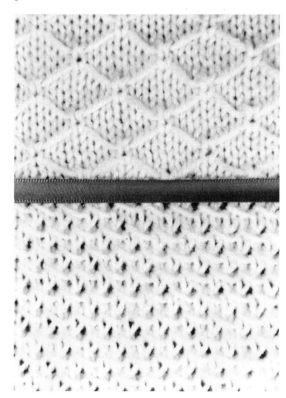

386 (*Top*) Quilted lattice pattern.
(*Bottom*) Barred blocks

Scallop stitch (see fig. 375 *Bottom*)

This pattern is created in the easiest possible way, by your leaving strands on the right side exactly where they are wanted. They are left after you have worked slipped stitches, and many other patterns can be made in the same way. It is also very easy to build up patterns in two or more colours using the colour for the slipped row only and returning to the background colour for the other rows.

Worked over a number of stitches divisible by 5, plus 2.

1st and every alt row (WS facing), P.
2nd row K.
4th, 6th and 8th rows P2, * sl3 with yarn forward, P2, rep from * to end.
10th row As 2nd row.
Rep 1st–10th rows as required.

Barred blocks

The strand in this pattern is not left in place as the row is worked but is lifted over three other stitches in just the same way that a slipped stitch is lifted over a knit stitch in a SKPO decrease (fig. 386b).

Worked over a number of stitches.

1st and every alt row (WS facing), P.
2nd row K1, * yon K2, pass yon over the 2 sts just knitted and off the needle tip using the left needle tip to lift the stitch up and over, rep from * to last st, K1.
4th row * yon, K2, pass yon over the 2 sts just knitted and off the needle tip using the left needle tip to lift the stitch up and over, rep from * to end.

Two-colour dip stitch

Here two factors are used to make the pattern. Purled loops on the right side contrast against the background colour, and the shapes are drawn together by your bringing a stitch or loop of yarn through from the wrong side to the right side.

Worked over a number of stitches divisible by 8, plus 3.

1st and 3rd rows (WS facing), With B, P.

2nd and 4th rows With B, K.
5th row With A, K.
6th row With A, K1, * insert right needle from front under the purled loop of the next st 6 rows below, K an extra st in this loop and then K a st in the st on the left needle and with the left needle lift the 2nd last st on the right needle over the last st and off the right needle tip, K7, rep from *, ending last rep K1.
7th–10th rows With B, rep 1st–4th rows.
11th row With A, K.
12th row With A, K5, rep from * as given for 6th row to last 5 sts, K5.
Rep 1st–12th rows as required.

Contrast shell stitch

This is another pattern that draws a loop through from the wrong side. The difference is that to make even, long stitches a crochet hook is used, not to work crochet stitches but simply to make the finished stitch more even and the entire pattern easier to knit (colour plate 10(b)).

Worked over a number of stitches divisible by 14, plus 2.

Cast on with A.

Preparation row K.
1st, 2nd, 3rd, 4th, 5th and 6th rows With B, K.
7th row (RS facing) With A, K9, * [insert crochet hook into the front of the st 5 rows below the 3rd st along the left needle and draw through a long loop and place it on the right needle, K next st on left needle] 6 times, taking all 6 loops from the same st 5 rows below, K8, rep from *, ending last rep K1 in place of K8.
8th row With A, K1, * [P2 tog tbl] 3 times, P1, [P2 tog] 3 times, K7, rep from * to last st, K1.
9th, 10th, 11th, 12th, 13th and 14th rows With B, K.
15th row With A, K2, rep from * of 7th row to end.
16th row With A, K8, * [P2 tog tbl] 3 times, P1, [P2 tog] 3 times, K7, rep from *, ending last rep K1 in place of K6.
Rep 1st–16th rows as required.

Swedish knitting

Sweden's contribution to knitting is large and varied, unusual for a country also involved in weaving and embroidery. Early knitting history is difficult to ascertain, for like Finland, Swedish knitters used a coiling method to make thick woollen garments, making the need for knitting less important.

Coloured knitting

Each area in Sweden where knitting was dominant had its own characteristic, sometimes reflecting the local weaving or embroidery. In the extreme north small brilliant patterns seem to be knitted extensions of the vivid woven braids, while in the south east patterns are so very like early Fair Isle patterns that one wonders which came first or whether their similarily is incidental (see fig. 388).

From the extreme south came thick fisherman's sweaters worked in the natural yarn patterned with dyed wool in the same pinkish light purple colour found in the Faroe Islands,

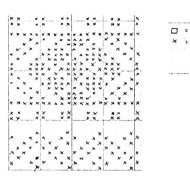

389 Chart for Swedish pattern

while from a less rural area came patterned sleeves and large counterpoint designs worked into jacket fabrics.

Caps

Swedish caps are a delight and traditionally made in many patterns, all of which are double, self-lined and therefore very comfortable to wear. With their thick, folded-back brims, they fit the head better and are warmer than other caps.

Begun at one end, the lining is worked in one colour and the pattern begins less than half way to the other end so that it shows on the turned-back brim. The patterns are banded and extend from brim to tip, often swirling round the top decreasing (fig. 390).

388 Swedish pattern from Halland area

390 Swedish cap

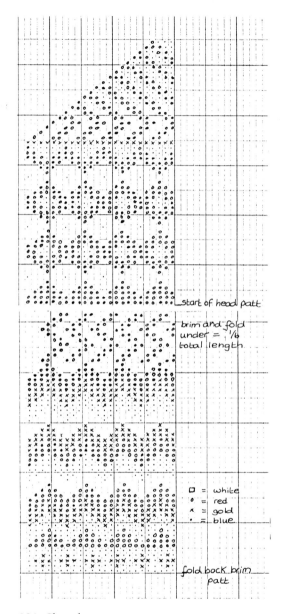

391 Chart for cap pattern

The fiddle player's cap or spelemansmossa is traditionally worked with a cream lining, patterned in white, gold, red and blue and charted in a repeat that gives the sectional pattern for the top, formed by decreasing. The top is trimmed with a large multicoloured pompon or a pompon attached to a cord and stitched to the centre top.

Cottage industry

As in other countries Swedes knitted to add to their incomes as well as clothe their families. Many old illustrations show the same busy life as found in the rural, knitting areas of England and Wales during the late eighteenth and early nineteenth century when people filled up any spare time with knitting, as they walked to market or to the fields, when they visited, or gathered round the fire on a winter's night.

This industry has lived on into the twentieth century; nowadays, the knitting is centrally organized to keep crafts alive and to create markets for the sale of high quality goods made by outworkers in their homes.

Swedish knitters also work two-end knitting, which is unlike knitting anywhere; two strands of yarn are used at the same time so an even self-coloured fabric is made. The fabric formed is warmer than single yarn knitting and was widely used for gloves, mittens and socks (fig. 392).

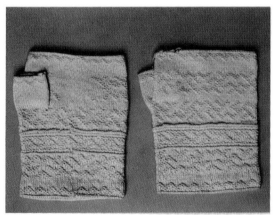

392 Two-end patterns

Two-end knitting

To cast on with two separate strands of yarn, by the thumb method, placing a slip knot in each yarn on the right needle (see figs 393a and b).

The diagrams show the movements in two colours but the actual knitting is carried out using two strands of the same yarn.

The third stitch is made by using the yarn and tail from the first slip knot (fig. 394a).

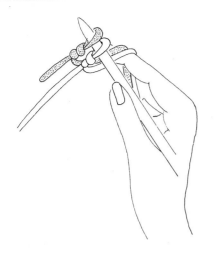

393a Place two slip knots on needle

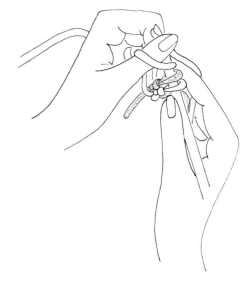

394a Use first yarn for third stitch

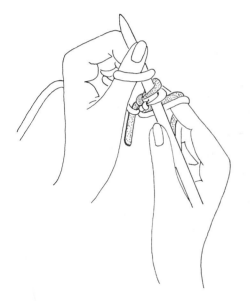

nd first yarn round thumb

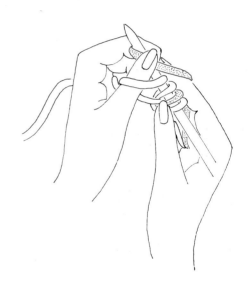

394b Use second yarn for fourth stitch

395a Continue for required number of stitches

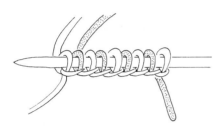

395b Finished cast on edge

The fourth stitch uses the yarn and tail of the second slip knot (fig. 394b).

Other stitches are made in the same way, by your alternating first one end and tail and then the other (figs 395a and b).

To knit
The stitches are worked in the usual way but both strands of yarn are controlled by the right hand, one over the first finger the other over the next finger tip (fig. 396a).

396a Work knitwise on all stitches with alternate yarns

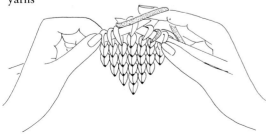

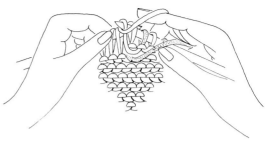

396b Work in same way purlwise

The one yarn is always carried over the other and alternate stitches are knitted with the same yarn.

When worked in rows the same applies to the purl row (fig. 396b).

In round knitting, stocking stitch is made using only knit stitches, purl stitches being used in pattern making.

Patterning
Patterns are made on the self-coloured fabric by your using the same two strands required for knitting. Work purl stitches on the knitted stocking stitch and accentuate it by carrying one yarn across the right side instead of the wrong side of the knitting.

Lines of ridges
A line of ridges on the right side is made by working the round in this way:
P the 1st st leaving yarn forward, with 2nd end K next st, P 3rd stitch with yarn left on right side, K 4th stitch with the yarn from the previous K st left at back. Continue in this way to the round end (fig. 397a).

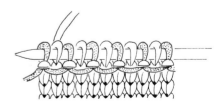

397a One yarn in front and one on the back

When a 2nd round is worked, reverse the stitches that are purled and knitted, so that a strand of yarn is taken across the stitch which

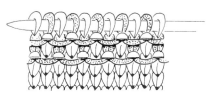

397b Alternated stitches on front

was purled in the previous round. The pattern will look like fig. 397b.

Rounds worked in this way over several rounds give a honeycomb pattern or woven slip stitch appearance (fig. 397c). Sock tops and glove and mitten gauntlets or wrist bands were often decorated with small motifs using this same purled technique, where the strand was carried on the right side before being returned to the wrong side after a second purled stitch.

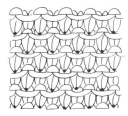

397c Finished self-coloured effect

Building a diamond begins with a single strand between two purl stitches (fig. 398a). The yarn used for the purled stitches is taken to the wrong side after the second stitch is worked, and the yarns are again alternated on the wrong side.

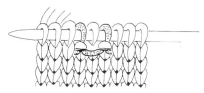

398a Strand on right side between purled stitches

On the second round, the first purl stitch is worked one stitch before the last round and is repeated so that two strands are left on the right side between three purl stitches (fig. 398b). On the following round the number of purl stitches becomes four but three stitches are worked in the centre knitwise.

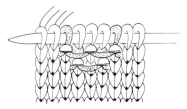

398b Wider second row

This round is worked as follows:
Work to 1 st before the 1st P st of previous round, take yarn to right side and P 1 st, K next st with other yarn still on wrong side, P next st with front yarn and take it back, K next 3 sts alternating yarns then take 1 yarn forward, P next stitch leaving the yarn forward, K 1 st with the back yarn, P next st with the front yarn and take it back, and complete the round alternating the yarn and knitting all the stitches (fig. 398c).

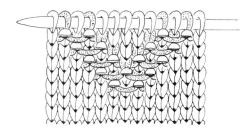

398c Building up motif

The finished effect is shown without the second colour in fig. 399.

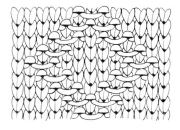

399 Finished self-coloured motif

Adapting for two needles

The adaptation is quite easy for working on two needles.

The *1st row* is worked as already given.

On the *next row* the stitch that would have been purled if on a round becomes a knit stitch and yarn to show on the right side is taken onto the right side before a knit stitch and is left there until after the following knit stitch.

Swiss darning

See **Embroidered knitting**

Tassels

Tassels, large or tiny, make a good finish to a cord or mitten ties and can be used to decorate garments or add a colourful touch to zipper ends.

Small tassels

Small tassels can be made by your winding yarn round several fingers but are tied and finished in the same way as large tassels.

Large tassels

The depth of the tassel is determined by the width of the card round which the yarn is wound and the number of strands round the card control whether it is to be lean and sleek or fat and bushy.

Cut a strip of firm card and wind the yarn round and round it, over the start of the yarn until there are sufficient strands. Cut off a long end and thread it into a wool needle. Thread the needle under the strands on one side of the card.

401 Making tassels

Take this strand over the top and under all the strands two or three times.

If the tassel is to be added to a cord it can be sewn through the cord end each time it is taken over the top of the tassel.

Slip the tassel off the card and draw the top firmly into shape, then take the yarn round the tassel just below the top, linking the yarn under itself to hold the yarn in place and wind it several times tightly round the tassel strands. Finish off securely and take the end down through the centre of the tassel.

Cut all the ends evenly and trim as required to obtain a good shape.

Coloured tassels

Wind yarn from two or three balls of yarn round the card at the same time for multicoloured tassels, or use two different textures of yarn.

Multiple tassels

Make tassels more interesting by threading several small tassels through a larger one to hang beneath like a bell clapper.

Alternatively, make a skirted or tiered tassel by hiding one partly under another. The same effect can be made by making one very large tassel and cutting its strands in two or more different lengths.

Combined tassels

Added to pompons, even more interesting ideas are possible with a long tassel hanging from a round, even pompon, or tiny pompons dangling below a bushy top.

Tension

Tension is both the most important factor and the most misunderstood factor in knitting. All printed instructions carry the tension that the garment has been made in and the warning that a sample swatch must be made so that the same tension is obtained, however, many sizes of different needles have to be tried on the way. It is not printed for the pattern writer's amusement,

but for the knitter to be able to make the garment successfully.

Sample swatches

A tiny swatch is not large enough to show that the tension may be out by a quarter or half a stitch per inch. To be certain that the swatch is serving its purpose, it must not be less than 10cm (4 in.). Preferably you should have a central area that measures this amount, allowing a margin all round for edge distortion. The simple message is that the *larger* the swatch is the more *accurate* the measurement will be.

Additional warning

Experience will probably have shown you that you work at quite a different tension over small numbers of stitches than you do over a larger number. Bearing this in mind, do see that there are sufficient stitches to give the feel of a reasonably-sized piece of knitting. One quarter or one half stitch seems far too little to be bothered about, but multiplied by 40 or even only 34 it can make all the difference between a fitting garment and something for a jumble sale.

Measuring tension

Place the swatch on a flat surface and let it remain there for a short time before measuring.

Use a firm rule and lay it evenly along the centre stitches. Mark the start of the area to be measured with a pin and mark the end in the same way.

Remove the rule and count the stitches between the pins.

Measure the number of rows in the same way.

Changing needle sizes

The size in any set of instructions is given only as a guide. Provided another size gives the correct tension, there is no reason to doubt that that is the best choice. People differ in every way; it is, therefore, not surprising that knitters' tension differs also. Be individual and start by getting it right.

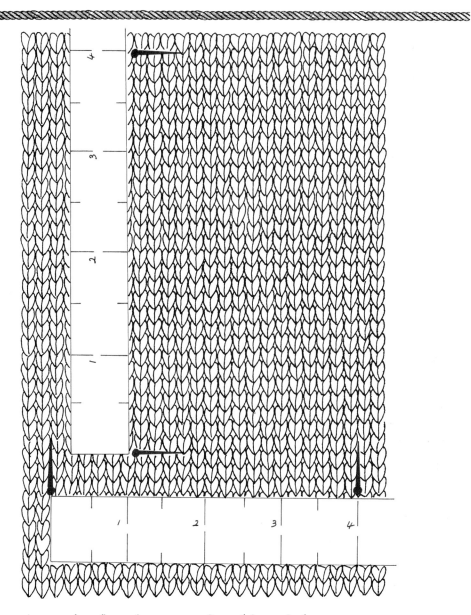

402 Measuring tension swatch on flat surface

Tied stitches

Stitches, like smocked embroidery, can be given a tied-together look by your drawing threads round them. You can do this by winding strands round a group of stitches by drawing strands through from the wrong side.

Smocking stitch

In this type of smocking, a ribbed fabric is tied at intervals to give a honeycomb effect. The tied stitch is a loop of yarn drawn through from the wrong side and is knitted together with another stitch to keep the strands horizontal (see fig 403a).

Worked over a number of stitches divisible by 8, plus 2.

1st and 3rd row (WS facing), K2, * P2, K2, rep from * to end.

403 (*Top*) Smocking stitch. (*Bottom*) Cluster stitch

2nd row P2, * K2, P2, rep from * to end.
4th row P2, * insert right hand needle from front to back between 6th and 7th sts on left needle and draw through a loop of yarn and slip this loop onto the left needle tip, then K it tog with the st to the left of it, K1, P2, K2, P2, rep from * to end (fig. 404).

404 Winding yarn round stitches on cable needle

5th and 7th rows As 1st and 3rd rows.
6th row As for 2nd row.
8th row P2, K2, P2, * draw loop between 6th and 7th sts on left needle, slip it onto left needle and K tog with next st on left needle, K1, P2, K2, P2, rep from *, ending K2, P2.
Rep 1st–8th rows as required.

Cluster stitch

Stitches that are clustered by having the yarn wound round them can be worked by your slipping them back and forwards from one needle to the other. At the same time, take the yarn round the stitches – it is easier to slip the stitches to be tied onto a cable needle or small spare double-pointed needle to wind the yarn freely round the stitches on the needle (fig. 403b).
Worked over a number of stitches divisible by 6, plus 5.
1st and every alt row (WS facing), P.
2nd row K.
4th row K4, * K next 3 sts and slip onto CN, wind yarn 6 times from left to right behind the stitches then in front finishing at the left side, slip the sts back to the right needle to complete the cluster, K3, rep from * to last st, K1 (fig. 405).

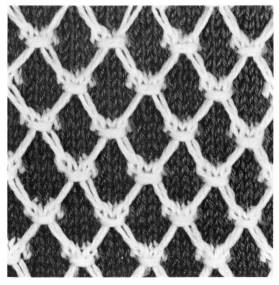

405 Cluster quilting

6th row K.

8th row K1, * cluster next 3 sts as on 4th row, K3, rep from * ending last rep K1 in place of K3.
Rep 1st–8th rows as required.

The pattern worked in this way can easily be re-arranged, grouped in different ways, worked round more stitches or fewer stitches or even have a coloured yarn in contrast carried along the back of the work just for the clustering.

Cluster quilting

One more pattern which uses the same method of clustering the stitches but links it with dropped stitches to form an interesting design (fig. 405).

Worked over a number of stitches divisible by 8, plus 1.

Cast on with A.

Preparation row (WS facing) With A, P1, * P1 winding yarn twice round needle, P5, P1 winding yarn twice round needle, P1, rep from * to end.

1st row With B, K1, * sl1 with yarn back dropping extra loop to make a longer st, K5, sl1 with yarn back dropping extra loop, K1, rep from * to end.

2nd row With B, P1, * sl1 with yarn forward, P5, sl1 with yarn forward, P1, rep from * to end.

3rd row With B, K1, * sl1 with yarn back, K5, sl1 with yarn back, K1, rep from * to end.

4th row With B, P dropping all lengthened A yarn sts off needle to right side of work.

5th row With A, K1, sl1 with yarn back, K1, * K up 1st dropped st, K1, K up next dropped st, with yarn at back slip last 3 sts just worked to CN and wind yarn round twice, ending at left edge of the 3 sts, slip them back to the right needle, K next st on left needle, sl3 with yarn back, K1, rep from * ending last rep sl1 with yarn back, K1 in place of sl3 with yarn back, K1 (fig. 406).

406 Picking up dropped stitch

6th row With A, P1, sl1 with yarn forward, * [P1, P1 winding yarn twice over needle] twice, P1, sl3 with yarn forward, rep from *, ending last rep sl1 with yarn forward, P1, in place of sl3 with yarn forward, P1.

7th row With B, K3, * sl1 with yarn back dropping extra loop, K1, sl1 with yarn back dropping extra loop, K5, rep from *, ending last rep K3 in place of K5.

8th row With B, P3, * sl1 with yarn forward, P1, sl1 with yarn forward, P5, rep from *, ending last rep P3 in place of P5.

9th row With B, K3, * sl1 with yarn back, K1, sl1 with yarn back, K5, rep from *, ending last rep K3 in place of K5.

10th row With B, P dropping all lengthened A sts off needle to right side.

11th row With A, K1, K up 1st dropped st, K1, sl3 with yarn back, K1, rep from * of 5th row, ending last rep K up last dropped st, K1.

12th row With A, P1, * P1 winding yarn twice round needle, P1, sl3 with yarn forward, P1, P1 winding yarn twice round needle, P1, rep from * to end.
Rep 1st–12th rows as required.

Tolerance

Tolerance is the amount added to a garment from the basic skin measurements to give it the ease and width required for it to hang as designed, to allow for movement and to provide room for garments which may be worn beneath it.

Fashion

Fashion dictates how much tolerance is needed, as does personal choice. When skinny-ribbed sweaters are in vogue the addition of tolerance may be quite unnecessary. Instead, the ribbing is stretched to obtain skin measurements and is designed not to outline the figure as knitted but to be worn in the stretched position. Large sloppy sweaters, however, may use twice as much rib, and you would wear them totally unstretched and 20 or more centimetres wider than your actual figure measurements.

Tools

See **Equipment,** *also* **Sheaths and sticks**

Travelling stitches

Stitches that are moved from one position to another are called travelling stitches. Their journey can be made by cabling, using a small needle to hold stitches while the position of one or more other stitches is changed or by twisting, which is working the stitches out of their original order.

For cabling methods *see* **Cables** and for twisting methods *see* **Twisted stitches.**

Travelling stitch patterns

Travelling stitches or crossed stitches, worked without the use of a cable needle, include many patterns, some using crossed stitches only, some combined with other techniques. Check with the abbreviation list and use the method of working recommended for each pattern.

Austrian block pattern

Chunky and satisfying, this pattern gives a robust pattern that is difficult to knit incorrectly, one row leading to the next so clearly (fig. 407 *Top*). Worked over a number of stitches divisible by 10, plus 1.
1st, 3rd, 5th, 7th and 9th rows (WS facing) P1, * K2, P5, K2, P1, rep from * to end.
2nd, 4th, 6th, 8th and 10th rows Kb1, * P2, TwR, K1, TwL, P2, Kb1, rep from * to end.
11th, 13th, 15th, 17th and 19th rows P3, * K2, P1, K2, P5, rep from * ending last rep P3 in place of P5.
12th, 14th, 16th, 18th and 20th rows K1, * TwL, P2, Kb1, P2, TwR, K1, rep from *, ending last rep P3 in place of P5.
Rep 1st–20th rows as required.

Wheatear rib

This old pattern can be used as a decorative rib as an allover pattern or as a single line on panels

407 (*Top*) Austrian block pattern.
(*Bottom*) Wheatear rib

or patterns, using other major vertical stitches such as cables (fig. 407 *Bottom*).
Worked over a number of stitches divisible by 5, plus 2.
1st row (RS facing) * P3, Tw2L, rep from * to last 2 sts, P2.
2nd row * K3, Tw2LP, rep from * to last 2 sts, K2.
Rep 1st and 2nd rows as required.

Lattice pattern

Lattice, on its own, as a central panel or as a frame for a different texture, provides many facets for pattern building. Worked in this way a clear line is made, although some methods of working a twist can leave a less perfect line and are sometimes better worked as a cable stitch (fig. 408 *Top*).

408 (*Top*) Lattice pattern.
(*Bottom*) Striped rib pattern

Worked over a number of stitches divisible by 16, plus 2.
1st row and every alt row (WS facing) P.
2nd row K1, * TwL, K4, TwR, rep from * to last st, K1.
4th row K2, * TwL, K2, TwR, K2, rep from * to end.
6th row K3, * TwL, TwR, K4, rep from * to last 7 sts, TwL, TwR, K3.
8th row K4, * TwR, K6, rep from * to last 6 sts, TwR, K4.
10th row K3, * TwR, TwL, K4, rep from * to last 7 sts, TwR, TwL, K3.
12th row K2, * TwR, K2, TwL, K2 rep from * to end.
14th row K1, * TwR, K4, TwL, rep from * to last st, K1.

16th row * TwL, K6, rep from * to last 2 sts, TwL.
Rep 1st–16th rows as required.

Striped rib pattern

This travelling stitch is also slipped which increases the size of the stitch making the pattern more noticeable (fig. 408 *Bottom*).

Special abbreviation
STw2 means pass needle behind the first stitch and knit the second stitch in back of the loop; then slip the passed stitch purlwise onto right needle and slip the knitted stitch also onto the right needle.
Worked over a number of stitches divisible by 7, plus 2.
1st row and every alt row (WS facing), K2, * P5, K2, rep from * to end.
2nd row P2, * STw2, K3, P2, rep from * to end.
4th row P2, * K1, STw2, K2, P2, rep from * to end.
6th row P2, * K2, STw2, K1, P2, rep from * to end.
8th row P2, * K3, STw2, P2, rep from * to end.
Rep 1st–8th rows as required.

Tucks
See **Ridged stitches**

Tunisian knitting

Tunisian knitting is awkward for westerners because it is worked so differently. Stitches to be knitted must be knitted through the back of the loop, and stitches to be slipped are slipped knitwise not purlwise when they are part of a piece of knitting that is to continue and are not being worked as a decrease.

Like a brioche pattern Tunisian knitting makes yarn over needle stitches, which are worked together in the next row. The order of working is important, and the pattern made by the stitches is completely lost if the stitches become out of order.

Horizontal Tunisian stitch

This pattern has a longer slanted stitch than the oblique Tunisian stitch and is worked over any number of stitches.

1st row * sl1 knitwise, yon, rep on every stitch ending with a yon. Because this row is not worked the last yon must be held in place when the row is turned. The yarn must be taken forward after every slipped st, taken over the needle to the back where it is in position for the next slipped stitch.

2nd row * K2 tog tbl, taking together the strand of the yon with the loop of a slipped stitch.

Repeat these 2 rows for the required length (see fig. 409).

409   Tunisian stitch

Oblique Tunisian stitch

This form places the yon before the slipped stitch which, although a very small alteration, gives a different appearance. Worked over any number of stitches (see fig. 410).

410   Oblique Tunisian stitch

1st row * Yon, sl1 knitwise, yarn forward, rep from * to end, taking care not to drop the last yon in turning.

2nd row * K2 tog tbl, rep from * to end.

Rep these 2 rows as required.

Examples of Tunisian knitting can be found in many museums. It was widely used in the making of coloured socks in Albania and surrounding countries.

Turkish knitting

Turkish knitting is as colourful as their carpets, and many of the same symbols and shapes are used. Stockings worked round with the heel added from a held opening are often made in turquoise and red, dark blue and white.

The knitting of the fez has been in the hands of Turkish knitters for countless years and is still knitted and felted as bonnets were in other countries.

Miss Pardoe, writing in her knitting book published in 1844 about a visit to a Fez factory says

> As we passed the threshold a most curious scene presented itself. About five hundred females were collected together in a vast hall, awaiting delivery of the wool which they were to knit and a more extraordinary group could not perhaps be found in the world. There was a Turkess with her yashmak folded closely over her face, and her dark feridjhe falling to the pavement; the Greek woman with her large turban and braided hair, covered loosely with a scarf of white muslin, her gay coloured dress and large shawl; the Armenian, with her dark eyes flashing from under the jealous screen of her carefully arranged veil, and her red slippers peeping out under the long wrapping cloak; the Jewess, muffled in a coarse linen cloth, and standing a little apart, as though she feared to offend by more immediate contact; and among the crowd some of the loveliest girls imaginable.

She thus provides a glimpse back in time to different cultures, beliefs and ways of life with the one common point, knitting.

Turned knitting

See **Darts**.

Twisted stitches

One way of working travelling stitches without the aid of a cable needle is to twist them. The twist does not turn the stitch as knitting through the back of the loop does but works them out of order, therefore moving the position of the stitch on the fabric.

Twisted stitches can be worked on knitted or purled fabric; they move stitches from knitted areas onto purled areas and the reverse, from purled areas onto knitted fabric. There are also different methods of twisting, each giving its own effect.

Round knitting

Twisted stitch patterns are easiest to work on round knitting because only half the abbreviations are required and only the forms of twisting that apply to the right side of the work are required.

Flat knitting

Twisted stitches, if they are to be moved on every row, do need two sets of working instructions for both right and wrong side movements for each type of stitch.

Adapting

Adapting is not difficult, it only looks more complicated. Flat knitting instructions usually only make use of right side rows and limit the knitter to moving stitches on every other row. However, every right side move does have a purled or wrong side copy, and the use of both allows complete freedom of design potential.

Twisting stitches on stocking stitch

Stocking stitch twisted stitches can be moved to left or to right. For both right and left moving stitches two versions are given: one is the standard movement, which can be found illustrated in older books; the other is a more modern method, which for most knitters gives a cleaner line and is easier to work. This latter method is particularly useful when stitches are moving across the fabric in diagonal lines.

Standard method to left, Tw2L
This abbreviation is also sometimes abbreviated to Tw2B because the right needle passes behind the first stitch. Take the right needle tip behind the first st and insert it knitwise through the back of the second stitch on the left needle (see fig. 411a).

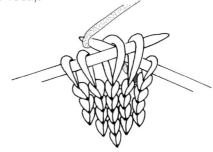

411a Knit into back of second stitch

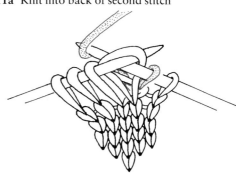

411b Knit into front of first stitch

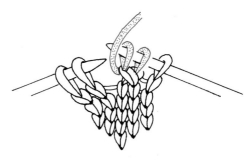

411c Slip both stitches to right needle

Knit it and draw the new stitch onto the right needle then insert the right needle knitwise into the first stitch on the left needle (fig. 411b). Knit it and slip both stitches onto the right needle where the stitch which was the first stitch is now the 2nd and crosses to the left in front of the other stitch (fig. 411c).

Easy method, TwL
Take the right needle tip behind the first stitch on left needle and insert it into the second stitch knitwise and through the back of the loop (fig. 412a).

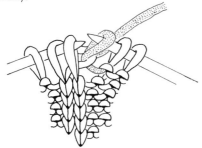

412a Knit second stitch through back of loop

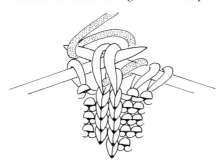

412b Knit both stitches together

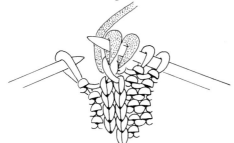

412c Slip both stitches to right needle

Knit the second stitch and then insert the right needle tip into both first and second stitches together, through the backs of the loops (fig. 412b).

Knit the stitches in this position and slip both stitches onto the right needle (fig. 412c).

Standard method, Tw2R
This is sometimes abbreviated to Tw2F because the right needle is taken across the front of the first stitch.

Take the right needle tip across the front of the first stitch on the left needle and insert it into the second stitch knitwise (fig. 413a).

Knit the stitch and then knit the first stitch (fig. 413b).

Slip both stitches to the right needle. The second stitch is now the first and lies on top of the other stitch sloping to the right (fig. 413c).

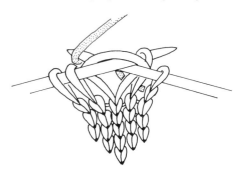

413a Knit second stitch

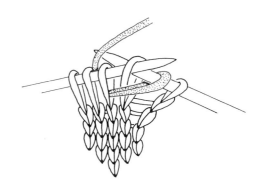

413b Knit first stitch

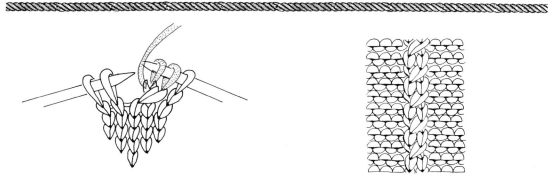

413c Completed Tw2R

415 Completed TWR

Easy method, TwR
Insert the right needle tip through both stitches knitwise and knit together in the usual way but do not slip them off the left needle (fig. 414a).

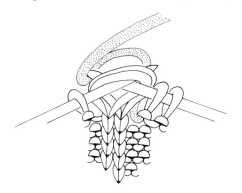

414a Knit both stitches together

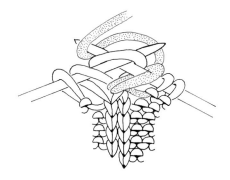

414b Knit first stitch again

Insert the right needle tip between the two stitches just knitted together and knit the first loop only again (fig. 414b). Slip both stitches off the left needle to the right (fig. 415).

Occasional alteration

The Tw2L or Tw2B may, in specific instructions, be worked by your knitting the second stitch without working it through the back of the loop, then knitting the first stitch in the usual way. This is only necessary if the pattern in use specifically states that this is the working method to be used.

Purl methods

Although the purl methods are less usual, they are worth knowing and can be used to give a variation on right side twists only. It is assumed that they are to be worked on the wrong side paired with right side twists, and the slope indication tells which way the twist will lie on the right side.

Purl twist to right, Tw2RP
Pass the right needle tip in front of the first stitch on the left needle and insert it purlwise into the second stitch (fig. 416a).

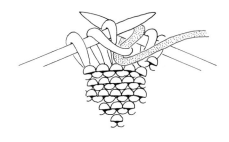

416a Purl second stitch

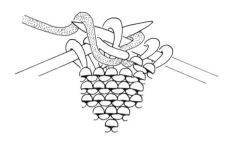

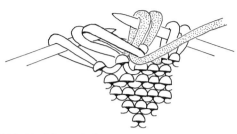

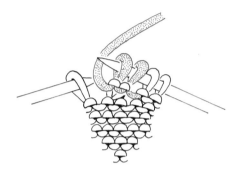

416b Purl the first stitch

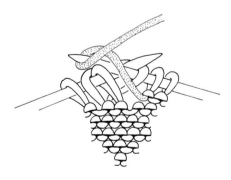

417b Purl first stitch

Purl it and then purl the first stitch (fig. 417b).
Slip both stitches onto the right needle to complete the twist.

Twisting ribbed stitches
Twisted stitches are often used to outline stocking stitch areas on purled backgrounds and you may use both purl and knit stitches in the process.

Work the actual twist as given in the various versions, working first or second stitch purlwise as required by the pattern.

416c Completed Tw2RP

Purl the stitch and then purl the first stitch (fig. 416b).

Slip both stitches to the right needle at the same time (fig. 416c).

Purl twist to left, Tw2LP
Pass right needle behind 1st stitch on left needle and insert it into the second stitch purlwise through the back of the loop (fig. 417a).

Tw2LPK, moving left
Pass the right needle behind the first stitch and purl into the back of the second stitch (fig. 418a).

Knit into the front of the first stitch and slip both stitches to the right needle (fig. 418b).

418a Purl into back of second stitch

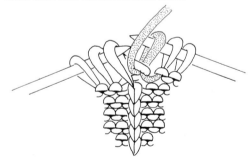

418b Knit into front of first stitch

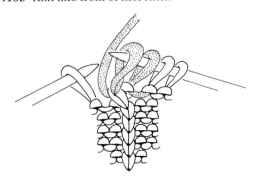

417a Purl second stitch through back of loop

Tw2RKP, moving right

Pass the right needle in front of the first stitch and knit the second stitch (fig. 419a).

Purl into the first stitch and slip both stitches to the right needle (fig. 419b).

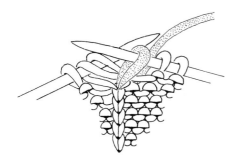

419a Knit the second stitch

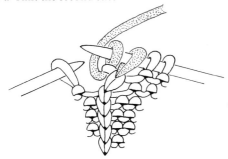

419b Purl the first stitch

Twisting three stitches

Three stitches can be twisted without the use of a cable needle by either a front twist or a back twist, that is either to right or to left (fig. 420).

420 Three stitches twisted to right

Tw3L or Tw3B

Pass the right needle tip behind the first and second stitches on the left needle and insert it into the third stitch knitwise, through the back of the loop (fig. 421a).

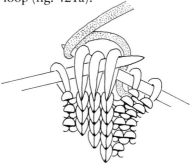

421a Knit third stitch through back of loop

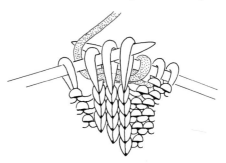

421b Knit second stitch through back of loop

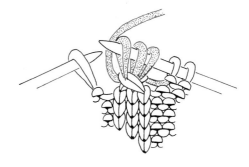

421c Then knit the first stitch

Knit the stitch then knit the second stitch (fig. 421b).

Then knit the first stitch (fig. 421c).

Slip all three stitches onto the right needle at the same time.

Tw3R or Tw3F

Pass the right needle tip in front of the first and second stitches on the left needle and insert the tip into the third stitch knitwise (fig. 422a).

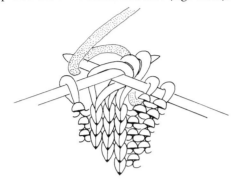

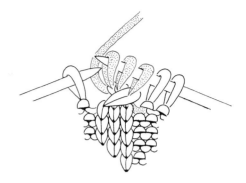

422a Knit the third stitch

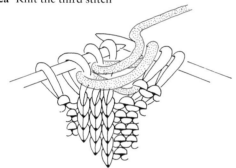

422b Knit the second stitch

422c Then knit the first stitch

Knit the stitch and then knit the second stitch (fig. 422b).

Knit the first stitch and slip all three stitches to the right needle at the same time (fig. 422c).

Charting twist stitch patterns

Twist stitch patterns are more easily dealt with on chart than by words. Charting the pattern also gives the more experienced knitter the alternative between working in rows or rounds, the chart showing the finished effect.

Uneven knitting

Stocking stitch often appears to be ridged and uneven, one row being wider than the other. To avoid this, use two different-sized needles. Check which row is the wider and use the smaller size for that row and one size larger for the other row to produce perfect stocking stitch.

Alternative method

Replace stocking stitch with continental stocking stitch where the twisted row disguises the unevenness of the knitting.
1st row (RS facing) K every st tbl.
2nd row P.
Rep these 2 rows throughout.

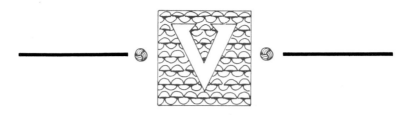

Victorian knitting

Victorian knitting provides a mine of information about forgotten stitches, ideas for textures and trims which have long been laid aside. In Victorian times, domestic knitting had reached its zenith. Tables were covered with lace work, and cushions and rugs abounded. Items that are nowadays fairly redundant, like dressing table tidies, penwipers and gaiters, were all knitted, patterned and decorated, along with one hundred and one other items.

The rise of the popular press was responsible for magazines such as *The Young Ladies' Journal* and *Weldon's pattern books*, *Godey's Ladies Book* and *The Ladies Newspaper*, all filled with idea upon idea.

425 Victorian knitting illustrations

Washing knitting

When you wash wool there are certain rules to be observed, although it is not as difficult as some people imagine.

Avoid friction and heat

Harsh rubbing of strands together and very hot water with undissolved soap particles in it must be avoided. Both will certainly damage the yarn, causing it to become thick and felted.

Cool water and dissolved soap

Cool water, with gentle soap thoroughly dissolved will not harm wool; gently squeeze the garment rather than twisting and scrubbing it.

Wool shampoo

A shampoo sold specifically for washing wool allows the dirt simply to fall out of the stitches and makes for a cleaner garment without endless squeezing or rubbing.

Rinsing

Rinse in cool water and continue to rinse, gently squeezing out as much water as possible until the water appears to be clean and free from any evidence of dirt or soap.

Machine-washable wool

Among the yarns available today, many are machine washable. This does not mean that they will stand up to boiling water, undissolved or harsh soap or detergents and agitating in a

427 Washing symbols

washing machine for as long as possible. Consult washing machine instructions and programmes and also the ball band of the yarn and use the information provided (see fig. 427).

Drying

Remove as much water as possible by squeezing the garment, then blot between dry towels to remove excess water.

Lay flat to dry, pulling into shape while wet. Dry out of direct sunlight or excessive heat and preferably on a slatted drying frame so that air can circulate all round the garment. *See also* **Blocking and pressing**.

Welts

The welt of a garment is often taken to mean the lower edge, whether ribbed, hemmed or worked in some other way, different from the pattern or fabric of the garment. Welt stitches are, however, not stitches that create vertical lines and tend to lengthen the area they are worked over, but horizontal lines formed by purl stitches against knit stitches, which shorten the number of rows over which they are worked.

428 (*Left*) Wager welt. (*Right*) Broken welt

Gurnsey welts

Many fishermen's guernseys were worked with a ridged welt of several rows of stocking stitch, followed by several rows of reverse stocking stitch giving an undulated surface known in many areas as rig and furrow because of its resemblance to a ploughed field.

One very effective welt has many names and is known in France as puzzle stitch, in Germany as dispute stitch and at one time in England was called all fools's welt, and all because at a first glance it would appear to be a simple arrangement of knit and purled stitches.

It is, in fact, a pattern which repeats over eight rows, of which only one is purled (fig. 428a).
To work it cast on any number of stitches.
1st, 3rd, 4th, 5th, 6th, 7th and 8th rows K.
2nd row P.
Rep these 8 rows as required.
Welt patterns can be built up with variations on the theme of one row knit and two rows purled or on even numbers if preferred.

Broken welt

The alternation of blocks of the welted stitches can make interesting designs, and again any number of stitches and rows can produce patterns (fig. 428b).

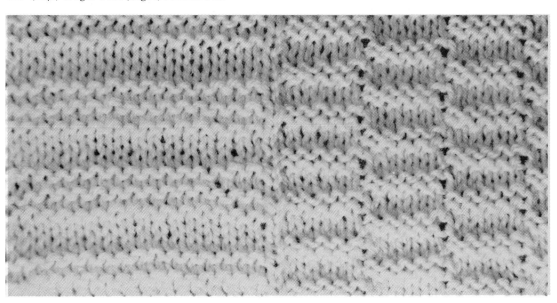

Worked over a number of stitches divisible by 10.

1st and 2nd rows * K5, P5, rep from * to end.
3rd and 4th rows * P5, K5, rep from * to end.
Rep these 4 rows as required.

White knitting

With the introduction of cotton in the seventeeth century came a new era of 'white' knitting, so named because the yarn was undyed. Fine yarn worked on very fine needles became the order of the day, and lace work of all types began to appear, particularly in European areas where there was not already a lace making industry.

Not all articles were small and many large items such as bedspreads were made and became heirlooms for many generations. Knitted samplers from the seventeenth and early eighteenth century show the variety and surprising number of lace patterns that were in use.

See also **Medallion knitting.**

Wool

See **Yarns**

Woven knitting

Woven knitting is not produced by leaving the strands formed by slip stitches on the right side of the fabric. These patterns often carry woven in their names but they only give the appearance of certain woven fabrics.

Instead, woven knitting is worked by placing a second yarn, usually in contrasting colour, but this is not essential, between the stitches. The contrast or woven yarn is never knitted or purled into place but lies between the other stitches.

To work weaving

This pattern uses an even number of stitches.
Cast on with the background colour.
Preparation row With A, P.

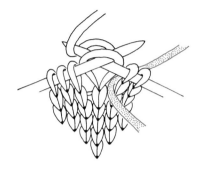

429a Bring weaving yarn to front

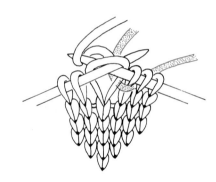

429b Carry yarn across front of next stitch then take it back

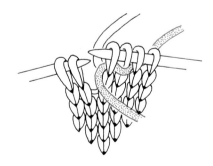

429c Knit next stitch with weaving yarn behind it, taking it forward when stitch is completed

1st (RS facing), K1A, bring B from back to lie across front of A st, * K1A, take B to back, K1A, bring B to front, K1A, rep from * to end.
2nd row P1A and bring B around edge to lie in front or on the purl side of the purled st, * take B to back, P1A, bring B to front, P1A, rep from * to end.
Rep these 2 rows that alternately pass the woven thread in front of and behind the stitches on both rows. Either side of the fabric can be used as the right side.

Patterning

Patterns can be built up by using the strand only in front of certain stitches, carrying it behind the other stitches to the next position where it is to be seen on the right side (fig. 430).

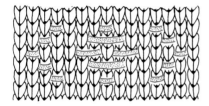

430 Woven motif

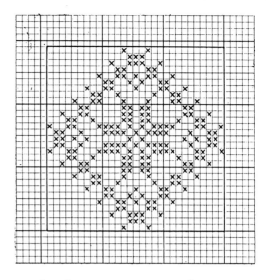

431 Chart for Estonian woven motif

The Estonian socks shown in fig. 216 use this method of weaving for the very ornate patterns used to outline the ankle and side leg shaping. They are worked from a chart and worked on every row to give an almost padded effect to the design (fig. 431).

Wrong side

The side that is not used as the right side when the garment is finished. In stocking stitch the purled side is used as the wrong side.

X and O pattern

See **Fair Isle knitting,** also fig. 372, **Shetland knitting.**

Yarns

Yarn list

Acrylic yarns

Stronger than wool, acrylic yarns are purely synthetic. They were first marketed around 1954. Since arylic is light and bulky, yarns made from it are much longer than wool yarns of the equivalent weight.

Alpaca

Alpaca is an expensive soft yarn, spun from the long woolly hair of llamas; it is often blended with cheaper fibres, but the mixed yarn still retains the softness of llama hair.

Angora

Angora is spun from the hair of the angora rabbit. It is extremely soft and retains its natural fluffiness. Pure angora is both difficult to obtain and expensive but there are several rabbit wool mixtures which are harder wearing, equally soft and fluffy and less expensive.

Cotton

Cotton is a natural fibre found in many fashion yarns today. For many years it has been used for household items and for fine crochet. Today it is available in the equivalent of 4 ply, double knitting and even Aran weights. It can be found in smooth soft yarns, more tightly twisted matt or polished yarns and many fancy surfaced yarns.

Courtelle

Courtelle is a high bulk acrylic yarn made by Courtaulds.

Linen

Linen is a natural fibre made from the flax plant. Not always available owing to fashion trends, it is usually blended with a proportion of another fibre for pliability.

Lurex

Shining, fine metallic yarns, now available in many shades as well as in metal colours.

Man-made fibres

This includes all yarns made from chemical or other than natural substances.

Mohair

Mohair is the hair of goats and is light, warm and fluffy. When dyed it has a beautiful sheen.

Natural fibres

Fibres which are grown on plants, fibres from the coats of animals, or as in silk, fibres which are spun by silkworms.

Nylon

A synthetic yarn discovered by Du Pont before the Second World War and initially used widely for fine spun stockings, before it was developed into suitable hand-knitting yarn.

Silk

Made from the spun threads formed by the silkworm.

Wool

Wool, the best of all knitting yarns, comes from
the fleece of the sheep. There are many different
qualities and mixtures to choose from.

If they are not perfect, tacking can easily be removed and altered – finished stitches take much longer to correct.

Once the position is correct, backstitch down each side of the zip with matching yarn. Wool is not strong enough nor fine enough and is difficult to draw through the zip tapes (fig. 436).

When the zip is sewn in, neaten the back edges by oversewing or hemming the tape edges through the back of the knitted stitches, taking care that no stitches pass through to the right side (fig. 435b).

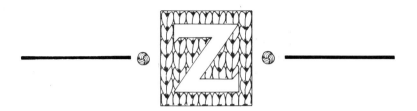

Zip fasteners

Zips can be awkward to sew into place once the garment has been seamed, when it no longer lies flat. If at all possible, sew the zip in before joining shoulder and side seams.

To place a zip

Place the section or sections to carry the zip on a flat surface and pin the zip into place. Tack it before sewing it in more firmly. Only pinned in, it can too readily move but tacked into place with not too large stitches it will lie flat, will not be distorted and will give a much clearer idea of whether the sides are even. There must be the same number of rows on each side with their lines running evenly across the fabric, not pulled out of true on one side or the other (fig. 435a).

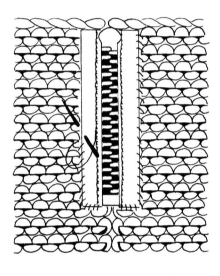

435b Hemming round tape edges on wrong side

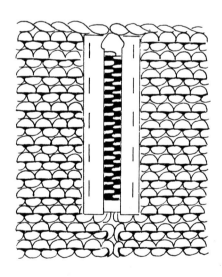

435a Tacked in position on wrong side

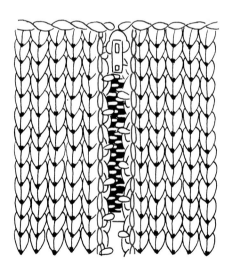

436 Zip stitching on right side